Date Due

FEB 2 3 2006			

SPORTS, EXERCISE, AND FITNESS

Recent titles in
Reference Sources in the Social Sciences

American Military History: A Guide to Reference and Information Sources
Daniel K. Blewett

Education: A Guide to Reference and Information Sources
Nancy Patricia O'Brien

Northern Africa: A Guide to Reference and Information Sources
Paula Youngman Skreslet

SPORTS, EXERCISE, AND FITNESS

A Guide to Reference and Information Sources

MARY BETH ALLEN

University of Illinois at Urbana-Champaign

Reference Sources in the Social Sciences

A Member of the Greenwood Publishing Group

Westport, Connecticut • London

Library of Congress Cataloging-in-Publication Data

Allen, Mary Beth.
    Sports, exercise, and fitness : a guide to reference and information sources /
Mary Beth Allen.
        p. cm.
    Includes bibliographical references and index.
    ISBN 1–56308–819–3 (alk. paper)
    1. Sports—Handbooks, manuals, etc.   2. Physical fitness—Handbooks, manuals, etc.
I. Title.
GV704.A55   2005
016.796—dc22   2004063835

British Library Cataloguing in Publication Data is available.

Library of Congress Catalog Card Number: 2004063835
ISBN: 1–56308–819–3

First published in 2005

Libraries Unlimited, 88 Post Road West, Westport, CT 06881
A Member of the Greenwood Publishing Group, Inc.
www.lu.com

Printed in the United States of America

The paper used in this book complies with the
Permanent Paper Standard issued by the National
Information Standards Organization (Z39.48–1984).

10 9 8 7 6 5 4 3 2 1

CONTENTS

V

ACKNOWLEDGMENTS

The author wishes to acknowledge the Research and Publication Committee of the University of Illinois at Urbana-Champaign Library, which provided support for the completion of this research.

Thanks go to Robert Burger for encouraging me to submit a book proposal to Libraries Unlimited, and to Barbara Ittner for patiently seeing it through.

The University of Illinois library holds an incredible collection, and working on this project has helped me tremendously to realize my goal of building one of the finest book collections in the areas I serve. However, I must acknowledge that this work has been greatly enhanced by the collections of many other libraries. I have borrowed freely and extensively through our fantastic interlibrary borrowing service, and the staff of that office ensured that all my requests for books at other libraries were satisfied quickly and efficiently.

Genuine thanks go to the many individuals who have worked with me in the Applied Life Studies Library at the University of Illinois at Urbana-Champaign during my involvement with this project. Thanks go to Amy Matzke, whose assistance laid the foundation for the initial database of sources. Perhaps the greatest thanks I owe is to the excellent students and permanent staff in the Applied Life Studies Library, who so enthusiastically and steadfastly continued their own work and took such dedicated care of the library while I was working on this project. The daily encouragement and positive support offered by Joan Sargent, Lil Morales, and especially Wendy Gregory are what made this idea a reality.

Thanks also go to my parents and other family members who gave their support. I especially want to thank my husband, Jaime, for his patience, good humor, and faith that I could do it, and my daughter, Emily, for being the best teacher yet.

INTRODUCTION

Of great societal interest, sport has grown to become a major-media market draw and economic power but also an academic pursuit with its own specialized literature. According to Ellis Cashmore, in *Sports Culture: An A to Z Guide*, "Sport as an institution is just too big economically, too important politically, too influential in shaping people's lives not to be taken seriously as a subject for academic inquiry. People kill in the name of sport; and, correspondingly, others die. Fans spend small fortunes in the pursuit of their sport. Bookies make and, occasionally, lose big fortunes. Corporations are built on what is now a sports industry. Elite sports performers can outgross many countries. This may have once been an exaggerated claim but, since the career of Michael Jordan, it is now literally true."[1] Sports are an interdisciplinary academic study, and scholars focus on aspects of sport as varied as economics, sociology, psychology, philosophy, history, physics, physiology, biomechanics, and medicine.

On an individual level, in our quest for the perfect body or media-generated idea of beauty, we often view an increased fitness level and better health as mere by-products. But the evidence is mounting that significant health benefits are to be gained from exercise at every stage of life, and especially as we approach old age. With reports that the rate of obesity is growing rapidly among children and evidence that a sedentary lifestyle is becoming ever more prevalent among many adults, America's newest fad is the low-carb diet and a daily exercise regimen. A recent study at Penn State University College of Medicine reported that exercise was more important than calcium in building bone strength in young women.[2] A growing body of scientific research conducted at many universities provides evidence that exercise not only improves physical health but also increases psychological well-being. At the University of Illinois a number of critical studies have shown that exercise improves cardiovascular fitness as well as "executive control," the complex multitask thinking that helps us react quickly in an emergency situation, and thus enhances cognitive function among older adults.[3] Another study demonstrates that increased cardiovascular fitness results in increased brain function, as measured by MRI scanning of the brain.[4] Studies such as these have tremendous public-health implications and provide clear, persuasive reasons for people to increase their fitness levels by exercising regularly and engaging in sports activities that are physically challenging throughout their life span.

This guide is intended to aid librarians in collection development and in general reference work and to assist readers with gaining access to the literature of sport, exercise, and fitness. The sources reviewed form the basis of a reference collection that will help librarians answer key questions about sports and exercise and will lead readers to instruction in a variety of fitness activities. Three basic types of information sources are included: traditional reference sources, instructional sources, and Web sites. The traditional reference sources are chosen for their quality and their comprehensiveness; they are appropriate acquisitions for college and university libraries that support programs in exercise science and all aspects of sport, as well as for larger public libraries. A number of the reference sources are also appropriate for high school libraries.

The instructional sources are included to provide further information on specific sports and activities. They offer a good introduction to an individual sport or activity, its history, techniques, strategies, terminology, and rules. The instructional sources provide basic playing specifications, as well as proper forms and techniques required for participation in the sport or activity, and they often contain excellent illustrations that can enhance understanding of technique. In addition, sport-specific instructional sources often contain a strong exercise and fitness component; such as a detailed plan for building fitness in the sport, so these resources can be a practical addition to any library's collection when there is such a demand.

The Web sites were chosen to provide continuing access to current information about specific sports and activities. Many of them are the work of official governing bodies and nonprofit associations that support a sport or activity, and the sites were chosen because they are stable and they provide comprehensive information. Many of the sites are popular with fans looking for current news and results, but their inclusion of history, rules, and much other information makes them valuable as educational sources as well.

The body of literature on sports, exercise, and fitness is extensive. This guide focuses specifically on the most important sources published between 1990 and May 2004, though some earlier, classic works have been included when a newer source did not duplicate the content. For the most part, sources were chosen to appeal to a wide audience: academic libraries, public libraries, and to some extent, high school libraries. Excluded were sources that are narrow in scope. For example, sources about just one athletic team were excluded, except when they were used as examples of typical types of sources. The focus is on English-language publications, with an emphasis on those from North America; important sources from Great Britain and many other areas of the world are also included, especially when they help balance the perspective culturally.

The guide is arranged chiefly by type of sport or activity, and similar sports and activities are grouped together in chapters. General sport sections include works on more than one sport. General sport sources are further divided by type of publication. Works that cover only one sport, regardless of type of reference work, are treated in the sport-specific sections and organized topically within chapters. For example, a biographical source that deals only with football players and personalities is listed under Football, rather than under Sport-Biographies.

Over 1000 entries are included, all with descriptive annotations that convey information about the nature and content of the information sources. Nearly all of the sources were examined by the author. Bibliographic information was verified using standard sources such as OCLC *WorldCat* and *Books in Print*. Standard review sources such as *Choice* and *American Reference Books Annual* were consulted where available.

In a work such as this, which represents many years of research within a large body of literature, inevitably there are omissions and errors. I accept responsibility for all of these, and I apologize to every author whose work is not included. There is indeed room for improvement, and I will gratefully accept such information and incorporate it in future works.

NOTES

1. Ellis Cashmore, *Sports Culture: An A to Z Guide* (New York: Routledge, 2000), ix–x.

2. Tom Lloyd, Moira A. Petit, Hung-Mo Lin, and Thomas J. Beck, "Lifestyle Factors and the Development of Bone Mass and Bone Strength in Young Women," *The Journal of Pediatrics* 144, no. 6 (2004): 776–782.

3. Charles H. Hillman, Artem V. Belopolsky, Erin M. Snook, Arthur F. Kramer, Edward McAuley, "Physical Activity and Executive Control: Implications for Increased Cognitive Health during Older Adulthood," *Research Quarterly for Exercise and Sport* 75, no. 2 (2004): 176–185.

4. Stanley J. Colcombe, Arthur F. Kramer, Kirk I. Erickson, Paige Scalf, Edward McAuley, Neal J. Cohen, Andrew Webb, Gerry J. Jerome, David X. Marquez, and Steriani Elavsky, "Cardiovascular Fitness, Cortical Plasticity, and Aging," *Proceedings of the National Academy of Sciences of the United States* 101, no. 9 (2004): 3316–3321.

Chapter 1

General Sport Sources

This chapter lists sport reference sources that each offer information on a variety of sports, or on sport in general. The types of resources included are almanacs, bibliographies, biographies, dictionaries, directories, encyclopedias, handbooks, indexes, abstracts, and databases, quotation books, rule books, statistics sources, and Web sites. These reference sources generally provide the reader with background information about sports, athletes and other important personalities in the world of sport, sporting events, results, rules, and terminology. They are important tools in reference work and are often the first place the reader or librarian will search for information. Naturally, there is a strong emphasis on the historical aspects of sport. Web sites of general sport associations and other stable information sources are also included to provide access to current information.

Sport Almanacs

1. Brown, Gerry, and Michael Morrison, eds. **ESPN Sports Almanac.** 2004 ed. New York: Hyperion ESPN Books, 2003. 960 pp. $12.99. ISBN 0-7868-8716-8.

This handy annual source begins with a review of the previous year in sports and includes a month-by-month calendar of major events that occurred. Major U.S. professional and college sports are given prime attention, but less popular sports such as bowling, horse racing, and auto racing are covered as well. Additional chapters provide data on the Olympic games, ballparks and arenas, halls of fame, and less-publicized sports such as soap-box derbies, fishing, and pro rodeo. It includes essays and analysis from ESPN personalities. Illustrated with hundreds of black-and-white photographs, graphs, and tables. Includes a review of the 2003 World Cup and World Series, and the Winter and Summer Olympics through the years.

2. Gross, Ernie. **This Day in Sports.** Jefferson, N.C.: McFarland, 2001. 286 pp. $35.00. ISBN 0-7864-0803-0.

This unique and entertaining reference source provides a day-by-day listing of major events that have occurred in sports history. Details are given for 365 days of the year and are arranged by date. Coverage is through 1998. Includes a bibliography and an index of persons named in the text. Not illustrated.

3. Smith, Ron. **The *Sporting News* This Day in Sports: A Day-by-Day Record of America's Sporting Year.** New York: Macmillan, 1994. 384 pp. $85.00. ISBN 0-02-897264-3.

With a page devoted to each day of the year, this source provides an entertaining account of the most notable events in the worlds of football, basketball, baseball, hockey, and other sports, such as boxing and track and field. Each date features three main events and includes a "Milestones in Sports" box with other sports news in brief. There are also listings of birth and death dates of notable sports figures. Illustrated with 570 historic photographs.

4. *Sports Illustrated* **Almanac 2004.** With the editors of *Sports Illustrated*. New York: Bishop Books, 2003. 895 pp. $12.99. ISBN 1-931933-79-0.

Filled with facts, statistics, and essays from *Sports Illustrated* writers, this popular sports almanac begins with a review of the year in sports. It then gives sport by sport coverage of baseball, pro football, college football, pro basketball, college basketball, hockey, tennis, golf, boxing, horse racing, motor sports, bowling, soccer, NCAA sports, the Olympics, track and field, swimming, skiing, figure skating, and other sports. It lists awards and provides brief profiles of athletes, as well as obituaries, and a look ahead to the major events of the next year.

5. Taaffe, William, and David Fischer, eds. **Sports of the Times: A Day-by-Day Selection of the Most Important, Thrilling, and Inspired Events of the Past 150 Years.** New York: St. Martin's Press, 2003. 416 pp. $40.00. ISBN 0-312-31232-6.

These 365 stories were originally published in the *New York Times*, and they come together to make this memory book of the most important sports events from the last 150 years, one from each calendar day. Three runners-up for each day are also included, and a five-star designation is given to the most significant events in sports history. Sports fans will delight in the vivid description of the facts and the historic black-and-white photographs. Arranged by date, from January 1 to December 31. Indexed.

Sport Atlas

6. Rooney, John F., and Richard Pillsbury. **Atlas of American Sport.** New York: Macmillan Reference USA, 1992. 198 pp. $150.00. ISBN 0-02-897351-8.

This unique source explores the geographical elements of American sport by mapping the distributions of facilities, players, and activities. The maps, photos, and essays illustrate regional differences in over seventy games and sports in which Americans are involved. Twenty-five major sports are examined in detail, and more than forty additional sports are reviewed more briefly. Appendices contain a list of associations and their addresses, a select bibliography, a general index, and a geographical index.

Sport Bibliographies

7. Arbena, Joseph, comp. **An Annotated Bibliography of Latin American Sport: Pre-conquest to the Present.** Bibliographies and Indexes in World History. Westport, Conn.: Greenwood Press, 1989. 324 pp. $105.00. ISBN 0-313-25495-8.

This important bibliography contains over 1300 entries on Latin American sports; all but forty of them are annotated. A variety of source types is included, and the entries are arranged in sections, the themes of which include theory and history, indigenous traditions, Iberian background, the colonial era, the national era, Hispanic sports and sportsmen in the United States, and current periodicals. The author has also completed a second bibliography that follows this one, entitled *Latin American Sport: An Annotated Bibliography, 1988–1998* (1999). Indexed by author and subject.

8. Arbena, Joseph, comp. **Latin American Sport: An Annotated Bibliography, 1988–1998.** Bibliographies and Indexes on Sports History. Westport, Conn.: Greenwood Press, 1999. 244 pp. $89.95. ISBN 0-313-29611-1; ISSN 1066-3746.

Following from the author's earlier work, *An Annotated Bibliography of Latin American Sport: Pre-conquest to the Present* (1989), this bibliography continues with sources the author has identified since 1988. It also includes a few items omitted from the earlier bibliography. Sections are arranged by topic and cover indigenous traditions, Iberian background, the colonial era, the National Period in countries of Middle America and in countries of South America, and Hispanic sports and sportsmen in the United States. Indexed by author and subject.

9. Clarke, Norman F. **The Recreation and Entertainment Industries: An Information Sourcebook.** 2nd ed. Jefferson, N.C.: McFarland, 2000. 286 pp. $59.95. ISBN 0-7864-0797-2.

In this revised and expanded second edition the author provides increased access points for information in the profit and nonprofit sectors of the recreation and entertainment industries. Arranged by topic and the North American Industry Classification System, sources are listed for the fitness industry, skiing, skating, bowling, and other sport-specific industries, sporting-goods industry, entertainment industry, and many other related types of industries. Basic reference sources are included. Each source is identified clearly and annotated briefly. Web addresses are included where appropriate. Indexed.

10. Cox, Richard William. **British Sport: A Bibliography to 2000.** Sports Reference Library. 2nd ed. 3 vols. Portland, Ore.: Frank Cass, 2003. $54.00 (v. 1);

$80.00 (v. 2); $54.00 (v. 3). ISBN 0-7146-5250-4 (v. 1); 0-7146-5251-2 (v. 2); 0-7146-5252-0 (v. 3).

Intended to provide comprehensive coverage of the history of sport in Britain, this second edition of this notable bibliography lists secondary works on the topic. The author indicates that this set is the second phase of his three-part project. The first phase identified types of sources for research on sport and was published as *History of Sport: A Guide to the Literature and Sources of Information* (Frodsham: Sports History Publishing, 1994). The third phase will document primary sources and build a comprehensive online source. Volume 1 is entitled *Nationwide Histories*; volume 2, *Local Histories*; and volume 3, *Biographical Studies of British Sportsmen, Sportswomen and Animals*. Each volume contains its own author index.

11. Cox, Richard William. **History of Sport: A Guide to the Literature and Sources of Information.** Frodsham, Cheshire: British Society of Sport History / Sports History Publishing, 1994. 101 pp. ISBN 1-898-010-03-X.

In this guide to the literature of the history of sport, the author identifies many types of sources that can serve as the basis for a research project on the development of sport in Britain. Sources are described and evaluated. Includes quick-reference sources, secondary sources, primary sources, and specialist areas of research. Indexed by name, subject, and title.

12. Cox, Richard William. **Index to Sporting Manuscripts in the UK.** Frodsham, Cheshire, U.K.: British Society of Sports History / Sports History Publishing, 1995. 129 pp. ISBN 1-898010-04-8.

This bibliography contains references to manuscripts related to sport in the United Kingdom. *Manuscript* is defined as any unpublished document and includes everything from photographs to a local golf club's minutes. Arranged in two sections, the first lists documents from the National Archives, and the second lists documents from local record offices. Each section is arranged geographically. The work includes an index to the repositories examined and a name index for the clubs, schools, leagues, and other sporting organizations that are identified.

13. Cox, Richard William. **International Sport: A Bibliography, 1995–1999, and Index to Sports History Journals, Conference Proceedings and Essay Collections.** Portland, Ore.: Frank Cass, 2002. 240 pp. $57.50. ISBN 0-7146-5260-1.

This bibliography of sources on the topic of international sport is the author's update for the years 1995 to 1999 and follows from his annual bibliography in the *International Journal of History of Sport*. This work is continued in a separate volume for the year 2000 alone. Basic bibliographic detail is included for books, articles, chapters, conference proceedings, and theses.

14. Cox, Richard William. **International Sport: A Bibliography, 2000, and Index to Sports History Journals, Conference Proceedings and Essay Col-**

lections. Sports Reference. Portland, Ore.: Frank Cass, 2003. 78 pp. $39.50. ISBN 0-7146-5364-0.

Intended for the sports historian or student of sport history, the bibliography compiled by this noted author covers the one-year period of January through December 2000 and includes books, articles, chapters, conference proceedings, and theses. It covers general reference sources, sport-specific ones, and those related to sport in individual continents or countries. Includes an author index, an index to journals, an index to conference proceedings, and a list of essay collections.

15. Cox, Richard William. **Sport in Britain: A Bibliography of Historical Publications, 1800–1988.** Manchester, U.K.: Manchester University Press; New York: St. Martin's Press, 1991. 285 pp. $59.95. ISBN 0-7190-2592-3.

This is the author's original work on the history of sport in Britain. This bibliography provides comprehensive coverage of the British literature by covering nationwide histories of sport, both general and sport-specific; local studies in the history of sport; and biographies, collective biographies within specific sports, and individual and family biographies, memoirs, and the like. A continuation of this work, entitled *British Sport: A Bibliography to 2000*, is published in three volumes by the same author and updates the content to 2000.

16. LeUnes, Arnold D. **Bibliography on Psychological Tests Used in Research and Practice in Sport and Exercise Psychology.** Mellon Studies in Psychology. Lewiston, N.Y.: Edwin Mellen Press, 2002. 388 pp. $119.95. ISBN 0-7734-7001-8.

This specialized bibliography on psychological tests used in sport psychology research includes citations for over 2,000 scholarly articles that report on research that has used such tests. The intended audience is sport researchers, practitioners, and graduate and undergraduate students in exercise and sport science. The author arranges the listing by the type of test category (what it measures), so research using tests that measure self-efficacy, for example, are grouped together. Indexed by sport and by author. Most appropriate for academic collections that support sport psychology programs.

17. Remley, Mary L. **Women in Sport: An Annotated Bibliography and Resource Guide, 1900–1990.** Boston: G. K. Hall, 1991. 210 pp. $40.00. ISBN 0-8161-8977-3.

This guide to the literature documents both the participation of women in sports and the increase in literature on the topic during the years 1900 to 1990. Arranged chronologically by year and then alphabetically by author, the books and other sources are given brief but useful annotations. The work also contains a chapter devoted to listing other sources of information. Indexed by author, subject, and title.

18. Shoebridge, Michele, ed. **Information Sources in Sport and Leisure.** Guides to Information Sources. London: Bowker-Saur, 1992. 345 pp. $50.00. ISBN 0-86291-901-0.

This comprehensive guide to the scholarly literature of sport and leisure brings together important essays written by experts in the field. The essays identify sources and describe the different types of information available. Topics include a general overview of sources; statistical and government information sources; sports science and sports medicine; history and sociology of sport; the Olympic games; leisure, physical education, physical fitness, and coaching; and sources specific to North America, Europe, and Australia. Appendixes provide additional information in the form of a list of international organizations and a list of acronyms. Indexed.

19. Wise, Suzanne. **Social Issues in Contemporary Sport: A Resource Guide.** Garland Reference Library of Social Science. New York: Garland, 1994. 789 pp. $40.00. ISBN 0-8240-6046-6.

Intended as a starting point for undergraduates and other beginning researchers in the sociology of sport, this annotated bibliography focuses on publications between 1970 and 1993 and includes over 2400 references to books, periodicals, conference papers, and other published sources. Each chapter contains references on a topical area, such as sport and education, sports law, or sport and politics. Includes lists of selected organizations and journals. Indexed by subject.

Sport Biographies

20. Aaseng, Nathan. **African-American Athletes.** A to Z of African Americans; Facts On File Library of American History. New York: Facts On File, 2003. 262 pp. $44.00. ISBN 0-8160-4805-3.

This source profiles over 155 African American athletes who have achieved prominence in major sporting events. Essays are arranged alphabetically by last name, and the career achievements of each athlete are highlighted. Most essays are approximately one page long and include a list of several other sources for further reading. Also includes a general bibliography and an appendix that lists entries by area of activity and year of birth. Indexed. Appropriate for high school and public libraries as well as academic collections.

21. Aaseng, Nathan. **Athletes.** American Indian Lives. New York: Facts On File, 1994. 118 pp. $25.00. ISBN 0-8160-3019-7.

This volume profiles the careers and accomplishments of eleven American Indian athletes. It is illustrated with twenty black-and-white photographs and includes an annotated bibliography. Indexed. Best for public or elementary, middle, or high school libraries.

22. Abbey, Cherie D., ed. **Biography Today: Sports Series.** Biography Today. Detroit, Mich.: Omnigraphics, 2002. 216 pp. $39.00. ISBN 0-7808-0463-5.

Intended for young researchers, this volume presents detailed biographies of ten major sports figures. The information relates to their careers in sports and also their personal lives, education and hobbies. Each entry includes a bibliography of sources for readers to consult for further information. Illustrated with black-and-white photographs. Most appropriate for elementary, middle, or high school libraries.

23. Ashe Jr., Arthur R. **A Hard Road to Glory: A History of the African-American Athlete.** Updated ed. 3 vols. New York: Amistad Press, 1993. $29.95 (v. 1); $39.95 (v. 2); $39.95 (v. 3). ISBN 1-56743-006-6 (v. 1); 1-56743-007-4 (v. 2); 1-56743-008-2 (v. 3).

Originally published in 1988, this is a comprehensive source that traces the history of African American athletes. Arranged chronologically by period (1619–1918, 1919–1945, and since 1946), the three volumes each contain chapters on individual sports and a reference section of championship statistics and individual athletes' records. Each volume is indexed and contains an extensive list of sources. Portfolios of historic photographs are interspersed within each volume. Also available are five separate paperback compendiums on individual sports—boxing, baseball, football, basketball, and track and field—excerpted from the original set.

24. Barnes, Dana R. **Notable Sports Figures.** 4 vols. Farmington Hills, Mich.: Gale Group, 2004. $375.00. ISBN 0-7876-6628-9 (set).

This four-volume biographical encyclopedia contains profiles of over 600 people who have been influential in the world of sport and on sport's impact on our culture and society; this includes the athletes, coaches, administrators, and media figures. It is international in scope and covers the nineteenth, twentieth, and twenty-first centuries. Entries are arranged alphabetically and include basic data, as well as the individual's personal background, early experiences in sport, and career highlights, and an explanation of why the person is considered notable. Illustrated with photographs and informative sidebars. Includes a time line of significant sports events in history, a glossary of terms, and a list of additional sources. Indexed by geographic home, sport/occupation, and general subject.

25. Christensen, Karen, Allen Guttmann, and Gertrud Pfister. **International Encyclopedia of Women and Sports.** 3 vols. New York: Macmillan Reference USA, 2001. $400.00. ISBN 0-02-864954-0 (set); 0-02-864951-6 (v. 1); 0-02-864952-4 (v. 2); 0-02-864953-2 (v. 3).

In this massive but easy-to-maneuver three-volume set, the history and present state of women's participation in international sport are covered more completely than in any similar source. Entries include over 130 biographies, nearly 150 articles on the sports and activities engaged in, over 60 country and region profiles, and additional articles on diverse topics of interest, such as aging, body composition, gender equity, self-defense, the International Women's Games, and the Women's Sports Foundation. Appendixes in volume three list women medalists; number of participants by sport, nation, and continent; and contact information for major women's sports organizations. Illustrated with black-and-white photographs, charts, and sidebars. Volume 1 contains a helpful reader's guide and a list of the articles. Indexed in volume 3.

26. Condon, Robert J. **Great Women Athletes of the 20th Century.** Jefferson, N.C.: McFarland, 1991. 180 pp. $32.50. ISBN 0-89950-555-4.

The author traces the development of women in sports then presents his selection of the top five women athletes, ten pioneers, and thirty-five more great women athletes. The fifty profiles focus on the athletes' sporting-career highlights, statistics, and honors but also include other details of the women's lives. The profiles average three pages in length and are illustrated with good black-and-white photographs of the athletes. References are not included. Indexed.

27. Edelson, Paula. **A to Z of American Women in Sports.** A to Z of Women set, 10 volumes; Facts On File Library of American History. New York: Facts On File, 2002. 278 pp. $44.00. ISBN 0-8160-4565-8.

This valuable biographical encyclopedia contains profiles of over 150 women who have been exceptional achievers in sports. Arranged alphabetically by the athlete's last name, each well-written essay contains a detailed description of the athlete's struggles and accomplishments throughout her career. Suggestions for further reading are included with each profile, and a general list of recommended books and Web sites is also given. Illustrated with fifty black-and-white photographs. Appendixes list the athletes by sport and by date of birth. Indexed. A great source for public and high school libraries as well as for college and university collections.

28. Hawkes, Nena Rey, and John F. Seggar. **Celebrating Women Coaches: A Biographical Dictionary.** Westport, Conn.: Greenwood Press, 2000. 281 pp. $49.95. ISBN 0-313-30912-4.

This unique source brings together biographical profiles of forty-two extraordinary women coaches from diverse sports backgrounds. The entries discuss their career accomplishments but also give family background and other factors that have helped shape their development in the coaching profession. The interview-style entries cover personal data, formative years, sports history, playing career, decision to coach, philosophy of coaching, memorable moments, role models, favorite books, hobbies, and achievements. Includes a list of suggested readings. Indexed.

29. Hickok, Ralph. **A Who's Who of Sports Champions: Their Stories and Records.** Boston: Houghton Mifflin, 1995. 904 pp. $29.95. ISBN 0-395-68195-2.

This ambitious reference source brings together biographical profiles of 2200 Canadian and U.S. individuals representing fifty different sports. Major college and professional sports feature prominently, but many lesser-known sports and individuals are also included, making this a very interesting source. Includes athletes, coaches, hall of fame members, Olympians, and many others. Indexed by sport.

30. Hine, Darlene Clark, and Kathleen Thompson. **Dance, Sports, and Visual Arts.** Vol. 3 of **Facts On File Encyclopedia of Black Women in America.** New York: Facts On File, 1997. 292 pp. $35.00. ISBN 0-8160-3644-6.

Part of an eleven-volume set, this volume is dedicated to black women in dance, sports, and visual arts. It contains a lengthy introduction, alphabetically arranged entries for individuals and groups, a chronology, and a bibliography. Illustrated with fifty black-and-white photographs. Indexed. This set is an updated version of an earlier work by Hine called *Black Women in America*. Appropriate primarily for high school and public libraries.

31. Johnson, Anne Janette. **Great Women in Sports.** Detroit, Mich.: Visible Ink Press, 1996. 552 pp. $17.95. ISBN 0-7876-0873-4.

This source provides detailed profiles of the sporting careers and describes facets of the personal lives of 150 of the most accomplished women athletes. Entries are arranged alphabetically by last name, and the table of contents lists each athlete's name and sport. For each athlete, basic biographical data, career highlights, and awards are outlined in a box alongside the descriptive essay. The essays are two to four pages in length. Most of the entries are illustrated with a good-quality black-and-white photograph of the athlete. Indexed.

32. Johnson, Rafer, special consultant. **Great Athletes.** Rev. ed. 8 vols. With the editors of Salem Press. Pasadena, Calif.: Salem Press, 2002. $475.00. ISBN 1-58765-007-X.

In this new edition of the original 1992 set, over 200 new biographical entries have been added and more than 500 entries have been revised. The total number of pages of text in the eight volumes is 3262. Entries follow a consistent format, and each is several pages in length. All the major American sports are covered, as are the less popular ones, such as tennis, swimming, skiing, and surfing. Each volume is indexed by sport, country, and athlete. Illustrated with photographs of the athletes. Most appropriate for school and public libraries.

33. King, C. Richard, ed. **Native Americans in Sports.** 2 vols. Armonk, N.Y.: M. E. Sharpe, 2004. $159.00. ISBN 0-7656-8054-8.

This two-volume reference work contains comprehensive information about Native American athletes and sports topics, including leagues and teams, organizations, and broader social and cultural themes. Includes a chronology of events and a bibliography for further research, and an index.

34. Layden, Joseph. **Women in Sports: The Complete Book on the World's Greatest Female Athletes.** Los Angeles: General Publishing Group, 1997. 272 pp. $29.95. ISBN 1-57544-064-4.

This biographical encyclopedia profiles more than 250 women athletes, in entries that include the athletes' career highlights and statistics, as well as personal stories. This book documents clearly the increase in women's participation in sports and includes a bibliography of frequently consulted sources. Illustrated with 150 photographs, some color. Indexed.

35. Markel, Robert, Susan Waggoner, and Marcella Smith. **The Women's Sports Encyclopedia.** New York: Henry Holt, 1997. 340 pp. $30.00. ISBN 0-8050-4494-9.

Arranged by type of sport and then by sport, this reference provides a brief history and overview of each major sport and focuses on women's participation throughout its development. Halls of fame, governing bodies, and major events and awards are identified for each sport, and boxes feature other special topics. Brief biographies of the most influential women athletes are provided for each sport, and awards and championship results are listed. Sources are not given. Contains an appendix of "fantastic firsts" and a full index. Written in a lively style, this book is appropriate for school, public, and academic collections.

36. Markoe, Arnold, ed. **The Scribner Encyclopedia of American Lives: Sports Figures.** 2 vols. Thematic Series. New York: C. Scribner's Sons/Gale Group, 2002. $250.00 (set). ISBN 0-684-80665-7 (set).

In this impressive two-volume set, 614 American sports figures are profiled, including many lesser-known yet significant persons. Arranged alphabetically, volume 1 covers A–K; volume 2 covers L–Z. The focus is on American athletes of professional stature, though others are also included. Entries include personal background, early influences and experiences in sport, and career highlights in the sport world as well as outside it. Most entries are illustrated with photographs and include sources for further reading or research. There is a list of entries by occupation or sport, and a full list of entries arranged alphabetically by name.

37. McGovern, Mike. **The Encyclopedia of Twentieth-Century Athletes.** Facts On File Sports Library. New York: Facts On File, 2001. 420 pp. $65.00. ISBN 0-8160-4242-X.

This volume celebrates the accomplishments of a selection of over 900 athletes who were prominent during the century. The brief profiles contain a mix of statistical information, career highlights, and personal stories that describe the character of each of these exceptional individuals. Entries are arranged by sport and then alphabetically by the athlete's name. Illustrated with black-and-white photographs of selected athletes. Appendixes contain a time line of major sporting events that occurred from 1900 to 2000; a directory of organizations, with contact info, arranged by sport and league; and a list of hall of famers and award winners for the major sports. Includes a glossary, a bibliography, and an index.

38. Oglesby, Carole A. **Encyclopedia of Women and Sport in America.** Phoenix, Ariz.: Oryx Press, 1998. 360 pp. $77.95. ISBN 0-89774-993-6.

Appropriate for the high school, college, or college/university library, this encyclopedia profiles over 140 outstanding American women athletes and includes essays on career opportunities for women in sports, about the sports themselves, and on other topics of importance in the world of women's sport. Some of the entries end with a list of references. Illustrated with black-and-white photographs. Contains a list of suggested readings by sport, a selected bibliography, and an index.

39. Page, James A. **Black Olympian Medalists.** Englewood, Colo.: Libraries Unlimited, 1991. 190 pp. $27.50. ISBN 0-87287-618-7.

This biographical source describes the lives and sporting careers of 472 African American Olympic athletes who won their medals between 1904 and 1988. Arranged alphabetically by athlete's name, the profiles are brief but informative. The work also provides additional information; for example, coverage of black managers in baseball, basketball, and football and a section of statistics by type of medal won. Illustrated with black-and-white photographs. Contains a bibliography and an index.

40. Platt, Jim. **Sports Immortals: Stories of Inspiration and Achievement.** With James Buckley Jr., editorial director. Chicago, Ill.: Triumph Books, 2002. 180 pp. $29.95. ISBN 1-57243-460-0.

This beautifully illustrated volume showcases Joel Platt's immense sports memorabilia collection. It contains a great deal of biographical information about the sports figures, as well as interesting stories of how the items were obtained. Covers selected major figures from baseball, basketball, boxing, football, and the Olympic Games, as well as a few examples from other sports. Also contains biographical information about Joel Platt, the collector. Indexed.

41. Porter, David L., ed. **African-American Sports Greats: A Biographical Dictionary.** Westport, Conn.: Greenwood Press, 1995. 429 pp. $70.95. ISBN 0-313-28987-5.

This excellent biographical dictionary covers 166 top African American athletes from twelve different sports: auto racing, baseball, basketball, boxing, cycling, figure skating, football, golf, horse racing, tennis, track and field, and wrestling. Arranged alphabetically, the signed (i.e., individually authored) entries are substantial, usually over two pages in length, and cover the person's career highlights as well as other interesting details; for each, a bibliography of sources is provided. Appendices contain additional information, such as an alphabetical list of entries with their sport indicated, a list of entries by major sport, and name cross-references for eleven married women athletes. Illustrated with a set of twenty-seven black-and-white photographs of the stars. Indexed.

42. Porter, David L., ed. **Biographical Dictionary of American Sports, 1989–1992: Supplement for Baseball, Football, Basketball, and Other Sports.** Westport, Conn.: Greenwood Press, 1992. 752 pp. $79.95. ISBN 0-313-26706-5.

This volume supplements the original four-volume set and includes 618 signed entries, listed alphabetically within each sport, cover athletes, coaches, promoters, and administrators who were influential in auto racing, baseball, basketball, bowling, boxing, communications, football, golf, horse racing, ice hockey, shooting, skating, skiing, swimming, tennis, track and field, wrestling, and miscellaneous other sports, such as cycling, equestrianism, gymnastics, and yachting. Thirty women are included. Most entries are one page in length and cover the person's career highlights as well as other interesting details; for each, a bibliography of sources is provided. Appendices contain a great deal of additional information, such as a list of entries by primary sport and by place of birth; women athletes by sport; major U.S. halls of fame; and sites of Olympic Games. Indexed.

43. Porter, David L., ed. **Biographical Dictionary of American Sports, 1992–1995: Supplement for Baseball, Football, Basketball, and Other Sports.** Westport, Conn.: Greenwood Press, 1995. 811 pp. $109.95. ISBN 0-313-28431-8.

In this second supplement to the original four-volume set, 616 signed entries, listed alphabetically within each sport, cover athletes, coaches, promoters, and administrators who were influential in auto racing, baseball, basketball, bowling, boxing, communications, football, golf, horse racing, ice hockey, shooting, skating, skiing, swimming, tennis, track and field, wrestling, and miscellaneous other sports, such as cycling, equestrianism, gymnastics, and yachting. Thirty women are included. Most entries are one page in length and cover the person's career highlights as well as other interesting details; for each, a bibliography of sources is provided. Appendices contain a great deal of additional information, such as a list of entries by primary sport and by place of birth; women athletes by sport; major U.S. halls of fame; and sites of Olympic Games. Indexed.

44. Porter, David L., ed. **Basketball and Other Indoor Sports.** Vol. 4 of **Biographical Dictionary of American Sports.** Westport, Conn.: Greenwood Press, 1989. 801 pp. $102.95. ISBN 0-313-26261-6.

In this book, yet another excellent reference source edited by Porter, over 550 signed entries, listed alphabetically within each sport, cover athletes, coaches, promoters, and administrators who were influential in basketball, boxing, swimming and diving, wrestling, ice hockey, gymnastics, figure skating, bowling, and weightlifting. Most entries are one page in length and cover the person's career highlights as well as other interesting details; for each, a bibliography of sources is provided. Appendixes contain a great deal of additional information, such as a list of entries by sport and by place of birth; women athletes by sport; ring names and real names of boxers; major U.S. halls of fame; major indoor sporting events; and sites of Olympic Games. Indexed.

45. Porter, David L., ed. **Outdoor Sports.** Vol. 3 of **Biographical Dictionary of American Sports.** Westport, Conn.: Greenwood Press, 1988. 728 pp. $99.95. ISBN 0-313-26260-8.

In this amazing reference source, over 500 signed entries, listed alphabetically within each sport, cover athletes, coaches, promoters, administrators, and others who were influential in auto racing, golf, harness and thoroughbred racing, lacrosse, skiing, soccer, speed skating, tennis, and track and field. Also covered are miscellaneous other sports such as bobsledding, cycling, equestrian, field hockey, and yachting. Most entries are one page in length and cover the person's career highlights as well as other interesting details; for each, a bibliography of sources is provided. Appendices contain a great deal of additional information, such as a list of entries by primary sport and by place of birth; women athletes by sport; major U.S. halls of fame; and sites of Olympic Games. Indexed.

46. Porter, David L., ed. **A Cumulative Index to the Biographical Dictionary of American Sports.** Westport, Conn.: Greenwood Press, 1993. 326 pp. $65.95. ISBN 0-313-28435-0.

This cumulative index covers the first five volumes of the *Biographical Dictionary of American Sports*.

47. Porter, David L., ed. **Latino and African American Athletes Today: A Biographical Dictionary.** Westport, Conn.: Greenwood Press, 2004. 448 pp. $85.00. ISBN 0-313-32048-9.

In this new reference source, the notable author and editor David L. Porter has collected profiles of 175 outstanding contemporary athletes who are notable in over eighteen different sports. One hundred thirteen African Americans and sixty-two Latino Americans are featured. The entries include the career athletic achievements of the selected individuals through 2002, including records, awards, and honors, but also include personal background information and details of the obstacles they have overcome. The work is illustrated with photographs and enhanced with quotes from the athletes. There is a general index, as well as lists of entries organized alphabetically and by sport.

48. Pruyne, Terry W. **Sports Nicknames: 20,000 Professionals Worldwide.** Jefferson, N.C.: McFarland, 2002. 423 pp. $75.00. ISBN 0-7864-1064-7.

This unique reference work identifies over 20,000 nicknames of athletes, teams, stadiums, and events from a range of major sports throughout the world. The first section of the book is arranged by sport, then by name of the athlete. Entries provide the person's position, team, and year of retirement and the story behind the nickname. The nicknames are gathered from all types of sport sources, and the sources are cited. Part two of the book is accessible by nickname, with the person's name and sport provided.

49. Robinson, Matthew J., Mary A. Hums, R. Brian Crow, and Dennis R. Phillips. **Profiles of Sport Industry Professionals.** Gaithersburg, Md.: Aspen, 2001. 485 pp. $29.00. ISBN 0-8342-1796-1.

This book profiles a diverse variety of sport management professionals at all levels, giving readers real examples of the many career opportunities available in the sport industry. Forty-eight persons are identified; their profiles describe how they reached their current position, their job responsibilities, pressures they face, their future aspirations and predictions for the sport industry, and career advice and strategies to those who are just getting started. The table of contents serves as an index to the type of careers and persons profiled.

50. Sherrow, Victoria. **Encyclopedia of Women and Sports.** Santa Barbara, Calif.: ABC-CLIO, 1996. 382 pp. $75.00. ISBN 0-87436-826-X.

This informative encyclopedia of women and sports contains hundreds of brief biographies of women who have been influential in sports, as well as essays on the sports themselves and on important topics, events, and associations pertaining to sport. Contains a unique time line that documents women's participation in sports, beginning with 776 B.C. Illustrated with black-and-white photographs. Includes a comprehensive bibliography and an index.

51. Siegman, Joseph. **Jewish Sports Legends: The International Jewish Sports Hall of Fame.** 3rd ed. Dulles, Va.: Brassey's, 2000. 278 pp. $27.95. ISBN 1-57488-284-8.

Written by the founder of the Jewish Sports Hall of Fame, this volume provides biographical information for every member of the hall of fame. Included for each individual is the date and place of birth, a black-and-white photograph, and a short essay on the significance of the person's accomplishments. Arranged by sport, then alphabetically within each sport. Appendices provide additional information, including description of the Maccabiah Games, with highlights from each year's games, through 1997. Indexed.

52. Silverman, B. P. Robert Stephen. **The 100 Greatest Jews in Sports: Ranked According to Achievement.** Lanham, Md.: Scarecrow Press, 2003. 188 pp. $26.95. ISBN 0-8108-4775-2.

In this ranking of the greatest Jewish athletes in major U.S. sports, the author offers a comparative ranking based on a number of performance categories. Entries contain the athletes' career highlights and statistics, stories of their personal lives, and black-and-white photographs of the athletes. Indexed.

53. Wiggins, David K., ed. **African Americans in Sports.** 2 vols. Armonk, N.Y.: M. E. Sharpe, 2004. $159.00. ISBN 0-7656-8055-6.

This reference source features over 400 articles written about African Americans in sports and includes entries for events, leagues, clubs, associations, and films, as well as the athletes, coaches, and other individuals who have distinguished themselves. Covers a wide range of sports at the amateur, college, and professional levels. The entries are presented in alphabetical order. The set includes a chronology of events from 1777 to the present, a bibliography of sources. Illustrated with photographs. Indexed.

54. Woolum, Janet. **Outstanding Women Athletes: Who They Are and How They Influenced Sports in America.** 2nd ed. Phoenix, Ariz.: Oryx Press, 1998. 412 pp. $68.95. ISBN 1-57356-120-7.

This balanced volume provides a history, biographical information, a bibliography, and statistics on women's participation in sport in the United States. It begins with the historical context and includes a chronological list of milestones in women's participation, beginning in 1804 and ending in 1997. It covers women's role in the Olympic games and reviews of their involvement in each Olympiad. Biographies are provided for eighty-six women who have made a significant contribution to women's sports; sources for further reading are sometimes included. A number of outstanding teams are also profiled. Appendices provide additional information, such as gold medal winners and a list of athletes by sport. Includes a selected bibliography and list of reference sources. Illustrated with photographs. Indexed.

Sport Dictionaries

55. Bernier, Julie N., ed. **Quick Reference Dictionary for Athletic Training.** Thorofare, N.J.: Slack, 2002. 352 pp. $24.00. ISBN 1-55642-461-2.

The first half of this reference contains a dictionary of 2100 terms; the second half of this pocket-sized volume contains twenty-two informative appendices illustrated with photographs and drawings. Official NATA documents are included. This book is intended for students and clinicians in athletic training and is most appropriate for libraries that support athletic training programs or trainers.

55a. Beyer, Erich, ed. **Dictionary of Sport Science: German, English, French.** Schorndorf, Germany: Verlag Karl Hofmann, 1992. 770 pp. $75.00. ISBN 3-7780-3502-9.

This trilingual dictionary was commissioned by the Federal Institute of Sport Science of the Federal Republic of Germany, and is based on the terms and definitions established in the *Sportwissenschaftliches Lexikon* (Schorndorf: Karl Hofmann, 1983), then expanded upon by an international panel of experts. Nine hundred and fifteen German terms appear alphabetically, with respective English and French definitions adjacent to these in the text. Cross-references are included within the entries, while English and French keyword indices are given at the end of the work. Includes a bibliography of sources.

56. Biesel, David B. **Can You Name That Team? A Guide to Professional Baseball, Football, Soccer, Hockey, and Basketball Teams and Leagues.** Metuchen, N.J.: Scarecrow Press, 1993. 239 pp. $29.95. ISBN 0-8108-4552-0.

In one unique collection, the author covers over 950 teams in thirty-six major professional leagues for baseball, football, soccer, basketball, and hockey. It offers a type of genealogy on the leagues and provides team franchise history. The first part of the work is an alphabetical listing by city, state, province, or region and includes an explanation of how each team's name was chosen. The second part contains a "family tree" that lists the teams in each of the thirty-six leagues, and their name changes. Contains an alphabetical listing of the team names, a bibliography, and an index.

57. Cox, Gerry, ed. **The Dictionary of Sport: The Complete Guide for TV Viewers, Spectators and Players.** London: Carlton Books, 1999. 400 pp. $16.00. ISBN 1-85868-748-9.

This unique dictionary covers over 130 sports, organized by general type of sport, such as motor sports or water sports, into twelve chapters. Each chapter begins with a paragraph defining the types of sports included and one page of more general terms and their definitions. The remainder of each chapter presents ten to twelve individual sports such as swimming, diving, water polo, a paragraph giving a basic definition for the sport, and a list of specific terms and idioms and their definitions. Illustrated with black-and-white photographs, this comprehensive and interesting resource covers everything from tug-of-war to pigeon racing. Includes a table of contents and an index.

58. Gendron, Celine. **Acrosport: Acronyms Used for Sport, Physical Education, and Recreation.** Gloucester, ON: Sport Information Resource Centre, 1993. 231 pp. ISBN 0-921817-05-3.

This unique source contains references to 2500 acronyms used in the world of sport. National and international organizations are the focus, but other types of terms are also included. The acronyms are arranged alphabetically and listed with their full name and the location of the organization's headquarters. Indexed by organizational name and by subject. A very useful source for the specialist sport and recreation library.

58a. Haag, Herbert, and Gerald Haag, eds. **Dictionary: Sport, Physical Education, Sport Science.** Kiel, Germany: Institute fur Sport and Sportwissenschaften, 2003. 768 pp. $39.00. ISBN 3-7780-3419-7.

This comprehensive international dictionary defines approximately 2000 of the most important English words and phrases that are found in the study of sport, physical education, and sport science. Arranged alphabetically, the English terms are defined in detail and cross-references are provided to related terms. An appendix offers indices in German, French and Spanish, while a CD-ROM is provided with indices in nine other languages.

59. Labriola, Patrick, and Jurgen Schiffer. **American Sports: Baseball, Football, Basketball: Wörterbuch Grosser Amerikanischer Sportarten: Englisch-Deutsch: Mit Einem Deutschsprachigen Index (Dictionary of Major American Sports: English-German: with a German Index).** Aachen, Germany: Meyer & Meyer Verlag, 1997. 423 pp. $25.00. ISBN 3-89124-437-1.

Intended primarily for the German reader who is interested in following American sports through the major news media, this English-German dictionary covers the vocabulary of baseball, football, and basketball. The three sports are covered separately in the volume, and each sport has an index in German. Following the indexes is a bibliography of sources that includes both English and German titles.

60. Matz, David. **Greek and Roman Sport: A Dictionary of Athletes and Events from the Eighth Century B.C. to the Third Century A.D.** Jefferson, N.C.: McFarland, 1991. 169 pp. $32.50. ISBN 0-89950-558-9.

Beginning with a history of Greek and Roman sport and a discussion of sources of information, this informative work then moves to the dictionary proper, where the athletes and events are defined. Entries include the athlete's name, events participated in, dates of activity, birthplace or place of origin, notable exploits, and a quick note on sources. The work also includes seven essays on particular aspects of the athletes and interesting questions, as well as a number of lists of Greek and Roman athletes and horses. Includes a list of classical texts cited, a glossary of places, and an index.

61. Palmatier, Robert A., and Harold L. Ray. **Sports Talk: A Dictionary of Sports Metaphors.** Westport, Conn.: Greenwood Press, 1989. 227 pp. $49.95. ISBN 0-313-26426-0.

This interesting source presents 1700 sports metaphors alphabetically, describing their meaning, use, and history. An appendix classifies the metaphors according to sport.

62. Phillips, Louis, and Burnham Holmes. **The Complete Book of Sports Nicknames.** 2nd ed. Los Angeles: Renaissance Books, 1998. 350 pp. $12.95. ISBN 1-58063-037-5.

Can you name that . . . nickname? The second edition of this fascinating tour of sports trivia can help. Divided into four sections, the first one lists the nicknames alphabetically, each with an explanation of the origin of the name. The second section contains histories of team names for the NHL, NBA, NFL, baseball's AL and NL, and major U.S. college teams and conferences. The third section contains nicknames of events, plays, and teams. The fourth supplies hundreds of additional nicknames. Contains an index of players' real names. Illustrated sparingly with black-and-white photographs. Earlier edition was titled *Yogi, Babe, and Magic: The Complete Book of Sports Nicknames* (1994).

63. Smith, Stephen L. J. **Dictionary of Concepts in Recreation and Leisure Studies.** Westport, Conn.: Greenwood Press, 1990. 372 pp. $69.50. ISBN 0-313-25262-9.

The author describes this work as a "map" of the field of recreation and leisure studies, and as such, it defines and discusses the path that major concepts in the field—such as amateur status, equity, holiday, mainstreaming, time, and volunteerism—have taken. Certainly, most concepts have continued to develop and change since this work was published, but it is still a good place to begin research. References are provided so that readers can extend their study further. Indexed by name and subject.

Sport Directories

64. Alsop, William L., and Geoffrey C. Fuller. **Directory of Academic Programs in Sport Management.** Morgantown, W.Va.: Fitness Information Technology, 2001. 305 pp. $24.00. ISBN 1-885693-23-0.

This directory compiles data on undergraduate and graduate sport-management programs in the United States and Canada, plus others in Spain, Korea, and Australia. The amount of information included for each entry varies but can include contact information, type of degree offered, admission requirements, faculty names with their rank and specializations, financial aid information, required courses in the program, internship requirements, and additional comments. Overall arrangement is by the name of the college or university, though the keyword alphabetical order can be confusing. Graduate and undergraduate programs are listed separately. An introductory section lists typical jobs that may be obtained by graduates of sport-management programs.

65. **Athletic Scholarships: A Complete Guide.** 2nd ed. Cleveland, Ohio: Conway Greene Publishing, 1998. 565 pp. $20.95. ISBN 1-884669-17-4.

In this very thorough and detailed directory, a great deal of practical information, such as a discussion of eligibility requirements, is given along with the directory of schools. The directory is arranged alphabetically by name of school and includes all the basic contact and identifying information, financial information, graduation rates, and a list of scholarships by sport. Contains separate men's and women's school locators by sport, a state-city locator, and an index.

66. Beazley, Chris, ed. **Blue Book of College Athletics: For Senior, Junior and Community Colleges.** 2003–2004 ed. Montgomery, Ala.: Athletic Publishing, 2003. 826 pp. $44.95. ISBN 1067-750X.

The *Blue Book* is the standard annual directory of college athletic departments. Now in its seventy-third year of publication, it includes over 2400 colleges and more than 49,000 coaches. Athletic departments are listed alphabetically within the following groups: senior colleges, Canadian colleges, and junior colleges, and associations, organizations, and conferences. For each school, detailed contact information is given, including name and phone number of all athletic personnel and many other related personnel, such as band director, events manager, and so forth. Indexed by state and by organization and association. The publisher also offers customized access to its database of coaches' names and athletic-department listings.

67. Blevins, Dave. **Halls of Fame: An International Directory.** Jefferson, N.C.: McFarland, 2004. 320 pp. $49.95. ISBN 0-7864-1509-6.

In addition to sport halls of fame, this reference work identifies many other physical halls of fame, related to such diverse subjects as rock-and-roll music, furniture, crayons, and cartoons. Identifies over 450 halls in the United States, Canada, and other parts of the world. Indexed.

68. Blum, Laurie. **Free Money for Athletic Scholarships.** Henry Holt Reference Book. New York: Henry Holt, 1993. 194 pp. $35.00. ISBN 0-8050-2659-2.

This directory offers a very brief introduction and some advice, then presents the directory of college and university scholarships, arranged alphabetically by state and then school name. For each school, a brief description and contact information is provided, along with the name of the athletic director and the approximate amount of scholarship money awarded. Contains a bibliography of other sources to consult. Indexed.

69. Brooks, Dana, and Ronald Althouse. **The African American Athlete Resource Directory.** Morgantown, W.Va.: Fitness Information Technology, 1996. 200 pp. $19.00. ISBN 1-885693-07-9.

This directory lists sources of information that focus on the African American athletic experience, and specifically, racism in collegiate sports. It includes references to books, periodical articles, newspapers, and films. Some of the lists are composed of references on a topic, such as economic forces or civil rights, while others are grouped by format, such as African American films or halls of fame. It also includes several sample course outlines to assist in the development of a high school or college course on African American sport.

70. Clark, Andy, and Amy Clark. **Athletic Scholarships: Thousands of Grants—and Over \$400 Million—for College-Bound Athletes.** 4th ed. New York: Facts On File, 2000. 338 pp. \$35.00. ISBN 0-8160-4308-6.

This guide to athletic scholarships explains the process for awarding athletic scholarships and describes a "game plan" for completing the process successfully. The directory is arranged by state, and schools are listed alphabetically for each state. Contact information is provided for all relevant offices at the campus, and athletic/sports programs for which scholarships are awarded for men and women are listed. The schools' Web sites are also provided. A sport-by-sport appendix lists all schools that offer the sport, whether or not financial assistance is available.

71. Danilov, Victor J. **Hall of Fame Museums: A Reference Guide.** Westport, Conn.: Greenwood Press, 1997. 275 pp. \$82.95. ISBN 0-313-30000-3.

This source describes 274 halls of fame in the United States and ten other countries, over half of them in the area of sports. The book begins with five chapters that detail the history and development of halls of fame, then provides the directory, which is arranged by subject area. Each entry describes the history and content, facilities available, and type of displays and exhibits and provides contact information, hours of operation, and admission policies. Illustrated with black-and-white photographs. Contains a selected bibliography and an index.

72. Gelbert, Doug. **Sports Halls of Fame: A Directory of Over 100 Sports Museums in the United States.** Jefferson, N.C.: McFarland, 1992. 176 pp. \$38.50. ISBN 0-89950-660-7.

This volume describes over 100 museums and is divided into three sections: national sports museums, multisport museums and those devoted to the achievements of individual sports figures, and local sports museums. Listings include address, phone number, days of operation, fees, and directions for finding the museums from major interstate highways. Each entry contains historical information about the museum and includes special features and a section on other historical attractions in the vicinity. An appendix lists sports museums by state.

73. Gietschier, Steve, comp. **Chase's Sports Calendar of Events 2000.** Chicago: NTC/Contemporary Publishing Group, 2000. 363 pp. \$29.95. ISBN 0-8092-2600-6.

In this annual day-by-day, chronological directory of sports events, the current year's most important events are listed and described briefly, and a selection of major athletes and other sports personalities who were born on the day are mentioned. Type of events include sponsored events that are taking place on the day, historic anniversaries, and holidays that involve sports and recreation. The entries include contact information for current, organized events. Valuable appendices list professional sports league and team addresses, halls of fame, award winners, and major championship winners over time. Illustrated with black-and-white photographs and many lovely drawings. A single index includes names, events, places, sports, and other relevant topics.

74. Guide to ACA-Accredited Camps: 2,400-Plus Day and Resident Camps. Martinsville, Ind.: American Camping Association, 2003. 320 pp. $12.95. ISBN 0-87603-186-6.

This comprehensive guide to camps provides many tips for parents and lists camps according to a Physical and Mental Challenges Index, a Special Clientele Index, a Specific Philosophies Index, and a Targeted Focus Index. The main directory is arranged alphabetically by state. A full index of camps, arranged by name, is provided at the end of the volume. Entries list contact information, the year the camp was established, activities offered, session lengths and capacity, clientele and fees, sponsoring association, facilities, and group-rental information.

75. International Council of Sport Science and Physical Education (ICSSPE). **Vade Mecum: Directory of Sport Science.** 2nd ed. Berlin, Germany: International Council of Sport Science and Physical Education, 2000. 318 pp. $20.00. ISBN 3-7780-7893-3.

This comprehensive, international reference lists fundamental information about the diverse group of sport-science disciplines and directs the reader to other sources for further study. Some examples of the nineteen disciplines include adapted physical activity; biomechanics, kinanthropometry; philosophy of sport; sport and exercise physiology; sport history; and sports vision. Information about each discipline is presented in a consist format: general information, information sources, organizational network, appendix materials, references. Contact information for each author is included. An expanded 3rd edition in CD-ROM format is available on the organization's Web site (http://www.icsspe .org; accessed November 30, 2004).

76. Kobak, Edward T. **The Sports Address Bible and Almanac: the Comprehensive Directory of Sports Addresses.** 16th ed. Santa Monica, Calif.: Global Sports Productions, 2004. 506 pp. $29.95. ISBN 1-891655-10-8.

This annual directory of over 7500 sports addresses covers professional and minor leagues, women's and independent leagues, junior leagues, and amateur leagues in the United States, Canada, Europe, and selected other areas. Comprehensive coverage is provided for organizations in baseball, basketball, football, hockey, soccer, and lacrosse, and more selective coverage is provided for many other sports. Other listings include sports-career development, the media, museums and halls of fame, facilities, sports agencies, collecting, Olympic sports, intercollegiate athletics, state high school organizations, and senior-games organizations. Contact information is provided for each entry, along with a Web or e-mail address when available.

77. Lidor, Ronnie, Tony Morris, Nicole Bardaxoglou, and Benno Becker Jr., eds. **The World Sport Psychology Sourcebook.** 3rd ed. With the International Society of Sport Psychology. Morgantown, W.Va.: Fitness Information Technology, 2001. 240 pp. $29.00. ISBN 1-885693-35-4.

This unique work is a collection of international reports that summarize academic and applied sport-psychology activities taking place in forty-eight countries around the globe. Though there is some variation in the entries, most include general background on the development of sport psychology in the country, national activities, communication channels, academic programs, institutions, certification, relationships among organizations in the country, and contact persons. Includes a list of sport psychology journals and a subject index.

78. McMillin, Challace Joe, and Corey Reffner. **Directory of College and University Coaching Education Programs.** Morgantown, W.Va.: Fitness Information Technology, 1999. 237 pp. $19.00. ISBN 1-885693-14-1.

In the directory of educational programs, 158 undergraduate and twenty-one graduate programs in athletic coaching education are identified. There are separate listings for undergraduate programs that maintain coaching majors, those that offer minors only, and for graduate programs. For each, the authors include contact information, a brief description of the program, and a list of courses offered. Appendices provide a listing by state, tables that compare programs, Web sites, and a reading list.

79. Morgan, Bradley J., ed. **Sports Fan's Connection: An All-Sports-in-One-Directory to Professional, Collegiate, and Olympic Organizations, Events, and Information Sources.** With Peg Bessette, associate editor. Detroit, Mich.: Gale Research, 1992. 584 pp. $86.00. ISBN 0-8103-7954-6; ISSN 1059-0862.

This reference provides coverage of approximately fifty competitive spectator sports played at the professional, collegiate, and Olympic levels. Includes full descriptive and contact information for professional teams and leagues, college and university athletics programs and conferences, organizations, associations, fan clubs, halls of fame, radio and television stations, and other sources of information. Includes master name and keyword indexes.

80. **National Directory of High School Coaches.** 2004–2005 ed. Montgomery, Ala.: Athletic Publishing, 2004. 916 pp. $69.95.

Now in its forty-second year of publication, this annual directory contains listings for over 19,500 high schools in the United States. Entries include the state athletic associations, school name, address, phone numbers, athletic directors, coaching staffs (men and women's) and the names of the sports they coach. All sports are included, and the information is arranged in state, city, and school order. Over 240,000 coaches are identified in this directory.

81. Paciorek, Michael J., and Jeffery A. Jones. **Disability Sport and Recreation Resources.** 3rd ed. Carmel, Ind.: Cooper Publishing Group, 2001. 312 pp. $35.00. ISBN 1-884125-75-1.

This excellent directory of sport and recreation opportunities for individuals with disabilities presents forty-six separate sport and recreation activities. For each, the authors provide national governing bodies, disability sport national governing body, official sport listing, primary disability, sports overview, historical overview, adapted equipment/modified rules, equipment suppliers/manufacturers, and additional resources, including Internet resources. Seven disability sport organizations are also profiled, and appendices provide additional information.

82. **Peterson's Summer Opportunities for Kids and Teenagers.** 20th ed. New York: Peterson's, 2002. 1588 pp. $29.95. ISBN 0-7689-0844-2; ISSN 0894-9417.

This comprehensive directory contains information about nearly 3000 summer camps, visual and performing arts programs, sports programs and clinics, academic courses, internships, volunteer opportunities, travel tours, language programs, and wilderness adventures. Brief profiles contain basic information, including dates and cost and contact addresses with e-mail and a URL for the camp, if available. Primary arrangement of brief profiles is geographic by state and by country when outside the United States. Illustrated with black-and-white photographs and time-saving tables of information that compare programs. Also provides in-depth descriptions of approximately 300 of the offerings and a directory of special-needs accommodations. Date on outside cover of the 20th edition is 2003.

83. Sachs, Michael L., Kevin L. Burke, and Diana C. Schrader, eds. **Directory of Graduate Programs in Applied Sport Psychology.** 6th ed. With the Association for the Advancement of Applied Sport Psychology. Morgantown, W.Va.: Fitness Information Technology, 2001. 334 pp. $24.00. ISBN 1-885693-26-5.

A directory of over 100 institutions that offer masters and doctoral degree programs in applied sport psychology in the United States, Canada, Australia, Great Britain, and South Africa, this source highlights the unique features of each program, as well as the faculty's research interests. Provides contact information, internship and financial aid opportunities, admissions information, and an overall program rating that indicates whether the program offers primarily a research or applied orientation.

84. Smith, Darren L., ed. **Sports Phone Book USA.** Detroit, Mich.: Omnigraphics, 1998. 535 pp. $65.00. ISBN 0-7808-0191-1.

This useful directory provides detailed contact information for major sports organizations, facilities, and services primarily in the United States, with some coverage of Canada. It includes listings for professional, collegiate, amateur and community sport leagues, teams, and organizations, as well as halls of fame, media sources, and sporting-goods manufacturers and retailers. Web sites and e-mail addresses are often identified. Arranged in two sections, the first is alphabetical by organization name, and the second is arranged by subject classification. The classified listing is indexed.

85. **Sports Scholarships and College Athletic Programs.** 4th ed. New York: Peterson's. 876 pp. $26.95. ISBN 0-7689-0273-8.

The most comprehensive sports scholarship guide, Peterson's contains entries for over 1700 colleges and universities, and it includes all NCAA-sanctioned sports. It provides several chapters that offer advice on the process of finding financial aid and includes separate listings for four-year and two-year institutions. Indexed by sport, sports association, and state. A 5th edition is expected in 2004.

86. Wheeler, Dion. **A Parent's and Student-Athlete's Guide to Athletic Scholarships: Getting Money Without Being Taken for a (Full) Ride.** Lincolnwood, Ill.: Contemporary Books, 2000. 458 pp. $14.95. ISBN 0-8092-2443-7.

This guide to finding appropriate athletic scholarships presents practical information for parents and students. In the first part of the book, the entire process is described in clear terms, from writing a cover letter to assembling critical documents to visiting colleges to negotiating an agreement. Contains a glossary of terms and a directory of colleges and universities that offer athletic scholarships. The directory is arranged by state and then alphabetically by college name. Each entry contains contact information (address and phone), the school's athletic affiliation, and lists of the men's and women's sport programs that are available.

Sport Encyclopedias

87. Arlott, John, ed. **The Oxford Companion to Sports and Games.** New York: Oxford University Press, 1975. 1143 pp. ISBN 0-19-211538-3.

Though dated, this dictionary is still a complete and very useful reference source. It includes entries for sports, people, and teams and includes bibliographical references for most sports.

88. Bell, Daniel. **Encyclopedia of International Games.** Jefferson, N.C.: McFarland, 2003. 591 pp. $75.00. ISBN 0-7864-1026-4.

This unique encyclopedia describes 175 international multisport competitions (similar to the Olympics) that have been held since 1896. Included are regional games (for example, Nordic Games and Central African Games) and games for specific populations or professions (for example, World Games for the Deaf and World Police and Fire Games). Entries contain an essay describing the history and unique features of the games, then listed for each is the host city, host nation, and dates of the games and the number of athletes, sports, and nations participating. Additional tables list the medals won. Substantial appendices show games by year, by nation, and by host city; the 100 largest games, by number of athletes and number of nations; the fifty-four largest games, by number of sports; and other games. Contains a significant bibliography and an index. Appropriate for college and university collections as well as public libraries.

89. Brucato, Thomas W. **Major Leagues.** American Sports History. Lanham, Md.: Scarecrow Press, 2001. 283 pp. $55.00. ISBN 0-8108-3908-3.

This source provides a register of major league teams in baseball, football, basketball, hockey, soccer, indoor soccer, arena football, tennis, roller hockey, and lacrosse. First, teams are arranged geographically by city or location, with a brief profile of each team's history. Next, teams are listed by league, with the years each one played in the league. It also contains a chapter that lists every team name ever used in the major leagues and another with information on the origins of team names, arranged alphabetically. Current through the summer of 2000. Also contains a bibliography.

90. **Canada: Our Century in Sport, 1900–2000.** Markham, ON: Fitzhenry & Whiteside, 2002. 592 pp. $60.00. ISBN 1-55041-636-7.

In this commemorative volume, Canada's most noteworthy athletes and sport accomplishments are presented. Beautifully illustrated, the encyclopedia contains Sports Hall of Fame members, a full record of Olympic participation, and various other Canadian award winners and historic events. Contains results and records, but also athlete biographies and essays on a wide range of related sport topics.

91. Cox, Richard William, Grant Jarvie, and Wray Vamplew, eds. **Encyclopedia of British Sport.** Santa Barbara, Calif.: ABC-CLIO, 2000. 463 pp. $75.00. ISBN 1-85109-344-3.

This comprehensive encyclopedia contains over 300 signed entries that define and describe individual sports, controversies, issues and concepts, key individuals, famous clubs, competitions, events, and incidents of importance in the world of British sport. It includes everything from the Admiral's Cup to St. Andrews to wrestling. The entries are arranged alphabetically, and each entry contains an essay, a brief list of references, sources for further reading, Web sites and cross-references. Illustrated with a selection of carefully chosen black-and-white photographs. Indexed.

92. **The Encyclopaedia of Sports Medicine.** 10 vols. Malden, Mass.: Blackwell Science, 1988–2003. $130.00/vol. ISBN 0-632-01963-8 (v. 1); 0-632-05348-8 (v. 2); 0-632-05911-7 (v. 3); 0-632-03331-2 (v. 4); 0-632-03785-7 (v. 5); 0-86542-904-9 (v. 6); 0-632-05094-2 (v. 7); 0-632-05084-5 (v. 8); 0-632-05392-5 (v. 9); 0-632-05813-7 (v. 10).

This multivolume IOC Medical Commission set is published in collaboration with the International Federation of Sports Medicine. Each volume presents state-of-the-art information on current topics of interest to the clinical and scientific sports-medicine community. Topics in the ten existing volumes include nutrition, endurance, strength and power, biomechanics, women in sport, children and adolescents in sport, Olympic athletes, rehabilitation, and other aspects of sports-injury prevention and care. Volume 1, *The Olympic Book of*

Sports Medicine (1988), edited by A. Dirix, H. G. Knuttgen and K. Tittel; volume 2, *Endurance in Sport* (2000), edited by R. J. Shephard and P.-O. Astrand; volume 3, *Strength and Power in Sport* (2003), edited by P. V. Komi; volume 4, *Sports Injuries: Basic Principles of Prevention and Care* (1993), edited by P.A.F.H. Renstrom; volume 5, *Clinical Practice of Sports Injury Prevention and Care* (1994), edited by P.A.F.H. Renstrom; volume 6, *The Child and Adolescent Athlete* (1996), edited by O. Bar-Or; volume 7, *Nutrition in Sport* (2000), edited by R. J. Maughan; volume 8, *Women in Sport* (2000), edited by B. L. Drinkwater; volume 9, *Biomechanics in Sport* (2000), edited by V. Zatsiorsky; volume 10, *Rehabilitation of Sports Injuries: Scientific Basis* (2003), edited by W. R. Frontera.

93. Fortin, Francois. **Sports: The Complete Visual Reference.** Buffalo, N.Y.: Firefly Books, 2000. 372 pp. $39.95. ISBN 1-55209-540-1.

This incredible resource covers 127 sports, including traditional Olympic events as well as many sports that are featured less often, such as rock climbing, netball, and parachuting, surfing, and motor sports. A beautifully illustrated guide, it provides an accurate point of reference for the history, rules, and playing environment for each sport. Details cover the equipment, playing area, techniques, and essential facts about competition in each sport. Indexed.

94. Franck, Irene M., and David M. Brownstone. **Famous First Facts about Sports.** Bronx, N.Y.: H. W. Wilson, 2001. 903 pp. $105.00. ISBN 0-8242-0973-7.

Ever wonder what the first U.S. croquet club was called? Wonder no more with this marvelous source. With over 5400 entries that cover over 100 sports, this fascinating reference work is a great addition to the reference shelf and is appropriate for casual browsing as well as finding rarely known first facts. Modeled after the traditional *Famous First Facts*, entries in this volume are organized chronologically under each sport, following from a list of the sports that is presented at the beginning of the text. There are no illustrations, but the very extensive indexes occupy two-thirds of the volume and are arranged by subject, year, month and day, personal name, and geographic place (nation, state/ province, or city). Checking the subject index, I quickly found that the Park Place Croquet Club was founded in Brooklyn, New York, in 1864.

95. Golden, Mark. **Sport in the Ancient World From A to Z.** The Ancient World from A to Z. New York: Routledge, 2004. 208 pp. $75.00. ISBN 0-415-24881-7.

This comprehensive historical work contains over 700 entries, arranged alphabetically. Topics include a good variety of Greek and Roman sporting activities, such as ancient athletic festivals and major festival locations, the athletes, the role of women, equipment used, prizes won. Each entry contains references to additional sources of information. Includes a map showing significant places and a time line of important events and developments.

96. Hickok, Ralph. **The Encyclopedia of North American Sports History.** 2nd ed. Facts On File Sports Library. New York: Facts On File, 2002. 594 pp. $75.00; $24.95 (pbk.). ISBN 0-8160-4660-3; 0-8160-5071-6 (pbk.).

This comprehensive reference is arranged alphabetically and provides quick access to 1600 brief essays on the history and development of Canadian and U.S. sports. Entries cover not only the sports themselves but also related sporting events, awards, and information on the athletes, cities, stadiums, organizations, and governing bodies. Includes address and Web site information where appropriate. This is an important reference for every library. Illustrated with black-and-white photographs. Indexed.

97. Hoffmann, Frank W., and William G. Bailey. **Sports and Recreation Fads.** New York: Haworth Press, 1991. 397 pp. $49.95; $14.95 (pbk.). ISBN 1-56024-056-3; 0-918393-92-2 (pbk.).

This review of sports-and-recreation fads that have occurred in American popular culture provides brief coverage of over 100 fads. It is arranged alphabetically by the name of the fad and includes many traditional sports, such as baseball, ping pong, and volleyball but also many other recreational activities such as charades, hula hoops, the Ouija board, and yo-yos. Each entry is one to two pages and contains a bibliography. Illustrated with poorly reproduced photographs and drawings. Indexed.

98. Kirsch, George, Othello Harris, and Claire E. Nolte, eds. **Encyclopedia of Ethnicity and Sports in the United States.** Westport, Conn.: Greenwood Press, 2000. 530 pp. $143.95. ISBN 0-313-29911-0.

Recommended for all types of libraries, this comprehensive reference source examines, from a sociological perspective, the sporting experience of Native Americans, African Americans, and other immigrant groups in the United States. Entries are in alphabetical order and include people, racial and ethnic groups, ethnic games, mainstream sports, and ethnic and racial institutions. Some examples are Michelle Kwan, Lacrosse, Hungarians, National Indian Athletic Association, and Baseball. Entries range in length from one page to several pages, and each contains its own selected bibliography. Also includes a general, selected bibliography at the end of the volume, and an index.

99. LaBlanc, Michael L., and Mary K. Ruby, eds. **Professional Sports Team Histories.** 4 vols. Detroit, Mich.: Gale Research, 1994. $49.00/vol. ISBN 0-8103-8859-6 (v. 1); 0-8103-8860-x (v. 2); 0-8103-8861-8 (v. 3); 0-8103-8862-6 (v. 4).

This multivolume set focuses on the history and evolution of the teams in four of the United States' major spectator sports: baseball, basketball, football, and hockey. A general essay in each volume traces the development of the sport over time. Each team is then profiled in an essay that highlights significant leaders and players, other personnel, franchise moves, name changes, team performance, and overall growth of the team. Provides a "Team Information at a Glance" section for quick facts. Each volume is illustrated with many black-and-white photographs of the sports' best; each volume is also indexed.

100. Levinson, David, and Karen Christensen, eds. **Encyclopedia of World Sport.** New York: Oxford University Press, 1999. 488 pp. $45.00. ISBN 0-19-513195-9.

A condensation of the same authors' three-volume work published by ABC-CLIO in 1996. Includes a bibliography and an index.

101. Levinson, David, and Karen Christensen, eds. **Encyclopedia of World Sport: From Ancient Times to the Present.** 3 vols. Santa Barbara, Calif.: ABC-CLIO, 1996. $275.00. ISBN 0-87436-819-7 (set).

A useful reference source for any type of library, this important three-volume work serves as a historical and cross-cultural survey of world sport but also contains articles on social issues in sport, such as aggression, ethnicity, gambling, religion, and technology. Each of nearly 300 sport entries describes the origin, development, and practice of the sport and includes a bibliography. Arranged alphabetically, entries in volume 1 cover acrobatics to gymnastics; entries in volume 2 cover handball to rugby union; and volume 3 covers sail boarding to yachting. Each volume includes a contents list for all three volumes; and the last volume includes a bibliography and an index. Also available from the publisher as an electronic book.

102. Liponski, Wojciech. **World Sports Encyclopedia.** St. Paul, Minn.: MBI, 2003. 596 pp. $50.00. ISBN 0-7603-1682-1.

With over 3000 entries that cover sports and games across the world, this reference source is appropriate for both public and academic libraries. In addition to all the Olympic sports, entries cover ancient and traditional sports as well as exercise-related topics such as aerobics. The book is unique in that it also provides information on the origin, etymology, cultural background, history, attire, equipment, and rules of so many international sports and games. Illustrated with over 1200 photographs, charts, and tables.

103. Messina, Lynn M. **Sports in America.** The Reference Shelf. New York: H. W. Wilson, 2001. 200 pp. $30.00. ISBN 0-8242-0999-0.

This slim volume is divided into six sections, each looking at sports from a different perspective: America's pastimes; youth sports; college and semipro sports; the good, the great, and the ugly; the business of sports; and the Olympics. The brief articles in each section are reprinted primarily from popular news sources such as *Sports Illustrated* and *Newsweek*. Most appropriate for high school and public libraries. Includes a bibliography and an index.

104. Miller, Ernestine G. **Making Her Mark: Firsts and Milestones in Women's Sports.** Chicago: Contemporary Books / McGraw-Hill, 2002. 401 pp. $16.95. ISBN 0-07-139053-7.

With over 1500 entries—from archery to dogsled racing to track and field to wrestling—that chronicle American women's achievement in fifty sports, this source presents the history of those milestone events and records. Arranged by sport, the achievements are described briefly and listed in chronological order, making it easy to chart the progress women have made over the years. Illustrated with occasional black-and-white photographs.

105. Mohr, Merilyn Simonds. **The New Games Treasury: More Than 500 Indoor and Outdoor Favorites with Strategies, Rules and Traditions.** Enlarged ed. New York: Houghton Mifflin, 1997. 432 pp. $23.00. ISBN 1-57630-058-7.

This is an enlarged edition of *The Games Treasury* (1993), by the same author. And it is indeed a treasury of history, rules, and little-known facts about new and old games. Divided into five sections, each deals with a different category of games: board games, those with playing pieces, card games, games of guessing and deduction, and outdoor games. Included in each entry is information such as other names for the game, number of players needed, equipment, duration, complexity, and a full description of rules and the object of play. Well illustrated with many drawings. Indexed.

106. Pollak, Mark. **Sports Leagues and Teams: An Encyclopedia, 1871 through 1996.** Jefferson, N.C.: McFarland, 1998. 708 pp. $65.00. ISBN 0-7864-0252-0.

This reference describes all the recognized professional leagues in baseball, basketball, bowling, football, golf, ice hockey, lacrosse, rodeo, roller hockey, softball, tennis, and volleyball, including women's and senior leagues. Detailed information is provided for individual teams as well. Entries include the city, nickname, home arena or playing field, championships won, and current status when appropriate.

107. Sparhawk, Ruth. **American Women in Sport, 1887–1987: A 100-Year Chronology.** Metuchen, N.J.: Scarecrow Press, 1989. 149 pp. $31.00. ISBN 0-8108-2205-9.

This chronology of American women's role in sport begins with the 1887–1916 era and continues through Title IX. Each of the entries is usually a sentence stating a particular individual's role during a given year, or a description of an event that took place. The only drawback is that the research ended in 1987. Illustrated with black-and-white photographs of a number of prominent leaders. The book also contains a list of references, a list of organizations, an index of names, and an index of sports.

108. Zumerchik, John. **Encyclopedia of Sports Science.** 2 vols. New York: Macmillan Library Reference USA, 1997. $295.00 (set). ISBN 0-02-897506-5 (set); 0-02-864665-7 (v. 1); 0-02-864666-5 (v. 2).

This unique encyclopedia introduces the physical, biological, medical, and scientific principles of sports in a well-organized and understandable format. Whether the question is in physics or physiology, this reference will help answer it. Organized in two parts, the encyclopedia first treats the sports and associated skills themselves, then in the second part deals with the body's physiological systems and topics. Cross-references lead the reader to related articles. Illustrated with black-and-white photographs and many drawings and diagrams that show why and how the scientific principles work. Each chapter contains a bibliography of sources so the reader may extend the study. Indexed in volume 2.

Sport Guides and Handbooks

109. Ashley, Clifford W. **The Ashley Book of Knots.** New York: Doubleday, 1993. 620 pp. $75.00. ISBN 0-385-04025-3.

This incredible bible of knots, originally published in 1944, is the masterful result of the author's forty-year collection of notes on knots that serve a prescribed purpose, such as for a sailor's use. The author eloquently described 3854 different knots and clearly illustrated them with over 7000 drawings. Includes a list of books that contain information on knots, and an index.

110. Barbarash, Lorraine. **Multicultural Games: 75 Games from 43 Cultures.** Champaign, Ill.: Human Kinetics, 1997. 137 pp. $15.95. ISBN 0-88011-565-3.

Intended for physical-education teachers, this source helps teachers meet content standards for multicultural awareness developed by the National Association for Sport and Physical Education. Games are arranged by area of the world and then by country. Information for each game includes the country of origin, number and age of participants, gross motor rating of the game, competitive level, and play area and equipment required. Also included for each game are a cultural fact and a cultural question, meant to encourage discussion about cultural differences.

111. Berlow, Lawrence H. **Sports Ethics: A Reference Handbook.** Santa Barbara, Calif.: ABC-CLIO, 1994. 204 pp. $39.50. ISBN 0-87436-769-7.

This book tackles some of the major questions in sports ethics and provides resources for additional investigation of the issues. Essays identify and describe the controversies, excerpts from documents provide evidence, and annotated lists of other sources offer an opportunity for further study. Includes a chronology of major sports ethics issues, from 1869 to 1994, and brief profiles of twenty individuals who have been major players on ethical issues. Covers issues such as racism, drug abuse, women in sports, and media relations.

112. Bull, R. Charles, and William O. Roberts. **Bull's Handbook of Sports Injuries.** 2nd ed. New York: McGraw-Hill, 2004. 834 pp. $64.95. ISBN 0-07-140291-8.

A comprehensive guide to sports injuries, this source is intended for use primarily by health professionals, but its concise entries are valuable for general reference also. It covers anatomy, diagnostic considerations, management, complications, and prevention of the most common sports injuries, as well as typical injuries for specific sports. Also includes discussion of other topics such as drugs and ergogenic aids, muscle training and conditioning, and endurance training. This is a revised edition of *Handbook of Sports Injuries* (1999). Includes bibliographical references and an index.

113. Carroll, Bob. **The Sports Video Resource Guide: A Fan's Sourcebook for All the Best in Sports Videos.** New York: Fireside / Simon & Schuster, 1992. 254 pp. $12.00. ISBN 0-671-73446-6.

This guide to videos is arranged by sport and covers baseball, basketball, football, hockey, soccer, boxing, tennis, golf, and other sports. In the sport-specific listings are instructional, historical, team, and individual biographical videos. Most of the entries are brief and contain a short sentence of description, along with year of release, running time, and price. Entries in the category "movies" have additional detail. Indexed by sport and by title.

114. Chalip, Laurence H., Arthur T. Johnson, and Lisa Stachura, eds. **National Sports Policies: An International Handbook.** Westport, Conn.: Greenwood Press, 1996. 442 pp. $125.95. ISBN 0-313-28481-4.

This collection of essays compares and examines the national sports policies of fifteen countries around the world. From Canada to India to Norway to the United Kingdom, the public policymaking with regard to sports is contrasted. Topics such as funding, organization, administration, education, and legal and social aspects are all present in this interesting, scholarly analysis. Illustrated with figures and tables. Indexed.

115. Chandler, Timothy, Mike Cronin, and Wray Vamplew. **Sport and Physical Education: The Key Concepts.** Routledge Key Guides. New York: Routledge, 2002. 252 pp. $19.95. ISBN 0-415-23142-6.

Intended for students of sport studies and physical education at any level, this handbook introduces major concepts and defines terminology in the discipline. Arranged alphabetically with cross-references and with other suggested reading at the end of each entry. The diverse entries cover such topics as ageism, amateurism, body, cultural imperialism, energy, leadership, martial arts, nationalism, special Olympics, and violence. Includes a full bibliography and an index.

116. Corbett, Doris, John Cheffers, and Eileen Crowley Sullivan, eds. **Unique Games and Sports Around the World: A Reference Guide.** Westport, Conn.: Greenwood Press, 2001. 407 pp. $70.95. ISBN 0-313-29778-9.

This source describes and includes the rules for over 300 games and sports from around the world. Arranged geographically, the six chapters include games from Africa, the Americas, Asia, Europe, the Middle East, and Oceania. There is also an index of games by continent, country, and contributor. The description of each game includes information on age and number of players; object of the game; costume or apparel and equipment required; arena, field, or space required; time length of the game; symbolism; and rules of play, including scoring. This interesting source is intended to be used to compare patterns of culture and to examine play and games from the sociological and anthropological perspective.

117. Craig, Steve. **Sports and Games of the Ancients.** Sports and Games through History. Westport, Conn.: Greenwood Press, 2002. 271 pp. $49.95. ISBN 0-313-31600-7.

Divided into seven chapters representing geographic regions of the world, this work describes sports and games in ancient times. Each chapter begins with a historical overview of sports, games, and play in the region. In-depth information is then provided on the most significant sports and games. Each sport or game is defined, a history is provided, and for most, equipment is described, brief rules or instructions are given, variations of the sport or game are explained, and a bibliography is included. Entries vary in length, depending on the amount of information discovered. Illustrated with black-and-white photographs and diagrams. Contains a general bibliography and an index.

118. Crego, Robert. **Sports and Games of the 18th and 19th Centuries.** Sports and Games through History. Westport, Conn.: Greenwood Press, 2003. 274 pp. $49.95. ISBN 0-313-31610-4.

Divided into seven chapters representing geographic regions of the world, this work describes sports and games in the eighteenth and nineteenth centuries. Each chapter begins with a historical overview of sports and games in the region. In-depth information is then provided on the most significant sports and games. Each sport or game is defined, a history is provided, and for most, equipment is described, brief rules or instructions are given, variations of the sport or game are explained, and a bibliography is included. Entries vary in length, depending on the amount of information discovered. Illustrated with black-and-white photographs and diagrams. Contains a general bibliography and an index.

119. Davidson, Judith A., ed. and comp. **Sport on Film and Video: The North American Society for Sport History Guide.** With Daryl Alder, comp. Metuchen, N.J.: Scarecrow Press, 1993. 194 pp. $36.50. ISBN 0-8108-2739-5.

This useful volume is a filmography of productions appropriate for educational use (e.g., in a sport-history course or in elementary school). It does not include how-to or commercial films. Topics range from general to historical, sociological, and psychological coverage of sport. Arranged alphabetically by title, this book briefly describes each film's content and indicates its date, running time, format, color format, age appeal, chronological placement regarding its subject (for example, Depression era or post-WWII), and distributor. Indexed separately by topic, name, and distributor, this filmography offers multiple access points.

120. Deardorff II, Donald L. **Sports: A Reference Guide and Critical Commentary, 1980–1999.** American Popular Culture. Westport, Conn.: Greenwood Press, 2000. 361 pp. $99.95. ISBN 0-313-30445-9.

This excellent guide to the literature of sports in American culture is an academic reference source and focuses on cultural and social aspects of sports. Each chapter covers a broad topic, such as popular culture, education, or sociology, and presents a lengthy essay describing the most significant sources on the topic. At the end of each chapter, a bibliography is given, listing books and journals. Appendices provide a chronology of important American sports events from 1980 to 2000; and additional sources of information such as halls of fame, libraries, museums, and Web sites. Indexed.

121. **Entertainment, Media and Advertising Market Research Handbook.**
6th ed. Norcross, Ga.: Richard K. Miller & Associates, 2004. 499 pp. $385.00.
ISBN 1-57783-049-0.

This publication was previously published as the *Entertainment, Sports and Leisure Market Research Handbook* (2002). It presents data and information on media transnational corporations and consolidation, branding, licensing, naming rights, sponsorship, cable networks and direct broadcast satellite, major sports events, spectator sports, sports broadcasting, professional team sports, sports marketing, extreme sports, and sports venues.

122. Field, Shelly. **Career Opportunities in the Sports Industry.** 3rd ed. New York: Checkmark Books / Facts On File, 2004. 288 pp. $49.50. ISBN 0-8160-5091-0.

This guide to careers contains profiles of over seventy job titles related to sports. The entries show the potential career ladder of the job, provide a detailed description of the work, indicate a salary range and the educational or experience prerequisites, best geographical locations for this type of position, and other advice on entering the field. Useful appendices provide additional information on degree programs, associations, and trade unions. Includes a bibliography and a glossary. Indexed.

123. Hastings, Penny. **Sports for Her: A Reference Guide for Teenage Girls.** Westport, Conn.: Greenwood Press, 1999. 264 pp. $49.95. ISBN 0-313-30551-X.

Along with the basic information on a variety of sports that are popular with and available to high school girls, and more detailed information on ten sports, this source also covers issues and challenges that typically accompany participation in sports, such as nutrition, drugs, tryouts, interactions with coaches, athletic scholarships, and careers in sports. Illustrated with photographs, diagrams, and tables. Includes a list of resources and an index. Best for middle school, public, and high school libraries.

124. Hillstrom, Kevin, Laurie Hillstrom, and Roger Matuz. **The Handy Sports Answer Book.** Detroit, Mich.: Visible Ink Press, 1998. 594 pp. $19.95. ISBN 1-57859-075-2.

This general sports trivia source answers 1000 questions that most of us never dreamed of asking, such as, "How much champagne does the Stanley Cup hold?" For trivia buffs, or just an entertaining browse, this is a good source. Includes chapters on auto racing, baseball, boxing, basketball, extreme sports, football, golf, hockey, horse racing, the Olympics, soccer, tennis, and volleyball. Illustrated with 150 photographs.

125. Loeffelbein, Robert L. **The Recreation Handbook: 342 Games and Other Activities for Teams and Individuals.** Jefferson, N.C.: McFarland, 1992. 237 pp. $27.50. ISBN 0-89950-744-1.

A unique handbook that features 342 informal, spontaneously created sports, games, and other recreational activities for children and teens, this is a recreation leader's dream. The games are arranged by type and include aquatic games, basketball-type, bat and ball, bowling-type, kicking-type, combative, hand striking and throwing, mallet-club-stick, paddle-and-racquet, and table games and more. Each entry includes age level, organizational level, number of players, supervision needed, playing time, space needed, equipment needed, and the directions for playing. Most entries include an illustration, usually a drawing or a photograph.

126. Mellion, Morris B., Margot Putukian, and Christopher C. Madden. eds. **Sports Medicine Secrets.** The Secrets Series. 3rd ed. Philadelphia: Hanley & Belfus, 2003. 618 pp. $34.95. ISBN 1-56053-548-2.

This popular series of medical books uses the question-and-answer approach to explain 110 prevalent medical conditions encountered by athletes. Intended primarily for care providers, the concise chapters are written by physicians and experts in sports medicine. Each topic is covered in fifteen to thirty questions and answers; a bibliography of scientific literature is provided for each. Topics are arranged by subject category, including medical supervision of the athlete, special populations, conditioning, environmental concerns, protective equipment, nutrition, behavioral concerns, general medical problems that apply to athletes, overuse injuries, rehabilitation, and imaging, as well as twenty-eight specific sport activities.

127. Mellion, Morris B., W. Michael Walsh, Christopher Madden, Margot Putukian, and Guy L. Shelton. **Team Physician's Handbook.** 3rd ed. Philadelphia: Hanley & Belfus, 2002. 804 pp. $69.95. ISBN 1-56063-441-9.

Arranged in outline format for quick scanning of the content, this medical handbook covers a wide range of topics and considerations for advising and treating the injured athlete. Specific activities such as bicycling, dance, gymnastics, rowing, rugby, wrestling, and many more are also covered in individual chapters. Illustrated with black-and-white photographs, charts and drawings. Indexed.

128. Pawson, Des. **The Handbook of Knots.** New York: Dorling Kindersley, 1998. 160 pp. $17.00. ISBN 0-7894-2395-2.

This guide to knots features over 100 different knots and clearly demonstrates how they are tied. Includes introductory material on rope construction, terms, and basic knot-tying techniques. The instructions are illustrated with excellent step-by-step color photographs. The entries contain quick-reference symbols for *camping*, *fishing*, *sailing*, *climbing*, *decorative*, or *general*, to identify the purpose of the knot. Contains a glossary and an index.

129. Postman, Andrew, and Larry Stone. **The Ultimate Book of Sports Lists.** New York: Black Dog & Leventhal, 2003. 432 pp. $14.95. ISBN 1-57912-277-9.

In this very browsable book of sports trivia, the authors cover the gamut of topics in creating their lists of the best, worst, classiest, biggest, most dramatic, most exciting, most memorable, and most moving moments in sports.

Arranged by general topic in sixteen sections, the book contains 283 lists that will entertain readers and bring them back for more. Indexed.

130. Puhalla, Jim, Jeff Krans, and Mike Goatley. **Sports Fields: A Manual for Design, Construction, and Maintenance.** Chelsea, Mich.: Ann Arbor Press, 1999. 464 pp. $65.00. ISBN 1-57504-070-0.

A comprehensive technical reference source for those who design, construct, renovate, or maintain sports facilities, this work will be most appropriate in academic libraries or public libraries. Contains complete information on the principles of turf grass culture, including selection of grass, soil science, aeration, thatch, mowing, irrigation, drainage, and chemicals; on sports fields for specific sports such as baseball and softball, football and rugby, soccer, croquet, tennis, track and field, volleyball, and playgrounds; and on quality, evaluation, and safety of sports facilities. Additional information is provided on surveying, sand fields, stadiums, paints, and covers. References are provided with each chapter. Illustrated with black-and-white photographs, tables and diagrams. Contains an extensive glossary and an index.

131. Scarrott, Martin, ed. **Sport, Leisure and Tourism Information Sources: A Guide for Researchers.** Boston: Butterworth-Heinemann, 1999. 267 pp. $62.95. ISBN 0-7506-3864-8.

This research guide is aimed at the needs of undergraduates who are beginning to work within the interdisciplinary field of sport, leisure, and tourism. It contains articles on various aspects of research, such as using libraries, finding statistics, navigating the Internet, and accessing the periodical literature of these disciplines. It utilizes major U.K. and European sources. An appendix contains a selection of books, and there is also a glossary of terms and an index.

132. Siekmann, Robert C. R., and Janwillem Soek. **Basic Documents of International Sports Organizations.** With T.M.C. Asser Instituut. Boston: Kluwer Law International, 1998. 626 pp. $175.00. ISBN 90-411-1069-0.

A useful tool for legal practice as well as for academic research in sport and the law, this work offers the basic documents (statutes, rules, and constitutions) governing general international sport organizations, such as the International Olympic Committee, the International Paralympic Committee, and the Association of National Olympic Committees. It also includes constitutions, bylaws, and statutes of the International Olympic Federations for specific sporting activities, such as the International Baseball Federation, the International Rowing Federation, and the International Triathlon Union. Indexed by subject.

133. Singer, Robert N., Heather A. Hausenblas, and Christopher M. Janelle, eds. **Handbook of Sport Psychology.** 2nd ed. New York: John Wiley, 2001. 876 pp. $95.00. ISBN 0-471-37995-6.

Contributors from around the world present the latest theories, research, and applications in the field of sport psychology. Thirty-three chapters address the most pertinent information on the following topics: skill acquisition, psychological characteristics of high-level performance, motivation, psychological techniques for individual performance, life-span development, exercise and health psychology, and future directions. Indexed by author and by subject.

134. **Sports in North America: A Documentary History.** 7 vols. Gulf Breeze, Fla.: Academic International Press, 1992–. $100.00/vol. ISBN 0-87569-188-9 (v. 1, pt. 1); 0-87569-189-7 (v. 1, pt. 2); 0-87569-136-6 (v. 2); 0-87569-156-0 (v. 3); 0-87569-135-8 (v. 4); 0-87569-148-X (v. 5); 0-87569-197-8 (v. 6); 0-87569-224-9 (v. 8).

Using primary-sources, this scholarly series brings alive the history of sports in North America from the colonial era to today. Expected to be complete in ten to twelve volumes, there are seven volumes available at the time of this writing: vol. 1, *Sports in the Colonial Era, 1618–1783/Sports in the New Republic, 1784–1820*, edited by Thomas L. Altherr; vol. 2, *Origins of Modern Sports, 1920–1840*, edited by Larry Menna; vol. 3, *The Rise of Modern Sports, 1840–1860*, edited by George B. Kirsch; vol. 4, *Sports in War, Revival and Expansion, 1860–1880*, edited by George B. Kirsch; vol. 5, *Sports Organized, 1880–1900*, edited by Gerald R. Gems; vol. 6, *Sports in the Progressive Era, 1900–1920*, edited by Steven A. Riess; vol. 8, *Sports in the Depression, 1930–1940*, edited by Douglas Owen Baldwin. Each volume contains a selected bibliography and name, subject, institution, and geographic place name indexes.

135. Wilkins, Sally. **Sports and Games of Medieval Cultures.** Sports and Games through History. Westport, Conn.: Greenwood Press, 2002. 325 pp. $49.95. ISBN 0-313-31711-9.

This work describes sports and games in medieval times. Divided into seven chapters representing geographic regions of the world, each chapter begins with a historical overview of sports and games in that region. In-depth information is then provided on the most significant sports and games. Each sport or game is defined, a history is provided, and for most, equipment is described, brief rules or instructions are given, and variations of the sport or game are explained. Entries vary in length, depending on the amount of information discovered. Illustrated with black-and-white photographs and diagrams. Contains a general bibliography and an appendix that contains information on finding and making sports equipment. Indexed.

136. Zucker, Harvey Marc, and Lawrence J. Babich, comps. **Sports Films: A Complete Reference.** Jefferson, N.C.: McFarland, 1987. 612 pp. $39.95. ISBN 0-89950-227-X.

This extensive scholarly reference includes descriptions of approximately 2000 films on spectator sports. It is arranged by sport, and the entries contain the title of the film, variants of the title, year of release, where the film was made, if not in the United States, distributor, and running time. A note is made if the film is in color. Then the cast is listed and the plot or content of the film is described. Illustrated with black-and-white photographs depicting dramatic scenes from selected films. Includes a bibliography, a general index, and a title index.

Sport Indexes, Abstracts, and Databases

137. Kehde, Ned, comp. and ed. **Index to the** *Sporting News*: **A Subject Index from 1975–1995.** 1975–1995 ed. Evanston, Ill.: John Gordon Burke, 1998. 518 pp. ISBN 0-934272-51-4; ISSN 1041-2859.

Because it is organized by subject, this index to the *Sporting News* is a valuable research tool. Each subject category includes titles of articles from the journal, giving the volume number, page number, date, and number of pages. Subjects are entered for the most specific entry possible. *See* and *see also* references are utilized.

138. **Leisure, Recreation and Tourism Abstracts.** Cambridge, Mass: CABI, 1976–. Quarterly. $610.00/year. ISSN 0261-1392.

LRTA's coverage of research and strategic development of leisure, recreation, sport, tourism, and hospitality activities, facilities, products, and services makes it an indispensable academic search tool for these areas. It taps the literature of leisure theory and policy but also covers aspects of sport and fitness related to management, economics, sociology, psychology, marketing, training, and education. Abstracts of book chapters, journal articles, conferences, and reports are included within subject categories; book reviews are presented separately. Indexed by author, subject, and by serials cited. CABI also offers an online version, as part of the complete CAB Abstracts database; the leisure-and-tourism database is also available as a separate online portal product and has additional features (go to http://www.leisuretourism.com, accessed December 1, 2004).

139. **The Lifestyle Information Network (LIN).** Toronto, ON. http://www.lin.ca/ (accessed December 1, 2004).

The Lifestyle Information Network is a nonprofit organization that provides knowledge management services to the leisure sector in Canada. One of their projects is the National Recreation Database, which is supported by the Interprovincial Sport and Recreation Council in Canada. The National Recreation Database contains full text documents and other sources and can be searched free of charge. The focus is on practical literature not available from traditional sources and it covers all aspects of leisure and recreation. The LIN offers a range of additional Web services on a subscription basis.

140. **Physical Education Index.** Bethesda, Md.: Cambridge Scientific Abstracts, 1970–present. Quarterly. $275.00. ISSN 0191-9202.

P.E. Index is a comprehensive subject index to international publications on dance, health, physical education, physical therapy, recreation, sports, and sports medicine. It covers many aspects of these subjects, including administration, facilities and law, history, philosophy, psychology and sociology, fitness, biomechanics, motor learning and perception, education, coaching and training, measurement and evaluation, and research. It indexes a wide variety of periodicals, both scholarly and popular, and also includes book reviews and descriptions of patents for sport and exercise equipment. The print index is updated quarterly, with an annual cumulation on CD-ROM. Indexed by author, subject, and geographic area. An electronic version is also offered and includes abstracts. Previously published by BenOak Publishing (1970–2000).

141. SIRCThesaurus: The Thesaurus of Terminology Used in the SPORT-Discus. 2001 ed. Ottawa, ON: Sport Information Resource Centre (SIRC), 2001. 536 pp. $149.00. ISBN 0-921817-50-9.

SIRCThesaurus represents the controlled vocabulary of over 25,000 descriptors used by the indexers who create the SPORTDiscus database. Using terms from the thesaurus enables researchers to achieve more precise search results. It contains sport and nonsport terminology, personal-name descriptors, geographical terms, names of teams, clubs, and associations, corporate names, and bibliography codes. It also provides reference to broader terms, narrower terms, and related terms. The title page of the book indicates that it was "previously published as a serial under the title: *Sport Thesaurus*." The thesaurus is also integrated within the online SPORTDiscus database. It can be purchased on CD-ROM in PDF format, and in print.

142. SPORTDiscus. Ottawa, ON: Sport Information Resource Centre (SIRC), 1975.

SPORTDiscus is a comprehensive international database containing over 650,000 records, with 28,000 new records added annually, in over 50 languages. It includes citations and usually abstracts of periodical articles, books, book chapters and essays, conference papers, theses, dissertations, reports, videotapes, and URLs to sources online. Subject coverage includes all aspects of sport science, sports medicine, psychology, administration, sociology, history, coaching, training, physical education, physical fitness, health, and recreation. Both popular and scholarly sources are included; to help users choose appropriate sources, each record is assigned a level of difficulty: advanced, intermediate, or basic. The database has its roots in the University of Oregon's Kinesiology Publications records from 1949 to the present; also included are the sociology-of-sport records from the discontinued SIRLS database, records from the Canadian sport history project of 1900–1995, and records from other projects. Records from indexing partner the Australia National Sport Information Centre, 1987 to the present, are also integrated. Other databases that have been incorporated into the SPORTDiscus database include Héraclès, the French database produced by the INSEP in Paris; the Catalogue du Musee Olympique, Lausanne, Switzerland; the Amateur Athletic Foundation of Los Angeles online catalogue; and Atlantes, the Spanish-language sport database. It is available as a CD or online subscription, for a single user or multiple users, through Silverplatter, OVID, EBSCO, Dialog, and DataStar. SIRC also offers SIRCExpress, its own fee-based document-delivery service via the database.

143. Sports Business Research Network (SBRnet). Princeton, N.J.: SBRnet, $279.00 (three-month trial); $750.00 (annual subscription).

SBRnet was founded in 1996 by Richard A. Lipsey, in Princeton, New

Jersey. It is a fee-based online source of data on the sporting-goods and sports-marketing industry. It combines market research from the largest single research supplier to the industry, the National Sporting Goods Association; the U.S. Department of Commerce; various sports governing bodies; and full-text articles from fourteen magazines and newsletters. In mid-1999, SBRnet added buyTRACK, an exclusive tracking study of sporting-goods purchases on the Internet. SBRnet's mission is to provide a continuously updated tool for finding market research and industry research on sports-equipment sales, sports participation, sports broadcasting, sports sponsorship, and sports-marketing.

144. **Sports Media Index 1997.** Hartsdale, N.Y.: American Sports Data, 1997. 804 pp.

The *Sports Media Index* reports the results of a national study that monitored magazine readership, TV viewership, sports spectatorship, and recognition of celebrity athletes. The purpose of the research was to provide the sport industry with media information that could be used for marketing. The publisher's Web site (http://www.americansportsdata.com) sells a number of similar current reports and also the results of a superb study on sports participation and reports on physical fitness trends, lifestyle trends, consumer attitudes toward fitness, and others.

Sport Quotation Books

145. DeVito, Carlo. **The Ultimate Dictionary of Sports Quotations.** Facts On File Sports Library. New York: Checkmark Books / Facts On File, 2001. 332 pp. $45.00; $34.95 (pbk.). ISBN 0-816-03980-1; 0-816-03981-X (pbk.).

This reference source contains more than 3000 quotes from persons from all walks of life, generally related to some aspect of sports. The quotes are arranged alphabetically by topic, and persons are included as topics also. Finding a specific quote is complicated by this arrangement, so it lends itself more to browsing. Listed under the topic "Food" is the following quote by boxer George Foreman: "I eat what I eat and I weigh what I weigh." Not illustrated. Includes a bibliography and an index.

146. Maikovich, Andrew J., and Michele D. Brown, eds. **Sports Quotations: Maxims, Quips, and Pronouncements for Writers and Fans.** 2nd ed. Jefferson, N.C.: McFarland, 2000. 237 pp. $39.95. ISBN 0-7864-0817-0.

Divided into twenty-seven major-sport categories, such as baseball, golf, soccer, and wrestling, this source contains nearly 3000 sports quotations. Each quotation is numbered and its speaker is identified, sometimes along with a bit of explanation of the context. The quotations are listed alphabetically by first word under the categories. Contains a speaker index, as well as a subject and keyword index.

147. Pickering, David. **Cassell's Sports Quotations.** 2nd ed. London: Cassell, 2002. 399 pp. $12.95. ISBN 0-304-36213-1.

Arranged alphabetically under themes (a sport, topic, attribute, or quotes by or about a person), this compendium of sports quotes contains over 3000 quotations. From archery to marriage to streakers to wrestling, this reference source covers the humorous and poignant moments in sports talk. Indexed.

Sport Rule Books

148. Diagram Group, The. **Rules of the Game: The Complete Illustrated Encyclopedia of All the Sports of the World.** New York: St. Martin's Press, 1995. 320 pp. $21.95. ISBN 0-312-11940-2.

A description on the front cover of this book reads: "Over 2500 illustrations in full color including 400 events, over 150 sports." The rules in this encyclopedia are authorized by over 300 official sports governing bodies. For each of 150 national and international sports, concise descriptions and authentic rules are provided. Indexed by sport and general topics.

149. Diagram Group, The. **Sports Rules on File.** Facts On File reference library. New York: Facts On File, 2000. $185.00. ISBN 0-8160-4117-2.

This rules source employs a consistent format and standard subheadings for all sports, allowing for ease of use. It provides a brief history, synopsis, general rules, and a description of playing area, equipment, scoring, competition overview, events, and specific rules. Intended for the high school and college audience, this source is issued in a three-ring binder with loose-leaf pages for easy reproduction. Illustrated with drawings and diagrams. Also available on CD-ROM.

150. Hanlon, Thomas W. **The Sports Rules Book.** 2nd ed. With Human Kinetics. Champaign, Ill.: Human Kinetics, 2004. 315 pp. $19.95. ISBN 0-7360-4880-4.

This concise rules book contains basic overviews and practical rule descriptions of forty-seven of the most popular U.S. and world sports. Following an alphabetical arrangement, included for each sport is a brief introduction that describes the origin and major features of the sport; a diagram of the playing field or area; definitions of important, unique terms; a description of the equipment required; rules; officials' signals, sometimes accompanied by illustrative drawings; rule adaptations for special players; and contact information for organizations that can provide additional rule interpretations. Also illustrated with one black-and-white photograph of typical play for each sport.

151. Peterson, Duncan. **The Book of Rules: A Visual Guide to the Laws of Every Commonly Played Sport and Game.** New York: Facts On File, 1998. 224 pp. $24.95. ISBN 0-8160-3919-4.

This guide to the rules provides all the essential information for over thirty international sports. Each entry includes a clear and concise step-by-step explanation of the competition, discussing rules as they occur within the context of play. The guide also includes information on the defined playing area, equipment, and other specifications as determined by the official governing body for the sport. Well-illustrated with abundant color photographs that assist the reader's understanding. A good choice for any library.

152. White, Jess R., ed. **Sports Rules Encyclopedia.** 2nd ed. Champaign, Ill.: Leisure Press, 1990. 732 pp. $44.95. ISBN 0-88011-363-4.

Arranged alphabetically, by name of sport, this encyclopedia provides the full rules for fifty-two sports. It offers the official rules of play, as determined by the official governing body for the sport; playing area specifications, including diagrams of the court, field, or area, where appropriate; equipment specifications; name, address, and function of the national governing body; and the top two journals or magazines for the sport.

Sport Statistics Sources

153. Brucato, Thomas W. **Major League Champions: 1871–2001.** American Sports History Series. Lanham, Md.: Scarecrow Press, 2002. 337 pp. $55.00. ISBN 0-8108-4480-X.

In this companion volume to *Major Leagues* (2001) by the same author, complete major league championship history is provided for arena football, baseball, basketball, football, hockey, lacrosse, indoor lacrosse, roller hockey, soccer, indoor soccer, and tennis. Lists year-by-year championship results; champions by year, league, and franchise; standings by franchise and city; and second-place teams, alphabetically by franchise. Contains a bibliography.

154. Gaschnitz, K. Michael. **Professional Sports Statistics: A North American Team-by-Team, and Major Non-Team Events, Year-by-Year Reference, 1876 through 1996.** Jefferson, N.C.: McFarland, 1997. 1338 pp. $85.00. ISBN 0-7864-0299-7.

With coverage of teams that are considered major league, this source provides statistics for baseball, basketball, football, hockey, and other sports. It is arranged chronologically, by year, so the reader can easily see what happened in the world of sports in any given year. Individual team statistics, arranged alphabetically by team name, are also provided in the last third of this substantial volume. Contains a bibliography of sources consulted.

155. Greenberg, Stan. **Guinness Book of Olympic Records: Complete Roll of Olympic Medal Winners (1896–1988, Including 1906) for the Sports (7 Winter and 25 Summer) Contested in the 1992 Celebrations and Other Useful Information.** New York: Bantam Books, 1991. 285 pp. $4.99. ISBN 0-553-29428-8.

A guide to the winter and summer games of 1992, including a timetable of the games in Barcelona and Albertville. Provides lists of all the medal winners since 1896, as well as many other statistics to delight the sports fan. Illustrated with black-and-white photographs.

156. Matthews, Peter. **The Guinness Encyclopedia of International Sports Records and Results.** 4th ed. Enfield, Middlesex, U.K.: Guinness Publishing, 1995. 416 pp. ISBN 0-85112-686-3.

Includes records and results for over 100 different international sports and championship games. Arranged by sport, this source contains table after table of data on the winners and record holders in each event. Illustrated sparingly with black-and-white photographs. Indexed.

157. Meserole, Mike. **The Ultimate Book of Sports Lists, 1998.** 1st American ed. New York: Dorling Kindersley Publishing, 1997. 224 pp. $24.95. ISBN 0-7894-2279-4.

This volume contains a variety of sports facts, statistics, and other information about athletes who led the way in baseball, football, basketball, hockey, golf, tennis, the Olympic games, track and field, swimming, soccer, horse racing, auto racing, and other competition. It is arranged alphabetically by sport; within each sport, a number of the best, most noted, highly rated, and all-time greatest athletes and teams are listed. Contains over 1000 lists. Illustrated with many black-and-white and color photographs. Indexed.

158. Wellner, Alison S. **Americans at Play: Demographics of Outdoor Recreation and Travel.** Ithaca, N.Y.: New Strategist Publications, 1997. 367 pp. $89.95. ISBN 1-885070-11-X.

From spending on air fares to participating in yard games, this reference book has the data to tell us how America plays. Tables throughout the book report on attendance, spending, and participation in a wide variety of the most popular sport and recreation activities. Data is based on the U.S. Forest Service's *1994–95 National Survey of Recreation and the Environment* and the Bureau of Labor Statistics' *1995 Consumer Expenditure Survey*. The author conveniently brings together in one volume the numbers that can otherwise be very difficult to locate for ready reference.

159. Young, Mark C., ed. **The Guinness Book of Sports Records.** 18th ed. Stamford, Conn.: Guinness Media, 1997. 256 pp. $12.95. ISBN 0-9652383-1-8.

Arranged alphabetically by sport, from archery to yachting, this records book covers over 100 sports. For each, there is a brief essay of the origins of the sport. Contains many tables of data and includes a chapter on the Olympic games. Well illustrated with black-and-white photographs.

Web Sites

160. **Amateur Athletic Foundation of Los Angeles.** http://www.aafla.org (accessed April 3, 2004).

Endowed with surplus funds from the 1984 Olympic Games in Los Angeles, this nonprofit foundation's mission is to serve youth through sport and increase people's knowledge of sport. The AAFLA operates the Paul Ziffren Sports Resource Center, a sports-research library. Among other activities, they are engaged in a significant project to digitize selected scholarly sport journals and historic Olympic publications. This virtual archive is available via their Web site.

161. **Amateur Athletic Union (AAU).** http://www.aausports.org (accessed January 19, 2004).

This nonprofit organization is devoted to the promotion and development of amateur sports and physical-fitness programs in the United States. Their Web site contains an events calendar, news, handbooks, information about the association and national programs, a photo gallery, hall of fame, and more.

162. **American Sport Education Program.** http://www.asep.com (accessed December 1, 2004).

A division of Human Kinetics Publishers, this group develops and implements coaching education programs and materials. Their Web site offers educational resources for coaches, athletic directors, teachers, and parents.

163. **Disabled Sports USA.** http://www.dsusa.org (accessed December 1, 2004).

This national nonprofit organization offers sport rehabilitation programs to anyone with a permanent physical disability. It provides activities in winter skiing, water sports, summer and winter competitions, general fitness, and special sports events. The Web site is very informative and includes links to regional chapters and detailed information on programs, championships, and the Paralympic Games.

164. **International Association of Sports Museums and Halls of Fame.** http://www.sportshalls.com/ (accessed December 1, 2004).

This association's Web site provides a searchable directory of worldwide sports museums and halls of fame. Indexed by sport and by region, the database is also searchable by keyword(s).

165. **National Association of Intercollegiate Athletics.** http://www.naia.org (accessed January 20, 2004).

This growing association Web site now contains an archive of NAIA championship history and records, along with full information on its programs and services.

166. **National Collegiate Athletic Association.** http://www2.ncaa.org (accessed December 1, 2004).

The NCAA is the primary governing body for collegiate sports in the

United States. Resources on the site include the NCAA News, databases, a sport library, statistics, eligibility information, championship results, and publications.

167. **National Disability Sports Alliance/formerly known as United States Cerebral Palsy Athletic Association.** http://www.ndsaonline.org (accessed December 1, 2004).

This organization serves all individuals with physical disabilities in the areas of sports, fitness and recreation. The Web site offers information on eligibility and classification, a listing of sports available, an athlete-of-the-month feature, a calendar of events, and news.

168. **National Federation of State High School Associations.** http://www.nfhs.org (accessed December 1, 2004).

This organization provides leadership and coordination for sports and other interscholastic activities offered in high school. The Web site provides news, a calendar of events, sports rules, educational programs, publications, and other information relevant to high school activities.

169. **Scholarly Sport Sites: A Subject Directory.** http://www.ucalgary.ca/library/ssportsite/ (accessed December 1, 2004).

A searchable directory of Web sites, arranged by subject, this source is valuable for sport researchers, librarians, and anyone else looking for Web resources on sports topics. It provides an index of subjects for easy browsing. Subjects include archives and special sport collections, associations, bookstores and booksellers, bibliographies of full text publications, databases, museums and halls of fame, publishers, serials, and many others. Most of these subjects are further divided into more specific categories.

170. **The *Sporting News*.** http://www.sportingnews.com/ (accessed April 3, 2004).

A sports fan's favorite address, the *Sporting News* Web site offers comprehensive facts and stats on all the teams and leagues. Also a source for fantasy sports, this site really does have it all. News, radio, books, magazines, history—it's there.

171. **The *Sporting News* Archives.** http://www.sportingnews.com/archives/ (accessed April 3, 2004).

The *Sporting News* has been America's leading sports weekly for over 100 years. Their online archive, called the Vault, contains several distinct collections: over 600,000 photographic prints; a 6000-volume collection of sports literature; team media guides from baseball, basketball, football, and hockey; a newspaper and magazine microfilm collection; clipping files on persons and subjects; and other publications. The archive features several historical exhibits, with an emphasis on baseball. It offers online scrapbooks of major stars, championship histories, an almanac, and much other great information. The Web site includes reference and research policies and services. Offers information about access to *Paper of Record*, the electronic version of all 117 years of the *Sporting News.*

172. **SPORTQuest: Virtual Resource Centre for Sport Information.** http://www.sirc.ca/online_resources/sportquest.cfm (accessed December 1, 2004).

SPORTQuest is a huge online directory of sport-related Web-site links. Online resources can be accessed by sport or by topic. It includes a wide variety of source types, from publishers of books on sport and sport-related associations to equipment retailers, colleges, universities, news sources, and statistics. A comprehensive directory for finding sport information.

173. **United States Association of Blind Athletes.** http://www.usaba.org (accessed December 1, 2004).

The mission of the USABA is "to increase the number and quality of grassroots-through-competitive, world-class athletic opportunities for Americans who are blind or visually impaired." The organization provides athlete and coach identification and support, program and event management, and national and international representation. The Web site offers a paralympic history, results and records of competition, information on camps and other sport and exercise opportunities, news, and an events calendar.

174. **USA Deaf Sports Federation.** http://www.usadsf.org (accessed December 1, 2004).

Recognized as the only national athletic association to coordinate the participation of American deaf and hard-of-hearing individuals in international competition, the USADSF is affiliated with the U.S. Olympic Committee. Their site contains information about the Deaflympics, the U.S. team, official documents, an archive, news, information about athletes and events, and more.

175. **World Stadiums.** http://www.worldstadiums.com/ (accessed December 1, 2004).

This commercial Web site aims to list every significant stadium in the world. Contains over 8500 stadiums in over 213 countries. Arranged geographically by area of the world and then by country and/or state, each entry lists the stadium name, the home club or team's name, the city, capacity, year it was built, and a photograph when available. Despite the advertising on this site, it provides a good directory of stadiums.

The Olympic Games

Chapter

2

The most celebrated of all sporting events, the Olympic Games generate intense excitement around the world. The Games are a rich example of our culture, no matter where we call home. The sources listed here provide a wealth of information on the history of the Games, the athletes who have participated, the contests themselves, and the results.

Reference Sources

176. Buchanan, Ian, and Bill Mallon. **Historical Dictionary of the Olympic Movement.** 2nd ed. Historical Dictionaries of Religions, Philosophies, and Movements. Lanham, Md.: Scarecrow Press, 2001. 367 pp. $65.00. ISBN 0-8108-4054-5.

This unique reference provides comprehensive coverage of the Olympic Games from their beginnings in ancient Greece, in the context of history and politics. Chronologies of the Olympic Movement and of the individual games are given at the start, and each set of games is described briefly, followed by an introduction to the Olympic Games. In the dictionary itself, events in the Olympic world are described and defined fully. Entries include the athletes, other important persons, countries, sports, and many related topics. Appendices list a great deal of additional information, such as presidents and members of the IOC, final Olympic torch bearers, most medals won in a variety of categories, and athletes who have tested positive for drug use. A lengthy bibliography is included.

177. **Chronicle of the Olympics, 1896–2000.** 1st American ed. New York: Dorling Kindersley, 1998. 330 pp. $29.95. ISBN 0-7894-2312-X.

With coverage of every Olympiad, from Athens in 1896 to Nagano in 1998, plus a preview of Sydney in 2000, this historical source offers brief information and abundant illustration. The highlights of each Olympiad are provided, along with images of the official Olympic poster, key athletes, and other significant moments. The statistics from each Olympiad are presented in a separate section. Illustrated with many striking historic photos, both black-and-white and color. Indexed.

178. Findling, John E., and Kimberly D. Pelle, eds. **Encyclopedia of the Modern Olympic Movement.** Westport, Conn.: Greenwood Press, 2004. 640 pp. $75.00. ISBN 0-313-32278-3.

In this edited volume of essays, the Olympic movement is examined in detail from the perspective of their historical, political, and economic context. Each of the Summer and Winter Games is covered in its own essay, in chronological order beginning with Athens in 1896, continuing up to Salt Lake City in 2002, and including plans for the 2004, 2006, and 2008 games. Important appendices provide additional information on the IOC, the U.S. Olympic Committee, television, films, and electronic sources for research. This is a revised and updated edition of the editors' earlier work, *Historical Dictionary of the Modern Olympic Movement.* Contains a general bibliography that describes Olympic-related collections and sources. Indexed.

179. Findling, John E., and Kimberly D. Pelle, eds. **Historical Dictionary of the Modern Olympic Movement.** Westport, Conn.: Greenwood Press, 1996. 460 pp. $85.00. ISBN 0-313-28477-6.

The same authors have now published a revised and expanded second edition of this reference work entitled *Encyclopedia of the Modern Olympic Movement* (2004).

180. Gafner, Raymond, ed. **1894–1994, The International Olympic Committee, One Hundred Years: The Idea, the Presidents, the Achievements.** 3 vols. With the International Olympic Committee. Lausanne, Switzerland: International Olympic Committee, 1994–1997. $144.00 (set). ISBN 92-9105-007-5 (v. 1); 92-9105-010-5 (v. 2); 92-9105-012-1 (v. 3).

This substantial scholarly set provides an extensive history of the IOC and of the Olympic Movement and its leaders. In volume 1, Yves-Pierre Boulongne, covered the presidencies of Demetrius Vikelas (1894–1896) and Pierre de Coubertin (1896–1925), and Karl Lennartz wrote about the presidency of Henri de Baillet-Latour (1925–1942). In volume 2, the presidency of Sigfrid Edström (1942–1952) is covered by Karl Lennartz, and the presidency of Avery Brundage (1952–1972) is written about by Otto Schantz. Volume 3 presents the presidencies of Lord Killanin (1972–1980) and of Juan Antonio Samaranch (1980–), written about by Fernand Landry and Magdeleine Yerlès. Illustrated throughout the three volumes with high-quality photographs from the IOC Archives, this work is a historian's dream. Also published in French.

181. Greenberg, Stan. **Whitaker's Olympic Almanack: The Essential Guide to the Olympic Games.** 2004 ed. London: A & C Black, 2003. 299 pp. $30.00. ISBN 0-7136-6724-9.

This detailed and all-inclusive encyclopedia of the Olympic Games contains extensive information on all Olympic sports and on all Games that have been held in the modern era. Provides a chronology of the Summer and Winter

Games, with essays for each, from Athens 1896 through Salt Lake City 2002, and includes brief comments on the games planned for 2004–2012. Next, the alphabetical entries are presented, covering sports and topics from A to Z. Olympic medals tables and results are presented by sport and year. A selection of color images illustrates the work, which is half encyclopedia and half record book. It contains an alphabetical name index for persons' names appearing in the encyclopedia part. Also contains contact information for international sporting organizations.

182. Lovett, Charlie. **Olympic Marathon: A Centennial History of the Games' Most Storied Race.** Westport, Conn.: Praeger, 1997. 192 pp. $68.95. ISBN 0-275-95771-3.

This interesting work examines the history of the Olympic marathon, providing a detailed account of each marathon from the first modern Olympics in 1896 through Atlanta in 1996. The Games are covered in chronological order, with additional chapters devoted to women's participation in the marathon. Each marathon's personalities are described in vivid detail. An appendix lists top marathon winners from each race. Well illustrated with photographs. Contains a select bibliography and an index.

183. Mallon, Bill. **The 1900 Olympic Games: Results for All Competitors in All Events, with Commentary.** Results of the Early Modern Olympics. Jefferson, N.C.: McFarland, 1998. 335 pp. $59.95. ISBN 0-7864-0378-0.

This work is the second in a series of reference volumes intended to document the results of early Olympic Games. The goal was to create a comprehensive record of those early games where none existed before. The author presents a general summary and analysis of the 1900 games held in Paris, France, and then treats each sport individually, starting with a short essay on the event and then following with the statistics and notes. All the results from 1900 are compiled from primary sources, as are other facts of the competition, including the dates, events, sites, athletes, and participating countries. Complete references are given for those sources. Appendices provide the 1900 program, a list of competitors by country, and a comparison of data found in other sources. Indexed.

184. Mallon, Bill. **The 1904 Olympic Games: Results for All Competitors in All Events, with Commentary.** Results of the Early Modern Olympics. Jefferson, N.C.: McFarland, 1999. 287 pp. $49.95. ISBN 0-7864-0550-3.

This work is the third in a series of reference volumes intended to document the results of early Olympic Games. The goal was to create a comprehensive record of those early games where none existed before. The author presents a general summary and analysis of the 1904 games held in St. Louis, Missouri, and then treats each sport individually, starting with a short essay on the event and then following with the statistics and notes. All the results from 1904 are compiled from primary sources, as are other facts of the competition, including the dates, events, sites, athletes, and participating countries. Complete references are given for those sources. Appendices provide the 1904 program, a list of competitors by country, and a comparison of data found in other sources. Indexed.

185. Mallon, Bill. **The 1906 Olympic Games: Results for All Competitors in All Events, with Commentary.** Results of the Early Modern Olympics. Jefferson, N.C.: McFarland, 1999. 232 pp. $49.95. ISBN 0-7864-0551-1.

This work is the fourth in a series of reference volumes intended to document the results of early Olympic Games. The goal was to create a comprehensive record of those early games where none existed before. The author presents a general summary and analysis of the 1906 games held in Athens, Greece, and then treats each sport individually, starting with a short essay on the event and following with the statistics and notes. All the results from 1906 are compiled from primary sources, as are other facts of the competition, including the dates, events, sites, athletes, and participating countries. Complete references are given for those sources. Appendices provide the 1906 program and a list of competitors by country. Indexed.

186. Mallon, Bill. **Total Olympics: The Complete Record and History of the Olympic Games.** Kingston, N.Y.: Total / Sports Illustrated, 2001. 1300 pp. $55.00. ISBN 1-930844-24-7.

A comprehensive view of the Winter and Summer Games is provided in this substantial work. It includes finalists and medal winners from every Olympiad, biographies of the greatest athletes in Olympic history, essays that chronicle the traditions, politics, and scandals surrounding the Olympics.

187. Mallon, Bill, and Anthony Th. Bijkerk. **The 1920 Olympic Games: Results for All Competitors in All Events, with Commentary.** Results of the Early Modern Olympics. Jefferson, N.C.: McFarland, 2003. 541 pp. $69.95. ISBN 0-7864-1280-1.

This work is the seventh in a series of reference volumes intended to document the results of early Olympic Games. The goal was to create a comprehensive record of those early games where none existed before. The authors present a general summary and analysis of the 1920 games in Antwerp, Belgium and then treat each sport individually, starting with a short essay on the event and following with the statistics and notes. All the results from 1920 are compiled from primary sources, as are other facts of the competition, including the dates, events, sites, athletes, and participating countries. Complete references are given for those sources. Appendices provide the 1920 program, essays on the scheduled 1916 games and the 1919 Inter-Allied Games, and a list of competitors by country. Indexed.

188. Mallon, Bill, and Ian Buchanan. **The 1908 Olympic Games: Results for All Competitors in All Events, with Commentary.** Results of the Early Modern Olympics. Jefferson, N.C.: McFarland, 2000. 516 pp. $69.95. ISBN 0-7864-0598-8.

This work is the fifth in a series of reference volumes intended to document the results of early Olympic Games. The goal was to create a comprehensive record of those early games where none existed before. The authors present a general summary and analysis of the 1908 games in London and then treat each sport individually, starting with a short essay on the event and following with the statistics and notes. All the results from 1908 are compiled from primary sources, as are other facts of the competition, including the dates, events, sites, athletes, and participating countries. Complete references are given for those sources. Appendices provide the 1908 program, coverage of controversies and protests, maps, the words and music of "Dorando" by Irving Berlin, and a list of competitors by country. Indexed.

189. Mallon, Bill, and Ture Widlund. **The 1896 Olympic Games: Results for All Competitors in All Events, with Commentary.** Results of the Early Modern Olympics. Jefferson, N.C.: McFarland, 1998. 152 pp. $49.95. ISBN 0-7864-0379-9.

This work is the first in a series of reference volumes intended to document the results of early Olympic Games. The goal is to create a comprehensive record of those early games where none existed before. The authors present a general summary and analysis of the 1896 games in Athens and then treat each sport individually, starting with a short essay on the event and following with the statistics and notes. All the results are compiled, as are other facts of the competition, including the dates, events, sites, athletes, and participating countries. Reprints of famous historical articles are included. Appendices provide the 1896 program, a list of competitors by country, and the Pindaric Ode that was read at the closing ceremonies. Indexed.

190. Mallon, Bill, and Ture Widlund. **The 1912 Olympic Games: Results for All Competitors in All Events, with Commentary.** Results of the Early Modern Olympics. Jefferson, N.C.: McFarland, 2002. 569 pp. $69.95. ISBN 0-7864-1047-7.

This work is the sixth in a series of reference volumes intended to document the results of early Olympic Games. The goal was to create a comprehensive record of those early games where none existed before. The authors present a general summary and analysis of the 1912 games in Stockholm and then treat each sport individually, starting with a short essay on the event and following with the statistics and notes. All the results from 1912 are compiled from primary sources, as are other facts of the competition, including the dates, events, sites, athletes, and participating countries. Complete references are given for those sources. Appendices provide the 1912 program, include essays on Jim Thorpe and others, and list competitors by country. Indexed.

191. Miller, David. **Athens to Athens: The Official History of the Olympic Games and the IOC, 1894–2004.** Edinburgh, U.K.: Mainstream Publishing Company, 2004. 528 pp. $61.00. ISBN 1-84018-587-2.

This substantial volume provides detailed accounts of both the Olympic Games and IOC history, presented in chronological order, and highlights the crises and scandals as well as the triumphs. Many significant individuals are profiled in the work, all of which is superbly illustrated with high-quality color photographs and historic black-and-white photographs from the IOC archives. Appendices provide additional information, including a list of IOC members from 1894 to 2003; Olympic Games results; medals tables; current National Olympic Committees; dates and statistics of Summer and Winter Games; IOC Sessions; Olympic Congresses; and Olympic logistics. Contains a bibliography and an index.

192. Olderr, Steven. **The Pan-American Games: A Statistical History, 1951–1999.** Jefferson, N.C.: McFarland, 2003. 392 pp. $75.00. ISBN 0-7864-1285-2.

This reference source provides a valuable history of the Pan-American Games and compiles the statistical results of the competition, beginning with the first, held in 1951, and ending with those held in 1999. The arrangement is alphabetical by sport, and for each sport a chronology of important events within the Pan-American Games is included. Provides a list of medal winners and a list of medals won by country. Also contains a general chronology of the Pan-American Games and information about the Pan-American Sports Organization (PASO). The book is a unique bilingual edition, in Spanish and English.

193. **The Olympic Century: The Official History of the Modern Olympic Movement.** 24 vols. Los Angeles, Calif.: World Sport Research & Publications, 1996–2000. $599.00 (set). ISBN 1-888383-00-3 (set).

This ambitious series was produced as a joint venture of the International Olympic Committee, the U.S. Olympic Committee, the 1st Century Project, and the publisher. It is the official history of the modern Olympic movement and an extremely important reference source on the topic. Well written and lavishly illustrated with historic photographs, it is an authoritative source that readers of all ages can enjoy. These are the individual volume titles: vol. 1, *The Ancient Olympiads and Bridges to the Modern Era*, James M. Lynch; vol. 2, *The I Olympiad: The Olympic Revival and Athens 1896*; vol. 3, *The II Olympiad: Paris 1900 and the Nordic Games*, Carl A. Posey; vol. 4, *The III Olympiad: St. Louis 1904 and Athens 1906*, Carl A. Posey; vol. 5, *The IV Olympiad: London 1908 and the International YMCA*, George M. Constable; vol. 6, *The V and VI Olympiads: Stockholm 1912 and the Inter-Allied Games*, George G. Daniels; vol. 7, *The VII Olympiad: Antwerp 1920 and Chamonix 1924*, Ellen Phillips; vol. 8, *The VIII Olympiad: Paris 1924 and St. Moritz 1928*, Ellen Phillips; vol. 9, *The IX Olympiad: Amsterdam 1928 and Lake Placid 1932*, George Russell; vol. 10, *The X Olympiad: Los Angeles 1932 and Garmisch-Partenkirschen 1936*, Ellen Galford; vol. 11, *The XI, XII and XIII Olympiads: Berlin 1936 and St. Moritz 1948*, George M. Constable; vol. 12, *The XIV Olympiad: London 1948 and Oslo 1952*, George G. Daniels; vol. 13, *The XV Olympiad: Helsinki 1952 and Cortina D'Ampezzo 1956*, Carl A. Posey; vol. 14, *The XVI Olympiad: Melbourne 1956 and Squaw Valley 1960*, Carl A. Posey; vol. 15, *The XVII Olympiad: Rome 1960 and Innsbruck 1964*, Ellen Phillips; vol. 16, *The XVIII Olympiad: Tokyo 1964 and Grenoble 1968*,

Carl A. Posey; vol. 17, *The XIX Olympiad: Mexico City 1968 and Sapporo 1972*, George G. Daniels; vol. 18, *The XX Olympiad: Munich 1972 and Innsbruck 1976*, George G. Daniels; vol. 19, *The XXI Olympiad: Montreal 1976 and Lake Placid 1980*, George M. Constable; vol. 20, *The XXII Olympiad: Moscow 1980 and Sarajevo 1984*, Roberta Conlan, contributing writer George M. Constable; vol. 21, *The XXIII Olympiad: Los Angeles 1984 and Calgary 1988*, Ellen Galford; vol. 22, *The XXIV Olympiad: Seoul 1988 and Albertville 1992*, Ellen Galford; vol. 23, *The XXV Olympiad: Barcelona 1992 and Lillehammer 1994*, George M. Constable; vol. 24, *The XXVI Olympiad: Atlanta 1996 and Nagano 1998*, Carl A. Posey. Each volume contains its own bibliography and index. Additional volumes are planned for the future.

194. The Olympic Games: Athens 1896–Athens 2004. Updated ed. New York: Dorling Kindersley, 2004. 372 pp. $30.00. ISBN 0-7566-0400-1.

This book, according to its front cover, includes "all the athletes, events and results since 1896." Timed to include a preview of the 2004 Olympic Games in Athens, this volume will appeal to most audiences, but especially those of public libraries. It is an updated version of *Chronicle of the Olympics*, first published in 1996 by Dorling Kindersley. Illustrated with many photographs, some color. Indexed.

195. The Olympics: Athens to Athens, 1986–2004. London: Weidenfeld & Nicolson, 2004. 360 pp. $34.94. ISBN 0-297-84382-6.

Produced by the Olympic Museum in collaboration with the International Olympic Committee and the French sports paper *L'Equipe*, this official volume features a historical examination of all twenty-six Olympic Games. Beautifully illustrated with over 600 photographs, many never seen widely, it includes biographical portraits of athletes, profiles of Olympic stadia, and many interesting details of the events and personalities that have captured the public's attention.

196. Searle, Caroline, and Bryn Vaile, eds. **The IOC Official Olympic Companion, 1996.** Atlanta ed. Washington, D.C.: Brassey's Sports, 1996. 490 pp. $18.95. ISBN 1-85753-128-0.

This companion to the Olympic Games presents a history of the 100 years of Olympic competition, focusing, though, on the 1996 Games in Atlanta. Includes a comprehensive guide to each Olympic sport program, with tables of medalists and results for each, from 1896 to 1992. Includes articles on many related topics, such as Olympic solidarity, marketing, the IOC, and other international games. Illustrated with black-and-white photographs, drawings, and diagrams.

197. Searle, Caroline, and Bryn Vaile. **The Official Olympic Games Companion: The Complete Guide to the Olympic Winter Games.** Nagano ed. London and Washington, D.C.: Brassey's Sports, 1998. 296 pp. $15.95. ISBN 1-85753-244-9.

This companion to the Olympic Winter Games presents a history of Winter Olympic competition between 1924 and 1998, focusing, though, on the 1998 Games in Nagano. Includes a comprehensive guide to each Olympic Winter sport program, with tables of medalists and results for each, from 1924 to 1994. Includes profiles of Olympic legends and contemporary heroes and heroines, as well as articles on many related topics, such as Olympic solidarity, host-city bidding, the IOC, and the fight against drugs in sport. Illustrated with black-and-white photographs, drawings, and diagrams.

198.   United States Olympic Committee. **Olympism: A Basic Guide to the History, Ideals, and Sports of the Olympic Movement.** An Official U.S. Olympic Committee Sports series. Torrance, Calif.: Griffin Publishing Group; distributed by Gareth Stevens Publishing, 2001. 152 pp. $22.60. ISBN 0-8368-2800-3.

Part of the USOC's Sports Series, this guide provides basic information intended to help the novice get started learning about the Olympic movement. Covers the history and fundamentals of Olympism and the Olympics, as well as information on all the Olympic sports. Illustrated with drawings and black-and-white photographs. Includes contact information for the national governing bodies.

199.   Wallechinsky, David. **The Complete Book of the Summer Olympics.** Athens 2004 ed. Toronto: Sport Media Publishing, 2004. 1172 pp. $37.95; $24.95 (pbk.). ISBN 1-894963-34-2; 1-894963-32-6 (pbk.).

Marketed as a companion volume to the 2004 Olympic Games in Athens, Greece, this respected compendium of essays and statistics is an essential reference for all libraries. Contains all the statistics for the summer games throughout modern Olympic history, 1896 through 2000. Also includes anecdotes and descriptions of events and people who have made their mark on Olympic history. Illustrated with classic black-and-white photographs and a color insert. A schedule is included for the 2004 games in Athens.

200.   Wallechinsky, David. **The Complete Book of the Winter Olympics.** 2002 ed. Woodstock, N.Y.: Overlook Press, 2001. 353 pp. $27.95. ISBN 1-58567-195-9.

This comprehensive and complete work covers the Winter Olympics, from the first one in Chamonix, France, in 1924 through Salt Lake City in 2002. Includes a brief general history of the games and further historical and descriptive detail on individual Winter Olympics events throughout the work. Each event is treated fully, including a list of the required elements of a program, then descriptions, winners, and rankings for each year. Various scandals of the games are also treated generously. Illustrated with black-and-white photographs of athletes in their element. The end of the book contains a special section of Winter Olympic records.

Web Sites

201. International Olympic Movement. http://www.olympic.org (accessed December 2, 2004).

The official Web site of the Olympic movement offers substantial opportunity for finding information on all aspects of the Olympics. It offers the latest Olympic news, links to international sports federations and national Olympic committees, a calendar of events, many interesting facts and images, a history of every Olympic sporting event, information on the International Olympic Committee itself, and links to upcoming Games. Provides links to the Olympic Museum and the Olympic Study Centre in Lausanne, as well as online educational document sets on topics such as the ancient Games, all the modern Games, the sports, athletes, and the organization of the IOC. Includes athlete biographies and the results of all medal winners in the modern Olympic Games.

202. International Paralympic Committee. http://www.paralympic.org (accessed December 2, 2004).

This comprehensive Web site offers news of paralympic competition, results, records, a calendar of events, information about past and future Paralympic Games, a glossary of terms, and a handbook.

203. National Senior Games Association. http://www.nsga.com (accessed December 2, 2004).

Dedicated to promoting healthy lifestyles for those who are aged fifty or older, the association also offers an informative Web site containing news, history, a hall of fame, events, results, rules, training programs, and more. Offers links to the state senior Olympic associations.

204. Special Olympics International. http://www.specialolympics.org (accessed December 2, 2004).

The mission of Special Olympics is to provide year-round sports training and athletic competition to individuals with intellectual disabilities in over 150 countries. Their Web site is a good source for information; it includes a directory of program locations, an events calendar, and information about the athletes, the sports, competition, eligibility, and information resources for coaches.

205. United States Olympic Committee. http://www.olympic-usa.org (accessed December 2, 2004).

The Web site of the USOC offers a great deal of information on their mission, programs, and documents, such as the USOC Constitution and Bylaws. It also provides profiles of the athletes, information on the U.S. Olympic Hall of Fame members, history of the Olympic Games, and links to more information on specific games. It posts the rules, equipment needed, history, prominent athletes, and a glossary for each sport. Also includes news on the bid process for future games, including New York City's bid for the 2012 games.

206. **U.S. Paralympics.** http://www.usparalympics.org (accessed December 2, 2004).

A division of the U.S. Olympic Committee, U.S. Paralympics sponsors the Paralympic Games for elite athletes with physical disabilities. Competition is offered in twenty-one sports, eighteen of which are contested in the Olympics. The Web site provides information about the sports and about qualifying, a calendar of events, news, and profiles of the athletes.

Chapter 3

Aquatic Sports

Swimming has its roots in the ancient world and is an excellent activity for health reasons, for competition, and even for transportation. Other aquatic sports and activities have grown in popularity over the years, along with swimming. This chapter covers reference sources, instructional sources, and Web sites on general aquatic topics, life guarding, surfing, swimming, diving, waterskiing, and water polo.

General Aquatic Sources

Reference Sources

207. **Aquatics International Directory.** Los Angeles, Calif.: Hanley Wood, 2004. 242 pp. $49.95. ISSN 1058-7039.

This annual directory features a two-year topical index of articles from the monthly *Aquatics International* magazine, as well as a calendar of events for the year and a list of swimming-industry associations, with contact information. The majority of the directory is devoted to aquatic products and manufacturers and is indexed by product classification and brand name. Also includes an extensive list of who's who in the aquatics industry and a list of Web sites, by product type.

207a. Griffiths, Tom. **Better Beaches: Management and Operation of Safe and Enjoyable Swimming Beaches.** Hoffman Estates, Ill.: National Recreation and Park Association, National Aquatic Section, 1999. 182 pp. $44.95. ISBN 0-929581-62-8.

A guide to managing and operating beaches as safe places for aquatic recreation, this reference source provides information on design factors, including accessibility, and offers a list of the twenty best beaches in the United States (including Hawaii). Provides detailed chapters on operation and maintenance of beaches, water quality, and other environmental concerns. Also provides significant information on water safety, with ten chapters on specific aspects such as weather, signage, lifesaving, and risk management. Appendices offer a selection of recreation agencies' documents that cover subjects such as beach and pool evaluation, routine procedures, water testing, and lifeguarding. Illustrated with color photographs and drawings.

207b. Johnston, Kevin, ed. **The Encyclopedia of Aquatic Codes & Standards.** Ashburn, Va.: National Recreation and Park Association, National Aquatic Section, 1999. 88 pp. $14.95. ISBN 0-929581-65-2.

Intended for aquatic recreation operators, pool managers, and other aquatic professionals, this practical encyclopedia provides information to assist with planning an aquatic facility. It includes detailed design considerations, information on facility safety, water treatment, life saving and emergency equipment, administrative standards, environmental considerations, and a section on spas. Throughout the work, United States maps are included to show variation in codes and standards by state.

208. National Collegiate Athletic Association. **NCAA Men's and Women's Swimming and Diving Rules.** 2004 ed. Indianapolis, Ind.: National Collegiate Athletic Association, 2003. 149 pp. $7.50. ISBN 0736-5128.

This official rule book pulls out the major rule changes for the year and then presents the full official rules for swimming and diving competition. Includes pool dimensions and equipment specifications, descriptions of events, the officials' duties, procedures of competition, and details on scoring and how records are recognized and registered. Illustrated with photos of NCAA committee members and diagrams.

209. Warshaw, Matt. **The Encyclopedia of Surfing.** Orlando, Fla.: Harcourt, 2003. 774 pp. $40.00. ISBN 0-15-100579-6.

This substantial surfing reference begins with a history of surfing, which is followed by 1500 entries, arranged alphabetically, on everything from California to hot curl board to zinc oxide. The entries vary in length and describe the people, places, events, equipment, culture, and language of the sport. Appendices contain an impressive bibliography of fiction and nonfiction surfing titles; surfing contest results from 1954 to 2002; a list of surfing movies; a list of magazines; and a surfer-music discography. Illustrated with 300 black-and-white photographs.

Instructional Sources

210. American Red Cross. **Lifeguard Training.** Boston: StayWell, 2001. 175 pp. ISBN 1-58480-075-5.

In this training manual for professional lifeguards, the characteristics and role of the lifeguard are fully described. In-depth information is provided on surveillance, emergency preparation, rescue skills, breathing and cardiac emergencies, first aid, caring for head, neck, and back injuries, specific needs of the waterfront and water park environments, defibrillation, oxygen administration, and preventing the transmission of disease. Well-illustrated with color photographs, drawings, and graphs. Includes a bibliography.

210a. Dixon, Peter L. **The Complete Guide to Surfing.** Guilford, Conn.: Lyons Press, 2004. 224 p. $17.95. ISBN 1-59228-292-X.

A very comprehensive instructional source on surfing, this guide provides a history of the sport, as well as detailed, step-by-step information on technique, a discussion of equipment, tips on surfing etiquette and essential terminology, and advice on how to improve performance regardless of one's skill level. Includes a list of resources, a glossary of terms, and an index. Illustrated with over 150 color photographs and drawings.

211. Ellis & Associates. **National Pool and Waterpark Lifeguard Training.** 2nd ed. With the National Safety Council. Sudbury, Mass.: Jones and Bartlett, 2001. 212 pp. $44.95. ISBN 0-7637-1733-9.

This lifeguard training program emphasizes teamwork and prevention strategies and integrates CPR, first aid, use of Automated External Defibrillators, and oxygen administration into one curriculum. Clearly written step-by-step instructions and guidelines are given for rescuing drowning victims on and below the water's surface, administering CPR and supplemental oxygen, and dealing with spinal-cord injuries, as well as other medical emergencies and injuries. A full chapter is devoted to the use of automated external defibrillators. Illustrated with color photographs and diagrams. Includes a glossary of terms and an index.

212. Favret, Ben, and David Benzel. **Complete Guide to Water Skiing.** Champaign, Ill.: Human Kinetics, 1997. 248 pp. $19.95. ISBN 0-88011-522-X.

This guide to the sport provides information on conditioning, equipment, safety, basic skills, and more advanced techniques in waterskiing. Illustrated with over 100 photographs that demonstrate proper technique in slalom, trick skiing, jumping, wakeboarding, and knee boarding.

213. Graver, Dennis K. **Aquatic Rescue and Safety: How to Recognize, Respond to, and Prevent Water-Related Injuries.** Champaign, Ill.: Human Kinetics, 2003. 249 pp. $24.95. ISBN 0-7360-4122-2.

This guide to lifesaving provides detailed information on identifying, treating, and preventing aquatic injuries. It presents the techniques for recognizing and responding to an emergency situation and includes physiological considerations such as water and body temperature, specific types of injuries (head, spinal cord, etc.), and injuries occuring during specific types of water activities (swimming, diving, boating, etc.). Discusses full first-aid procedures, evacuations, emergency action plans, and legal concerns. Appendices provide a first-aid equipment list, a sample action plan, and suggested readings. Illustrated with black-and-white photographs and diagrams. Includes a bibliography and an index.

214. YMCA of the USA. **On the Guard II: The YMCA Lifeguard Manual.** 4th ed. Champaign, Ill.: Human Kinetics, 2001. 341 pp. $31.00. ISBN 0-7360-3976-7.

Published for the YMCA of the USA, this is the organization's official lifeguard training manual. Essential safety and survival skills are described in detail and the information is illustrated with colorful photographs. Includes chapters on lifeguarding responsibilities, procedures, rules and regulations, as well as skills needed for rescue and first aid. New appendices in this edition include YMCA guidelines for resident camp, day camp, child care, and waterfront operations; waterfront safety; and basic management of pools. Includes a CD-ROM.

Web Sites

215. **International Surfing Association.** http://www.isasurf.org/ (accessed April 4, 2004).

The Web site of the surfing's world governing authority provides a rule book, history, mission statement, and directory of national governing bodies.

216. **USA Water Ski.** http://www.usawaterski.org (accessed December 2, 2004).

As the national governing body or organized waterskiing in the U.S., the organization's Web site offers club, camp, and school listings, bylaws, reports, an events calendar, athlete biographies, and much other information about waterskiing competition.

Diving

Reference Source

217. **Official Rules and Code of USA Diving, Inc.** Indianapolis, Ind.: United States Diving, 2001. $10.00.

This annual publication offers the official rules. It can be purchased from USA Diving, or viewed via their Web page: http://www.usdiving.org (accessed December 2, 2004).

Instructional Sources

218. **Encyclopedia of Recreational Diving.** 2nd ed. Rancho Santa Margarita, Calif.: Professional Association of Diving Instructors, 2001. $35.00. ISBN 1-878663-02-X.

This comprehensive, standard text on diving is available at local PADI-affiliated diving shops. There is a directory of these shops on the association's Web site: http://www.padi.com/ (accessed December 2, 2004).

219. **Go Dive: Open Water Diver Manual.** Rancho Santa Margarita, Calif.: Professional Association of Diving Instructors, 1999. 260 pp. ISBN 1-878663-16-X.

This is another standard diving instruction manual that is available at PADI-affiliated diving shops.

220. Graver, Dennis K. **Scuba Diving.** 3rd ed. Champaign, Ill.: Human Kinetics, 2003. 209 pp. $22.95. ISBN 0-7360-4539-2.

According to the book's cover, it is the "official scuba instructional manual of the YMCA of the USA." The concise explanations given in this comprehensive guide to the sport of scuba diving, introduce the reader to diving and move through the science behind it, the adaptations and planning required, and the opportunities available for learning more. Beautifully illustrated with color photographs and drawings. Appendices contain other sources of information, an equipment checklist. Contains a glossary of scuba diving terms, a bibliography, and an index.

221. O'Brien, Ron. **Springboard and Platform Diving.** 2nd ed. Champaign, Ill.: Human Kinetics, 2003. 226 pp. $22.95. ISBN 0-7360-4378-0.

Written by an acclaimed coach, this guide to diving presents all the fundamentals of body alignment and movement going into the dive, then the basic dives and more complex work for competition. Intended for both divers and coaches, it includes information on skill progressions and on training and peaking for competition, as well as the psychological aspect of the sport. The guide is illustrated with step-by-step drawings and black-and-white photographs. Includes a glossary of terms and an index.

Web Site

222. **United States Diving, Inc.** http://www.usdiving.org (accessed December 2, 2004).

USA Diving is the national governing body for diving in the United States. Its Web site provides rules, results, a calendar of events, and information on the organization's history, structure, and mission, on national teams, and training and developing coaches.

Swimming

Reference Sources

223. Costill, David L, Ernest W. Maglischo, and Allen B. Richardson, eds. **Swimming.** Handbook of Sports Medicine and Science. Malden, Mass.: Blackwell Science, 1991. 224 pp. $34.95. ISBN 0-632-03027-5.

This series is published under the auspices of the International Olympic Committee Medical Commission. This volume covers the epidemiology of injury in the sport, the physiology of nutritional issues related to swimming, preventive medicine, and the biomechanics of different swimming strokes. The articles in the handbook are intended for use by physicians, trainers, and coaches but would also be useful for athletes themselves or parents of children who are participating in athletics. Illustrated with diagrams, tables, and black-and-white photographs. Each chapter contains a list of references for further reading. Indexed. This series is most appropriate for college and university collections in sports medicine.

224. Gonslaves, Kelly, and Susan LaMondia. **First to the Wall: 100 Years of Olympic Swimming.** East Longmeadow, Mass.: FreeStyle Publications, 1999. 374 pp. $24.95. ISBN 0-9674171-0-4.

This history of Olympic swimming contains considerable trivia and anecdotal information about the athletes and the contests. It is illustrated with many black-and-white photographs. For each Olympiad, there is a chart that indicates the times, events, and finalists. Arranged chronologically and covers 1896–1996. Indexed.

225. Griffiths, Tom. **The Complete Swimming Pool Reference.** 2nd ed. Champaign, Ill.: Sagamore Publishing, 2003. 472 pp. $48.95. ISBN 1-57167-523-X.

This comprehensive book on swimming-pool safety and management contains thirty chapters of detailed information on first aid, lifeguarding, and pool maintenance. It uniquely combines the technical aspects of a pool-operations manual with the practical aspects of water safety. Covers all types of pools, including hot tubs and their mechanical and chemical properties and requirements. Illustrated with black-and-white photographs, diagrams, and graphs. Includes a glossary of terms and an index.

226. Haverland, Bill, and Tom Saunders. **Swimmers Guide: Directory of Pools for Fitness Swimmers.** 2nd ed. Stuart, Fla.: ALSA Publishing, 1995. 349 pp. $16.95. ISBN 0-9635960-1-2.

This directory of pools includes information on over 3000 year-round swimming facilities across the United States. Arranged alphabetically by state, then city, and within cities by numerical zip code, the guide provides state and city maps, name and address of the facility, telephone number, and a description of the pool, including the admission charge. It also includes 126 masters-club listings, a variety of clubs with reciprocal-use arrangements, and a select group of hotel pools. A great resource for planning travel to include swimming. An online version is also available.

227. **The Swimming in College Directory.** 7th ed. Fort Lauderdale, Fla.: American Swimming Coaches Association, 2001. $22.00.

Published every two years, this directory contains listings for 585 colleges and universities that offer men's and/or women's swimming. Information on diving and water polo is also included. Each listing provides facts about the school, personnel, and facilities and a guide to the top racing times for the year. The main listing is alphabetical by college name, with additional indexing by state and division. According to the cover, it is "the most current and complete collegiate directory available with information on college swimming and diving programs in the USA and Canada."

Instructional Sources

228. American Red Cross. **Swimming and Diving.** Boston: StayWell, 1998. 353 pp. ISBN 0-8151-0595-9.

This comprehensive guide to swimming and diving lays out the history and development of the sports and predicts future trends. Topics included in the guide are safety, hydrodynamics, basic skills and mechanics, opportunities for people with disabilities, lifetime fitness, training, competitive activities, and rescue techniques. Appendices list organizations that promote aquatic activities, equipment, tables for calculating heart rate, and lifesaving techniques. Illustrated with color photographs, drawings, and graphs. Includes a glossary, list of sources, and an index.

229. Colwin, Cecil M. **Swimming Dynamics: Winning Techniques and Strategies.** Chicago: Masters Press, 1999. 370 pp. $19.95. ISBN 1-57028-206-4.

This book contains excellent information on coaching, the techniques involved in all swimming strokes, and the history of swimming, including biographical information on and interviews with many important figures in modern swimming. It contains records and statistics, but they aren't organized in a way that makes them easily retrievable. Still, this is an important book on swimming. Colwin is also the author of *Breakthrough Swimming* (Human Kinetics, 2002).

230. Counsilman, James E., and Brian E. Counsilman. **The New Science of Swimming.** Englewood Cliffs, N.J.: Prentice Hall, 1994. 420 pp. $33.75. ISBN 0-13-099888-5.

Primarily for academic collections, this detailed and complete treatment of swimming covers the biomechanics and theory of movement in water, as well as physiology and other scientific aspects of the sport. A full chapter is devoted to each stroke, including thorough information on body position, leg and arm movements, breathing and timing. There also is extensive coverage of all aspects of training. Includes a glossary, an index, and black-and-white illustrations.

231. Freedman, Françoise Barbira. **Water Babies.** New York: Lorenz Books, Anness Publishing, 2001. 96 pp. $17.95. ISBN 0-7548-0793-2.

Beautifully illustrated with color photographs, this informative book advocates the "Birthlight" approach to water training, taking the reader through a sequence of exercises designed to encourage coordination, strength, and confidence in babies and toddlers. Includes a list of organizations, references for further reading, and an index.

232. Goldstein, Mel, and Dave Tanner. **Swimming Past 50.** Ageless Athlete. Champaign, Ill.: Human Kinetics, 1999. 203 pp. $16.95. ISBN 0-88011-907-1.

Devoted to the serious, mature swimmer, this book provides age-appropriate fitness and competitive-training information to help experienced swimmers improve their performance. Includes motivating profiles of masters swimmers over age fifty and provides the details of their workouts. Provides information on the aging process, injuries, goal setting, and using new technology and techniques. Illustrated with black-and-white photographs. Includes sample workouts, a bibliography, and an index. Appropriate for public or academic collections.

233. Juba, Kelvin. **Swimming for Fitness.** Fitness Trainers. London: A & C Black, 2001. 186 pp. $14.95. ISBN 0-7136-5825-8.

A comprehensive handbook on swimming, this volume provides information on how swimming develops fitness, the equipment needed, getting started, warming up, cooling down and stretching, goal setting and charting of progress, and nutrition. It also offers advice on improving speed, strength, and endurance. A variety of training programs are specified, based on desired objectives. Illustrated with drawings. The handbook also contains a good list of sources for further information and a list of masters swimming records (British, European, and world). Indexed.

234. Laughlin, Terry, and John Delves. **Total Immersion: The Revolutionary Way to Swim Better, Faster, and Easier.** Rev. and updated ed. New York: Simon & Schuster, 2004. 320 pp. $15.00. ISBN 0-7432-5343-4.

In the new edition of this popular book, the author teaches how improved technique can help train better swimmers. Includes step-by-step drills to encourage a smoother, easier stroke. A sampling of the topics include new moves, training versus trying, and swimming for life. Offers a holistic approach and also includes exercise for outside the water. An appendix includes six "skill-builder practices." Illustrated and indexed.

235. Maglischo, Ernest W. **Swimming Fastest.** Champaign, Ill.: Human Kinetics, 2003. 791 pp. $44.95. ISBN 0-7360-3180-4.

An epic work in swimming, for the coach and the serious athlete, this massive source explains the physiological basis for stroke technique and training methods. Includes thorough analysis of the four primary strokes—freestyle, backstroke, breaststroke, and butterfly—as well as detailed sample workouts. Illustrated with over 500 photographs and drawings. This work is a revised edition of *Swimming Even Faster* (Mayfield, 1993) by the same author.

236. Thomas, David G. **Swimming: Steps to Success.** Steps to Success Activity Series. 2nd ed. Champaign, Ill.: Human Kinetics, 1996. 160 pp. $17.95. ISBN 0-87322-846-4.

This instructional guide to swimming provides lessons in twelve clear steps, covering the basic strokes, dives, and other aquatic skills. It includes 132 drills that reinforce skills at any level and over 100 illustrations that show proper technique. It also provides instruction on basic diving into water, kicking and breathing properly, and using a mask and snorkel.

237. YMCA of the USA. **The Parent/Child and Preschool Aquatic Program Manual.** YMCA Swim Lessons. Champaign, Ill.: Human Kinetics, 1999. 198 pp. $32.00. ISBN 0-7360-0053-4.

Intended for swimming instructors who work with parents and their children, this guide presents information on the developmental characteristics of preschool children and introduces the skills appropriate for each level. Clear objectives and detailed lesson planning are provided. An appendix includes activities, games, and songs that can be incorporated into the lessons. Well illustrated with color photographs, drawings, and charts. Designed to be used with *Teaching Swimming Fundamentals* (1999), another YMCA/Human Kinetics publication.

238. YMCA of the USA. **Teaching Swimming Fundamentals.** YMCA Swim Lessons. Champaign, Ill.: Human Kinetics, 1999. 192 pp. $32.00. ISBN 0-7360-0044-5.

This text is used in the initial course taken by all YMCA swimming instructors. It establishes a structure and environment for learning and then presents the fundamentals of six strokes: front crawl, back crawl, breaststroke, side stroke, butterfly, and elementary backstroke. An appendix provides eighty-four aquatic-skill games arranged by skill, plus worksheets and checklists that can be used by instructors. Well illustrated with color photographs and drawings. Includes a bibliography and an index.

239. YMCA of the USA. **The Youth and Adult Aquatic Program Manual.** YMCA Swim Lessons. Champaign, Ill.: Human Kinetics, 1999. 202 pp. $32.00. ISBN 0-7360-0048-8.

This manual presents a teaching method for youth and adults. Seven different developmental levels of swimming skills are presented; for each, there is information on teaching personal safety, personal growth, stroke development, water games and sports, and rescue. Well illustrated with many color photographs. Appendices include drills for improving strokes and building fitness, plus rules for playing YMCA wetball. Indexed.

Web Sites

240. **International Swimming Federation / Federation Internationale de Natation Amateur (FINA).** http://www.fina.org (accessed March 4, 2004).

As the international governing body for aquatic activities, the comprehensive FINA Web site contains news, results of competition, records, rankings, a calendar of events, press releases, photos, lists of officials and judges, official rules and regulations for all activities, and publications that can be ordered. The site also contains athlete biographies and a directory of national federations.

241. **International Swimming Hall of Fame.** http://www.ishof.org (accessed March 23, 2004).

The ISHOF Web site provides full coverage of the world of swimming. It offers news, honoree biographies, information about their museum and the Henning aquatic library, and much more.

242. **Swimmers' Guide.** http://www.swimmersguide.com (accessed March 23, 2004).

This Web site provides an online version of *Swimmers' Guide*. With world-wide coverage, it is a descriptive directory of public swimming pools, searchable by location.

243. **United States Swimming.** http://www.usa-swimming.org (accessed March 21, 2004).

The national governing body for swimming competition in the United States maintains an informative Web site. It provides news and history, including all-time lists, meet results, records and rankings, an events calendar, and a great deal of other useful information.

244. **United States Synchronized Swimming.** http://www.usasynchro.org (accessed March 21, 2004).

This Web site represents the national governing body for synchronized swimming competition. It is informative, with news, recent coverage of people and events in synchronized swimming, an events calendar, photos and profiles of the national teams, club and collegiate news, a directory of summer camps, and more.

Water Polo

Reference Source

245. National Collegiate Athletic Association. **NCAA Men's/Women's Water Polo Rules.** 2003–2004 ed. Indianapolis, Ind.: National Collegiate Athletic Association, 2003. 86 pp. $7.50. ISSN 0736-5144.

This annual official rule book contains diagrams of playing areas, official signals, and the official rules and interpretations. Clearly shows changes in the rules for the year and points of emphasis. Indexed.

Instructional Sources

246. Nitzkowski, Monte. **United States Tactical Water Polo.** Pittsburgh, Pa.: Sports Support Syndicate, 1994. 376 pp. $45.00. ISBN 1-878602-93-4.

Intended for coaches and serious water polo athletes, this book is concerned primarily with the tactical aspects of the game. It provides detailed and thorough information on individual and team defense, counterattack, frontcourt offense, six-on-five, and other special situations in water polo. Drills are included to reinforce the skills being examined. Illustrated with many position diagrams and poorly reproduced black-and-white photographs. Includes a graphic glossary, a glossary of terms, and an index.

247. Nitzkowski, Monte. **Water Polo: Learning and Teaching the Basics.** Huntington Beach, Calif.: Water Polo Consulting Service, 1998. 130 pp. $29.95. ISBN 0-9662699-1-8.

This instructional source is intended to help young water polo players to learn the basic skills and their coaches to teach these skills effectively. With a focus on the swimming techniques required, as well as the throwing, passing, and shooting skills, it covers the entire range of practice. Includes a chapter on conditioning for the sport, and one on designing a practice schedule. The book is illustrated with small black-and-white photographs that could be improved upon. Contains a glossary of terms.

Web Site

248. **United States Water Polo Inc.** http://www.usawaterpolo.com (accessed March 26, 2004).

As the national governing body for water polo competition, this group's Web site is comprehensive and provides news, bylaws, athlete rights, championship information, a calendar of events, coach and referee information, and details of play at high school, collegiate, and other levels.

Chapter 4

Nautical Sports

Many early cultures navigated the water in boats powered only by the wind or by human-powered paddles and oars. In addition to being a mode of transportation, boats serve the utilitarian function of assisting in getting the catch of the day. In today's sporting world, nautical pursuits are for adventure as well as for competition. This chapter lists sources of information on a number of nautical sports, including canoeing and kayaking, rowing, sailing, and whitewater rafting. The majority of these are handbooks, which usually include a variety of information essential for the beginner and the experienced nautical enthusiast alike.

Canoeing and Kayaking

Reference Source

249. Ziegler, Ronald M. **Wilderness Waterways: The Whole Water Reference for Paddlers.** 2nd ed. Kirkland, Wash.: Canoe America Associates, 1991. 177 pp. ISBN 0-9631595-0-X; 0-9631595-1-8 (pbk.).

In this comprehensive listing of paddlers' resources, the author provides information on all aspects of the sport of paddling. Types of sources include guidebooks and articles, instruction books, competition books, history and biography sources, pictorial works, periodicals, videotapes, indexes and databases, maps and charts, government agencies, and private organizations. Includes over 1500 sources in all, from the years 1978 to 1990. Indexed by name, title, and subject.

Instructional Sources

250. Gordon, I. Herbert. **The Complete Book of Canoeing: The Only Canoeing Book You'll Ever Need.** 3rd ed. Old Saybrook, Conn.: Globe Pequot Press, 2001. 240 pp. $16.95. ISBN 0-7627-0900-6.

This canoeing handbook is a complete and informative guide to the sport. Chapters contain in-depth accounts of basic equipment, paddling skills, rapids and water level, onshore preparation, and learning to handle the water, wind and other factors. Includes a thorough discussion of liveries and outfitters and of special situations such as short trips, canoeing with kids, and wilderness travel. Includes sections on outdoor cuisine, field medicine, and protecting our rivers. Appendices contain a glossary of terms, a shopper's guide, a list of canoe and kayak schools with contact information, and a list of canoe clubs with contact information. Illustrated with photographs and drawings. Indexed.

251. Gullion, Laurie. **Canoeing.** Outdoor Pursuits. Champaign, Ill.: Human Kinetics, 1994. 146 pp. $14.95. ISBN 0-87322-443-4.

This guide to canoeing contains all the basic instructional information on paddling, maneuvering in the water, equipment, fitness, and safety. It also contains comprehensive information on planning a trip, including a thirty-page chapter on the best places to canoe, complete with maps that show good locations in North America, Europe, the United Kingdom, Australia, and New Zealand. Well illustrated with color photographs and diagrams. Appendices provide contact information for organizations, lists of publications, and a glossary of terms. Indexed.

252. Hutchinson, Derek C. **The Complete Book of Sea Kayaking.** 5th ed. Guilford, Conn.: Globe Pequot Press, 2004. 209 pp. $19.95. ISBN 0-7627-2825-6.

This fundamental guide to sea kayaking is a great all-around source for the beginner or a good reference for the advanced paddler. It covers the process of choosing equipment, boat design and history, basic and advanced techniques, weather and navigation, safety, rescue, and racing. It is well illustrated with drawings and color photographs. It is also approved by the British Canoe Union.

253. Jackson, Eric. **Whitewater Paddling: Strokes and Concepts.** Kayaking with Eric Jackson. Mechanicsburg, Pa.: Stackpole Books, 1999. 80 pp. $16.95. ISBN 0-8117-2997-4.

This book, which is sanctioned by the World Kayak Federation, introduces the strokes and concepts that are required to be successful in kayaking. The focus is on perfecting one's technique before moving into the whitewater environment. For each stroke, a similar format is used to describe, then illustrate, the technique so that the kayaker can visualize the result. Exercises and drills reinforce the information about each stroke. Further detailed instruction is given to apply the strokes and concepts to whitewater rafting. Illustrated with color photographs that show the steps being described.

254. Johnson, Shelley. **The Complete Sea Kayaker's Handbook.** Camden, Maine: Ragged Mountain Press / McGraw-Hill, 2002. 307 pp. $18.95. ISBN 0-07-136210-X.

In this comprehensive book on sea kayaking, the author introduces beginners to the sport and also provides a wealth of information for the seasoned sea kayaker. Includes good coverage of the preparation phase for a trip and also covers the skills and techniques used to control the boat and navigate the environment safely for an enjoyable trip. Includes sections on camping, maintenance of gear, and planning a dream drip, as well as on resources such as books, magazine, clubs, organizations, Web sites, schools, events, and lists of water trails. Illustrated with many photographs and diagrams. Indexed.

255. Kesselheim, Alan S. **The Wilderness Paddler's Handbook.** Camden, Maine: Ragged Mountain Press, 2001. 284 pp. $18.95. ISBN 0-07-135418-2.

Written by a noted canoeing author, this handbook of paddle sports is a combination of wilderness writing with practical aspects of canoe tripping. Provides detailed information on planning a trip, the skills and techniques required to survive the trip, and outfitting. Appendices provide a guide to "off-season puttering" and a resource list of books, periodicals, Web sites, schools, and other information. Illustrated with black-and-white photographs, maps, and charts. Indexed.

256. Kuhne, Cecil. **Canoeing: An Illustrated Guide to Equipment, Technique, Navigation, and Safety.** Paddling Basics. Mechanicsburg, Pa.: Stackpole Books, 1998. 150 pp. $15.95. ISBN 0-8117-2881-1.

This guide to the sport of canoeing presents the techniques that will enable the beginner to get started. Contains good information on the boat itself and other equipment required, on the techniques required for movement through the water, including basic and advanced paddling strokes, and on reading whitewater and other maneuvering tips. Also includes safety information and a chapter on tackling hazardous situations. Illustrated with excellent drawings by Cherie Kuhne. Appendices contain trip checklists, contact information for manufacturers and equipment sources, lists of periodicals and conservation associations, and a glossary of terms.

257. Lessels, Bruce. **AMC Whitewater Handbook.** 3rd ed. Boston: Appalachian Mountain Club Books / Globe Pequot Press, 1994. 288 pp. $14.95. ISBN 1-878239-01-5.

Includes all the basics of technique for both kayaking and canoeing, plus a guide to the terminology, equipment, strokes, and safety and rescue for the sport. Also contains a full range of advanced techniques and an introduction to racing. Appendices include information sources for learning more, finding clubs and outfitters, and joining conservation efforts. Illustrated with over 200 photographs and drawings. Indexed. Endorsed by the Appalachian Mountain Club and available for purchase on their Web site.

258. Ray, Slim. **The Canoe Handbook: Techniques for Mastering the Sport of Canoeing.** Harrisburg, Pa.: Stackpole Books, 1992. 210 pp. $16.95. ISBN 0-8117-3032-8.

In this standard source for canoeing information, the author provides the basics of preparation, instruction on the fundamental and advanced strokes, moving-water basics, and more complex maneuvers. Contains a good explanation of whitewater and other river features, including the anatomy of a river. Also covers equipment and safety. Illustrated with diagrams and action photographs.

259. Rounds, Jon. **Basic Canoeing: All the Skills and Tools You Need to Get Started.** Mechanicsburg, Pa.: Stackpole Books, 2003. 90 pp. $16.95. ISBN 0-8117-2644-4.

This basic guide to canoeing is exceptionally well illustrated, with color photographs throughout the text that guide the reader from one step to the next. It is a spiral-bound volume that could possibly be taken along for the adventure. It contains all the fundamentals of transporting the canoe, explanations of strokes both basic and more advanced, and descriptions of navigation techniques. It also contains excellent information on types of boats, paddles, and other gear, and on safety and rescue. Appendices provide the details of car topping and a list of resources. Indexed.

260. Saidman, David, and Roseann Beggy Hanson. **The Essential Sea Kayaker: The Complete Guide for the Open Water Paddler.** 2nd ed. The Essential Series. Camden, Maine: Ragged Mountain Press, 2001. 153 pp. $14.95. ISBN 0-07-136237-1.

This guide's easily understood format makes it a great source for beginners. It contains information on choosing a boat and other equipment, and transporting and maintaining it, then proceeds to teach the techniques needed for moving effectively in the open water. Includes safety and rescue information and in-depth information on navigation. Contains a section that lists other resources such as books, charts, clubs, and schools. Indexed.

Web Sites

261. **American Canoe Association.** http://www.acanet.org (accessed December 2, 2004).

A comprehensive site, with information on safety and instruction, conservation, events, and competition.

262. **American Whitewater.** http://www.americanwhitewater.org (accessed March 22, 2004).

According to its Web site, this organization "restores rivers dewatered by hydropower dams, eliminates water degradation, improves public land management and protects public access to rivers for responsible recreational use."

263. **International Canoe Federation (ICF).** http://www.canoeicf.com/ (accessed March 4, 2004).

The ICF is the international governing body for canoe/kayak competition, and it provides a great deal of information on its site, including a directory of national federations and a history of canoeing. The site also includes news and a calendar of events for each of the disciplines (flatwater, wildwater, canoe polo, etc.), information on international competition and on the structure of the organization, and many links to other sources of information.

264. **United States Canoe Association.** http://www.uscanoe.com/ (accessed December 2, 2004).

USCA is a nonprofit educational group that encourages the growth of recreational and competitive paddling. It publishes *Canoe News* and offers a basic canoeing instruction program for beginners.

265. **USA Canoe/Kayak.** http://www.usack.org/ (accessed December 2, 2004).

This group is the national governing body for canoeing and kayaking competition, and its Web site is informative. Contains athlete profiles, news, a schedule of events, bylaws, history, and much more.

Rowing

Reference Source

266. **Rules of Rowing.** 2002 ed. Indianapolis, Ind.: United States Rowing Association, 2002. 129 pp.

Edited by the Judge-Referee Committee of the United States Rowing Association, this volume contains the official rules of rowing and is updated annually. The same rules are available on the association's Web site (see "Web sites"). Call the U.S. Rowing Association at 1-800-314-4ROW (4769) to order a print copy.

Instructional Sources

267. Bourne, Gilbert C. **A Textbook of Oarsmanship: A Classic of Rowing Technical Literature.** Toronto, ON: Sport Books, 2002. 376 pp. $29.95. ISBN 0-920905-12-9.

This classic, comprehensive source, first published in 1925 and reprinted several times, covers the theory and historical context of the sport of rowing, as well as the techniques of movement required to excel. Other chapters detail the oars, boats, and other equipment used and describe the mechanics of racing, including the specific details of muscular action involved in rowing. Essays are also provided on racing techniques and coaching. Beautifully illustrated with over sixty black-and-white drawings and diagrams, plus several historic photographs.

268. Boyne, Daniel J. **Essential Sculling.** New York: Lyons Press, 2000. 141 pp. $16.95. ISBN 1-55821-709-6.

In this handbook of rowing the author discusses the health and fitness aspects of rowing but focuses more on developing one's stroke and technique, building boat-handling skill, and the mechanics of rigging and competition. Also covered in depth is the equipment of rowing, including advice on choosing a well-made boat. Regardless of age or fitness level, anyone can gain from reading about the fundamentals in this well-written and interesting source. Includes a glossary of common rowing terms. Indexed.

269. Churbuck, David C. **The Book of Rowing.** Updated ed. Woodstock, N.Y.: Overlook Press, 1999. 295 pp. $22.95. ISBN 0-87951-709-3.

Beginning with the history of rowing, this book provides nineteen informative chapters, covering such topics as how a crew works, off-the-water workouts, coaching, women in rowing, the Olympics, and recreational rowing. Illustrated with photographs and pen-and-ink drawings. Appendices contain a glossary, bibliography, and list of rowing clubs and teams in the United States, races and regattas, and sources of equipment. Indexed.

270. McArthur, John. **High Performance Rowing.** Ramsbury, Marlborough, U.K.: Crowood Press, 1997. 156 pp. $29.95. ISBN 1-86126-039-3.

Intended for coaches and crews training for competitive rowing, this book covers both the basics of the stroke and further training for higher performance levels. Includes detailed information on rigging, physiology, and technique. Describes how to write a training program. Explains strategies for improving technique and increasing power and endurance at various levels of competition. Well illustrated with many black-and-white photographs of rowers demonstrating the proper technique. Indexed.

271. Paduda, Joe. **The Art of Sculling.** Camden, Maine: International Marine / Ragged Mountain Press, 1992. 149 pp. $15.95. ISBN 0-87742-308-3.

Covers beginning technique, equipment, rigging, and advanced technique, as well as good discussion of exercise physiology, conditioning, nutrition, and energy sources. Also contains chapters on boating safety and on strategy and psychology of competition, including team racing. Includes a glossary of terms, a list of additional information sources, and an index. Illustrated with black-and-white photographs.

Web Sites

272. **International Rowing Federation / Federation Internationale de Societes d'Aviron (FISA).** http://www.worldrowing.com (accessed January 9, 2004).

FISA, the international governing body for the sport of rowing, provides an informative Web site. It includes the FISA rulebook, which is available for downloading. World results for Olympic qualifying rounds, archived race stories, information on top rowers, a photo gallery, a calendar of events, publications, and information on training and rowing equipment is all available on their comprehensive site.

273. **National Rowing Foundation.** http://www.natrowing.org (accessed December 2, 2004).

Promotes athletes and U.S. participation in international rowing competition, archives information related to rowing, and maintains the NRF hall of fame. Contains many links to Web sites of other rowing groups and museums devoted to rowing and its history. Members of the hall of fame are listed on the site; further development of member information is in development.

274. United States Rowing Association. http://www.usrowing.org (accessed March 21, 2004).

A comprehensive Web site appropriate to this national governing body, it includes member and association governance information, news, history, a regatta calendar, referee information and a referee directory, and the most current official rules of rowing. Also contains athlete and coach biographies, and many links to other rowing information.

Sailing

Reference Sources

275. Aak to Zumbra: A Dictionary of the World's Watercraft. Newport News, Va.: Mariners' Museum, 2000. 676 pp. $49.95. ISBN 0-917376-46-3.

This unique work contains over 5600 entries that define and describe the world's watercraft. Arranged in dictionary style, from A to Z, this is a source that will identify rare and extinct working watercraft. Entries contain information on the boat's origin, function, dimensions, crew size, and typical means of propulsion. It contains a geographical index by country and sources for further reading. Illustrated with over 400 detailed drawings.

276. Jeans, Peter D. **Ship to Shore: A Dictionary of Everyday Words and Phrases Derived from the Sea.** 2nd ed. Camden, Maine: International Marine / McGraw-Hill, 2004. 352 pp. $18.95. ISBN 0-07-144027-5.

More than a dictionary, this reference work provides a history of sailing, describing the language in lively detail. It describes how nautical terms have become such an essential part of everyday language. The original version of this noted dictionary was published in 1993 but is out of print, so this new version is a welcome discovery.

277. Krause, Soren, ed. **Paul Elvstrom Explains the Racing Rules of Sailing: 2005–2008.** 5th ed. Camden, Maine: International Marine, 2005. 208 pp. $24.95. ISBN 0-07-145626-0.

The first section of the book contains the complete text of the International Sailing Federation's (ISAF) official rules for 2005–2008. The second section is color coded to follow from the first section. It interprets the rules with the use of color illustrations. The third section summarizes the "case law," or the ISAF rulings on appeals. This source also provides a color chart of race signals, a graphic quick-reference locator for the rules, a summary of recent rule changes, and procedural notes for filing a protest.

277a. Lenfestey, Thompson, with Captain Thompson Lenfestey, Jr. **The Sailor's Illustrated Dictionary.** Guilford, Conn.: Lyons Press, 2004. 541 pp. $18.95. ISBN 1-59228-367-5.

Originally published as *The Facts on File Dictionary of Nautical Terms* (New York: Facts on File, 1994), this comprehensive dictionary covers terms from all aspects of the sport of sailing. The book's forty-four illustrations are useful, but one would expect more of them, considering that over 8000 terms are defined. The entries are concise, and many of them include a brief example of proper usage. Entries include "see" and "see also" references. Includes a list of abbreviations and a bibliography.

278. Mayne, Richard. **The Language of Sailing.** Chicago: Fitzroy Dearborn, 2000. 369 pp. $35.00. ISBN 1-57958-278-8.
   This rich dictionary defines the extensive language of sailing and also gives the origins of the words, with the *Oxford English Dictionary* used as the primary source. The definitions read as short essays and include abundant interesting detail and multiple examples of use. Contains a bibliography of sources quoted, but there are no illustrations.

279. Schult, Joachim. **The Sailing Dictionary: A Comprehensive Reference Book of Sailing Terms.** 2nd ed. With Jeremy Howard-Williams. Dobbs Ferry, N.Y.: Sheridan House, 1992. 331 pp. $29.95. ISBN 0-924486-37-6.
   This comprehensive specialized dictionary of over 4000 sailing terms is intended for persons who build, buy, equip, and sail boats, whether they are beginners or expert sailors. Arranged in traditional alphabetical order, the definitions are clear, concise, and illustrated with many excellent drawings. The International Code of Signals and the International Association of Lighthouse Authorities buoys are illustrated with color drawings.

Instructional Sources

280. Aarons, Richard N., ed. **Small-Boat Seamanship Manual.** Camden, Maine: International Marine / McGraw-Hill, 2002. 468 pp. $29.95. ISBN 0-07-138800-1.
   This complete manual contains the same information found in the U.S. Coast Guard's official 1200-page training guide. It provides in-depth coverage of boat handling, navigation, search and rescue, safety in extreme weather conditions, using knots properly, and emergency procedures. Illustrated with black-and-white photographs and drawings (some color). Contains a substantial glossary of terms and an index.

281. Bond, Bob. **The Handbook of Sailing.** Rev. and updated ed. New York: Alfred A. Knopf, 1997. 352 pp. $26.00. ISBN 0-679-74063-5.
   This thorough book begins with a history of the development of sailing. It covers all the basic elements, including choosing a boat, transporting it, other equipment, rigging, controls, basic seamanship, specific techniques, and rules of the road. Also covers advanced techniques, as well as cruising, navigation, meteorology, maintenance, and safety. Appendices provide aero- and hydrodynamics properties, rope work, and the essentials of boat ownership. Illustrated with many excellent photographs and diagrams. Indexed.

282. Braden, Twain. **The Handbook of Sailing Techniques.** Guilford, Conn.: Lyons Press, 2003. 192 pp. $19.95. ISBN 1-58574-644-4.

This handbook of sailing is intended to introduce most of the skills and techniques a beginning sailor will need. Skills are discussed in a systematic manner, from the basic environment of the water to essential equipment to survival tactics at sea. Includes sections on boat anatomy, equipment, navigational tools, knots and line, safety, and the mechanics of safely moving a sailboat through the water in various conditions. Illustrated with black-and-white drawings. Contains a glossary of terms and an annotated list of books and other sources for further reading. Indexed.

283. Calder, Nigel. **Boatowner's Mechanical and Electrical Manual: How to Maintain, Repair, and Improve Your Boat's Essential Systems.** 3rd ed. Camden, Maine: International Marine / McGraw-Hill, 2005. 832 pp. $49.95. ISBN 0-07-143238-8.

This hefty manual is considered by many to be an essential piece of boating equipment. Includes all the instructions needed to maintain mechanical and electrical systems on recreational boats of all sizes. Illustrated with many photographs, charts, and diagrams that show the detail of equipment and systems. A very technical source, but important for self-sufficiency when boating. Indexed.

284. Carr, Michael William. **International Marine's Weather Predicting Simplified: How to Read Weather Charts and Satellite Images.** Camden, Maine: International Marine / McGraw-Hill, 192 pp. $25.95. ISBN 0-07-012031-5.

This guide shows readers how to use satellite photos and weather maps to easily and accurately predict weather. Chapters detail how weather reports and charts are generated and provide specific information relevant for marine/coastal weather predicting. Appendices provide additional information. Includes a glossary and an index.

285. Leonard, Beth A. **The Voyager's Handbook: The Essential Guide to Bluewater Cruising.** Camden, Maine: International Marine / McGraw-Hill, 1998. 448 pp. $34.95. ISBN 0-07-038143-7.

This is a great handbook for those planning a long-term sailing adventure. This complete source offers information on the best equipment and techniques to make the voyage healthy, safe, and enjoyable. Provides excellent coverage of the leadership role women can take in sailing. Covers critical topics related to the crew, the yacht, finances, health, safety, weather, provisions, fresh water, and foreign port protocol during a long-term voyage. Appendices provide galley equivalents and substitutes and the contents of a medical kit. Illustrated and indexed.

286. Maloney, Elbert S., and Charles Frederic Chapman. **Chapman Piloting and Seamanship.** 64th ed. New York: Hearst Books, 2003. 927 pp. $49.95. ISBN 1-58816-089-0.

This classic source of recreational boating information is extremely comprehensive in its coverage. It includes Morse Code and flag signal dressings, new technologies, and all the boating essentials, such as seamanship, safety, piloting, electronics, charts and compasses, tides and weather, as well as official boating laws and government regulations. Illustrated with over 1500 photographs and drawings. Used as a text in many navigation and sailing schools, this edition is completely revised with new photographs, maps, and charts. Previously published under the title *Chapman Piloting, Seamanship & Boat Handling*.

287. Murrant, Jim. **The Boating Bible: An Essential Handbook for Every Sailor.** Dobbs Ferry, N.Y.: Sheridan House, 1991. 310 pp. $29.95. ISBN 0-924486-13-9.

A very comprehensive handbook filled with practical information, this source covers the basics as well as the complex in sailing. Beginning with sailboat construction and equipment, and continuing through knots and techniques for navigation, the author stresses safety and being prepared for anything that might arise along the way. Nicely illustrated with many drawings and photographs, some in color. Includes a dictionary of sailing terms. Indexed.

288. Sleight, Steve, and Morris Truman. **DK Complete Sailing Manual.** 1st American ed. New York: Dorling Kindersley, 1999. 320 pp. $30.00. ISBN 0-7894-4606-5.

Illustrated with over 750 color photographs, drawings, and diagrams, this reference source is a visual treat. It provides comprehensive coverage of sailing, from simple safety measures to basic ropes and knots to navigation and boat maintenance. Intended to provide basic training for beginners and also to serve as a reference for seasoned sailors. Includes suggestions for choosing a boat, navigating through rough weather conditions, and making emergency repairs. Contains a glossary of terms and an index.

289. Wing, Charles. **Boating Magazine's One Minute Guide to the Nautical Rules of the Road.** Camden, Maine: International Marine / Ragged Mountain Press, 1998. 104 pp. $14.95. ISBN 0-07-071094-5.

A practical guide, this work includes the fundamental principles of boating, how to communicate with other boats, what to do when encountering another boat, and international and U.S. inland rules for sailing, steering, shapes and lights, and signals. Written in an easy-to-understand style, with terms clearly defined. Includes a quick-reference guide for when critical decisions need to be made very quickly. Indexed.

Web Sites

290. **International Sailing Federation (ISAF).** http://www.sailing.org (accessed January 20, 2004).

The international governing body for sailing was formerly known as the International Yacht Racing Union. Their Web site contains everything you would expect: a history of the organization, news, events, manuals on training and development, sailor's information, a comprehensive listing of national sailing authorities, information on Olympic competition, rankings, and much more.

291. **United States Sailing Association (US Sailing).** http://www.ussailing.org (accessed March 21, 2004).

As the national governing body for yacht racing in the United States, this organization creates standards for sailing instruction, supports public-access programs, provides information for race officials, and prepares teams for the Olympic Games and Pan-American Games. This comprehensive site provides a calendar, rules, bylaws, an eligibility test, press releases, and much more. Formerly called the United States Yacht Racing Union.

Whitewater Rafting

Reference Sources

292. Armstead, Lloyd. **Whitewater Rafting in North America: More Than 100 River Adventures in the United States and Canada.** 2nd ed. Old Saybrook, Conn.: Globe Pequot Press, 1997. 268 pp. $16.95. ISBN 0-7627-0083-1.

This guide to whitewater rafting adventures describes 100 trips in the United States and Canada, plus an additional section on river adventures in Mexico and Costa Rica. The author begins with the basics of whitewater rafting and provides seven chapters that address aspects of trip preparation: accommodations, cost, clothing, equipment, outfitters and guides, whitewater classifications (includes a glossary), and tips on how to enjoy the river experience. The remaining chapters identify and describe trips in various geographic areas. For each area, there is a map, a river comparison chart, and detailed trip information for each river. Appendices supply a river index, a list of the best half-day trips for beginners, and the best intermediate one-day, advanced one-day, and multiday trips. Illustrated with photographs and maps.

293. Penny, Richard. **The Whitewater Sourcebook: A Directory of Information on American Whitewater Rivers.** 3rd ed. Birmingham, Ala.: Menasha Ridge Press, 1997. 319 pp. $24.95. ISBN 0-89732-245-2.

This directory of whitewater rivers includes full river descriptions arranged alphabetically by state. The entries include contact information needed to plan a trip, including sources for river levels, maps, guidebooks, and permits. There is also a summary of information at the end of each state's listing. Includes sources for hydrologic information, maps and literature, and contact information for schools, organizations, and festivals. Includes a bibliography and index of rivers.

Instructional Sources

294. Bennett, Jeff. **The Complete Whitewater Rafter.** Camden, Maine: Ragged Mountain Press / McGraw-Hill, 1996. 196 pp. $16.95. ISBN 0-07-005505-X.

This comprehensive manual is written by a professional guide and instructor, and it works from start to finish as a complete course on rafting. It contains a history of the sport, a full description of the equipment, gear, and crew, and a chapter on the dynamics of running water. Offers a primer on all the strokes, on captaining, and on running the rapids safely. Also offers a great deal of other information on planning a trip, career opportunities, and conservation. Illustrated with photographs and diagrams. Appendices supply the Safety Code of the American Whitewater Affiliation and a good list of other sources to consult. Includes a glossary and an index.

295. Kuhne, Cecil. **Whitewater Rafting: An Introductory Guide.** New York: Lyons & Burford, 1995. 168 pp. $16.95. ISBN 1-55821-317-1.

Appropriate for beginners or seasoned rafters, this guide to the sport of whitewater rafting includes chapters on equipment, rowing and paddling techniques, safety, and planning and preparing for a trip. It also describes the anatomy of a river and provides descriptions of major whitewater rafting rivers in North America, as well as a history of river preservation. Illustrated with color and black-and-white photographs and diagrams. Contains a glossary of terms and an index.

Precision and Accuracy Sports

Chapter

5

In this chapter are grouped a number of sports that require the skills of precision and accuracy. In all of them, an individual athlete performs solo, although several individuals may join together to form a team. They all require that specific equipment be utilized in play, such as arrows, specialized balls, and other objects. The precision-and-accuracy sports include archery, billiards, pool and snooker, bowling, curling, golf, and shooting.

Archery

Reference Source

296. Paterson, W. F. **Encyclopaedia of Archery.** London: Robert Hale, 1984. 202 pp. ISBN 0-7090-1072-9.

This comprehensive encyclopedia of archery is arranged in alphabetical order, with clearly written definitions of terms and explanations of the concepts of the sport. Excellent black-and-white photographs and drawings illustrate the text. Appendices contain the rules of archery, champions of a variety of archery competitions worldwide, equipment suppliers in the United Kingdom and the United States; and contact information for associations. Also includes a bibliography. Though this source is dated, it is still a very useful volume.

Instructional Sources

297. Bolnick, Helen, Richard Bryant, Margaret Horn, Robert Phillips, Don Rabska, Henry Williford, and Lura Wilson. **Archery Instruction Manual.** 4th ed. Dubuque, Iowa: Kendall / Hunt Publishing, 1993. 257 pp. $15.95. ISBN 0-8403-8402-5.

In this comprehensive guide to archery, the authors describe the history of archery, the health benefits of and conditioning required for the sport, facilities and equipment required, rules and officiating for archery competition, tournament organization, necessary techniques and strategies, safety, and bow tuning. Includes the official NAA rules and information on specialized forms of archery, such as field archery and bow hunting. The front cover of the book indicates that it is "presented by the National Archery Association of the United States."

298. Chase, Charles M. **Archery: Guidelines to Excellence.** Dubuque, Iowa: Eddie Bowers Publishing, 1997. 134 pp. ISBN 0-945483-73-2.

In this basic guide to the sport of archery, the author takes the reader step-by-step though an introduction to the sport, its equipment, techniques for shooting, strategies for better accuracy, and forms of competition. Each chapter contains a set of review questions to assess the reader's comprehension. Illustrated with black-and-white photographs and diagrams. Indexed.

298a. Engh, Douglas. **Archery Fundamentals.** Sports Fundamentals Series. Champaign, Ill.: Human Kinetics, 2005. 125 pp. $15.95. ISBN 0-7360-5501-0.

This source provides instruction in all the basic skills of archery. Topics include the essential techniques of shooting, taking aim, and scoring one's performance. The book also provides detailed information on bows, arrows, and accessories, and a chapter on repair of equipment. Includes a discussion of competition also. Illustrated with black-and-white photographs.

299. Fadala, Sam. **Traditional Archery.** Mechanicsburg, Pa.: Stackpole Books, 1999. 246 pp. $17.95. ISBN 0-8117-2943-5.

This excellent guide to the traditional form of archery provides a wealth of information on the history and present practice of the sport. It provides extensive description of technique, bow and arrow construction, selection and maintenance of equipment, and safety while practicing archery. Illustrated with black-and-white photographs. Appendices contain an annotated archer's buyer's guide, an annotated list of traditional bowyers in the United States, and an annotated list of magazines and books on traditional archery. Contains a good glossary.

300. Hamlett-Wood, Michael. **Field Archery: A Complete Guide.** London: Robert Hale, 2002. 350 pp. $40.00. ISBN 0-7090-6991-X.

This comprehensive volume covers the fundamentals of the sport as it is practiced in Great Britain. Chapters include detailed information on techniques of aiming and shooting a bow, laying out an archery ground, various types of targets, selecting and repairing equipment, setting up the wide variety of bows used; and the rules of the regulating organizations. Illustrated with black-and-white photographs and drawings. Includes an appendix of contact information for manufacturers and organizations in the United Kingdom and the United States; a glossary; and a bibliography.

301. Haywood, Kathleen M., and Catherine F. Lewis. **Archery: Steps to Success.** 2nd ed. Steps to Success Activity Series. Champaign, Ill.: Human Kinetics, 1997. 160 pp. $15.95. ISBN 0-87322-854-5.

For readers interested in developing the fundamental skills and techniques of archery, regardless of specific form or equipment. This illustrated handbook includes sections on the history of the sport, equipment and accessories, and safety. Each chapter includes drills for practice and specific keys to success. Also includes a glossary of terms. Not indexed.

302. Lawrence, H. Lea. **The Archer's and Bowhunter's Bible.** New York: Doubleday, 2001. 189 pp. $12.00. ISBN 0-385-42221-0.

This comprehensive handbook on the hunting aspect of archery provides a wealth of information on the choice and maintenance of equipment, strategies for learning the sport, and perfecting technique, as well as ethical considerations of bow hunting. Contains specific chapters on topics such as tree stands, stalking and driving techniques, competition, and typical and not-so-typical fish and game that are targeted by bow hunters. Appendices provide reference material such as names of major organizations, with contact and descriptive information; listings of hunting and shooting preserves and archery clubs in the United States and Canada, arranged by state or province; and government regulating agencies.

303. McKinney, Wayne C., and Mike W. McKinney. **Archery.** 8th ed. Madison, Wisc.: Brown & Benchmark, 1997. 252 pp. $12.80. ISBN 0-697-27983-9.

This comprehensive guide to archery begins with a full chapter on the history of the sport. What follows is an in-depth discussion of the arrow and bow, as well as other accessories, and their care. The fundamentals of the activity are explained in detail, and the use of archery in sport, hunting, and fishing is explained. The book also provides full information on fitness and conditioning for the archer, and a chapter on literature and art related to archery rounds out the work. Illustrated with many black-and-white photographs and drawings. Appendices list official wildlife agencies in the United States and Canada; archery organizations. A glossary of terms and a selected bibliography are provided. Indexed.

304. Onuma, Hideharu. **Kyudo: The Essence and Practice of Japanese Archery.** With Dan DeProspero and Jackie DeProspero. New York: Kodansha International, 1993. 160 pp. $35.00. ISBN 4-7700-1734-0.

The Japanese art of Kyudo is defined and described in this well-written source. Covers the history and development of the art, as well as the philosophy and spirit behind it. Defines the elements of the shooting place, equipment and accessories, and the eight stages of shooting. Further describes the technique in basic, intermediate, and advanced forms and provides detailed instruction on the practice of Kyudo. Well illustrated with many step-by-step drawings, photographs, and a set of color prints. A unique appendix reveals an enlightening conversation between teacher and student. Includes a bibliography, a directory, and an index.

305. Ruis, Steve, and Claudia Stevenson, eds. **Precision Archery.** Champaign, Ill.: Human Kinetics, 2004. 202 pp. $19.95. ISBN 0-7360-4634-8.

This guide to archery is intended for those who are approaching more advanced skill levels and want to prepare for competition; thus, it includes in-depth instruction. Chapters cover competition, advanced form, tuning bows, coaching and being coached, practice strategies, conditioning programs, and testing new equipment. Includes sources of further information, a bibliography, and an index.

306. United States Olympic Committee. **A Basic Guide to Archery.** Updated Olympic ed. An Official United States Olympic Committee Sports Series. Glendale, Calif.: Griffin Publishing, 1997. 114 pp. $7.95. ISBN 1-882180-88-7.

This guide provides basic information intended to help the novice user get started with the sport. Covers history, fundamentals of the sport, information on the Olympics and other competitions, equipment, safety, and nutrition and training. Illustrated with drawings and black-and-white photographs. Includes a glossary and information about the National Archery Association of the United States.

307. Wise, Larry. **Bow and Arrow: The Complete Guide to Equipment, Technique, and Competition.** Mechanicsburg, Pa.: Stackpole Books, 1992. 278 pp. $16.95. ISBN 0-8117-2411-5.

This guide to archery covers target archery, field archery, and unknown-distance archery for recreation, competition, and hunting. Provides detailed information on equipment, including instructions on how to make arrows and tune a bow, and coverage of the techniques and strategies required to improve shooting form, along with practice tips. Includes safety information too. Illustrated with line drawings. Appendices contain official archery tournament regulations and bylaws.

Web Sites

308. **International Archery Federation (FITA).** http://www.archery.org/ (accessed March 4, 2004).

FITA is the international governing body for archery, and as such its site contains news, press releases, results of competition, a calendar of events, rules to download, other publications, statistics, a world ranking list, photographs, and essays on the history of archery and of FITA, and much more. A directory of national member organizations is available as a PDF file. In French, the name is Federation Internationale de Tir a l'Arc.

309. **National Archery Association.** http://www.usarchery.org (accessed March 20, 2004).

The national governing body for archery competition in the United States maintains an informative Web site that contains a calendar of events, results, records, news, club information, rules and regulations, and much more.

310. **National Field Archery Association (NFAA).** http://www.nfaa/archery.org/ (accessed April 1, 2004).

The NFAA's Web site contains general information about field archery and its various styles and rules; about the organization and its purpose, programs, and tournaments; news; and links to other sites.

Billiards

Reference Sources

311. Billiard Congress of America. **Billiards: The Official Rules and Records Book.** New York: Lyons Press, 1992. 152 pp. $10.95. ISBN 1-55821-189-6.

This compact handbook contains all the official rules of play, as sanctioned by the Billiard Congress of America. It offers a brief history of the game, equipment specifications, information for referees and tournament play, and the detailed instructions that guide the play of many forms of billiards, including snooker. It also provides the fundamental techniques and strategies that are useful for beginners. Includes a list of BCA champions and a glossary of billiards terms.

312. Shamos, Michael Ian. **The New Illustrated Encyclopedia of Billiards.** Rev. and updated ed. New York: Lyons Press, 2002. 336 pp. $19.95. ISBN 1-58574-685-1.

In this comprehensive reference on snooker, billiards, pool, and other cue sports, the author covers the history of cue sports, the rules, records, statistics, and important players. With over 2000 entries and 200 illustrations, it is a treasure for those who are serious advocates of billiards. Appendices contain additional information, such as a list of billiard concepts indexed with numerical value; a list of over 400 billiard games; and names of over 100 billiard organizations. The work also contains a bibliography of sources cited in the text. Indexed.

Instructional Sources

313. Byrne, Robert. **Byrne's Complete Book of Pool Shots: 350 Moves Every Player Should Know.** San Diego, Calif.: A Harvest Original / Harcourt Books, 2003. 356 pp. $22.00. ISBN 0-15-602721-6.

Intended for pool players of every skill level, including the advanced, this comprehensive guide to pool shots describes 350 different shots. The noted author begins with a brief chapter reviewing the fundamentals for beginners. The shots are arranged according to twenty categories, such as back spin, banks, caroms, and jumps. The book contains illustrations. An appendix offers an essay on the culture of the game. Indexed.

314. Byrne, Robert. **Byrne's New Standard Book of Pool and Billiards.** Rev. ed. San Diego, Calif.: Harcourt Brace, 1998. 406 pp. $35.00. ISBN 0-15-100325-4.

Considered the bible of billiards by many, this reference is organized in two main sections: the first is on pool, and the second, on three-cushion billiards. Both begin with the fundamentals of play and progress to in-depth coverage of every shot imaginable. Each section contains its own glossary. The book includes chapters on eight-ball, nine-ball, trick shots, and collecting billiard memorabilia. With over 400 illustrations, the book clearly demonstrates the techniques and concepts that are described. Offers sources of additional information and an index.

315. Everton, Clive. **Snooker and Billiards: Technique, Tactics, Training.** Swindon, Wiltshire, U.K.: Crowood Press, 1991. 128 pp. $22.95. ISBN 1-85223-480-6.

Appropriate for players at any level, this guide is focused primarily on snooker, with a separate section devoted to billiards. It provides a brief history and objectives and rules of snooker, and a detailed view of the equipment and accessories, then provides detailed coverage of the skills, techniques, and strategies required to be successful. The book's color photographs and drawings contribute to the clear presentation of the skills and tactics. Contains both a general glossary and one devoted to snooker. Indexed.

Web Sites

316. **Billiard Congress of America.** http://www.bca-pool.com (accessed March 19, 2004).

This comprehensive Web site contains information on the history of billiards and of the BCA; news; the general rules of pocket billiards; information on equipment; dates of tournaments; results; a hall of fame; and a list of regional, national, and international periodical publications on billiards and related games.

317. **World Pool-Billiard Association.** http://www.wpa-pool.com (accessed March 31, 2004).

The Web site of this international organization devoted to billiard sports is comprehensive and informative. It contains the history of billiards as well as of the WPA, official world rules, a calendar of events, news, rankings, and tournament results. Offers many links to other information.

Bowling

Instructional Sources

318. Agne-Traub, Charlene E., Joan L. Martin, and Ruth E. Tandy. **Bowling.** Sports and Fitness. 8th ed. Boston: McGraw-Hill, 1998. 120 pp. $18.43. ISBN 0-697-34539-4.

This basic guide to bowling covers this sport's history, skills, scoring, rules, professional organizations and competitions, leagues, and equipment. Using a four-step approach, it teaches the fundamentals to beginning bowling students of any age, and it can be used to enhance the skills of experienced bowlers. Includes a chapter on the language of bowling. Indexed and illustrated with black-and-white photographs, diagrams, and drawings.

319. Grinfelds, Vesma, and Bonnie Hultstrand. **Right Down Your Alley: The Complete Book of Bowling.** The Wadsworth Activity Series. 5th ed. Belmont, Calif.: Thomson / Wadsworth, 2003. 162 pp. $21.95. ISBN 0-534-51575-4.

This comprehensive guide to bowling includes the basics of equipment, etiquette, safety, and orientation to the modern bowling environment. Provides detailed discussion of stance, approach, delivery, and body movement during play, as well as advanced techniques and suggested practice plans. Updated to include techniques for left-handed bowlers. Illustrated with black-and-white photographs and diagrams. Appendices include in-depth information on scoring, league bowling, rules, history, and a bowler's analysis chart. Contains a glossary of terms. Indexed.

320. Mullen, Michelle. **Bowling Fundamentals: A Better Way to Learn the Basics.** Sports Fundamentals. Champaign, Ill.: Human Kinetics, 2004. 127 pp. $14.95. ISBN 0-7360-5120-1.

This guide to bowling covers the basic skills and tactics required for success in the game, including offensive and defensive strategies. It provides instructions in a sequential order and is illustrated with photographs. Covers grip, stance, footwork, arm swing, timing, and release.

321. Strickland, Robert H. **Bowling: Steps to Success.** 2nd ed. Steps to Success Activity Series. Champaign, Ill.: Human Kinetics, 1996. 162 pp. $17.95. ISBN 0-87322-581-3.

This series of lessons is arranged sequentially, with 66 drills in all. At every step, performance goals are given, many times with instructions on how to increase or decrease the level of difficulty. Includes a brief history of the game, information on selecting equipment, and a score sheet. Illustrated with 145 drawings and diagrams. Contains a glossary of terms and a list of further references.

Web Sites

322. **Bowl.com.** http://www.bowl.com (accessed January 26, 2004).

This master bowling site provides links to all the major bowling organizations, including the American Bowling Congress and collegiate, junior, and women's membership groups. Provides news, a calendar of events, tournament results, and an online encyclopedia of bowling that includes records and statistics. Also includes an online directory of bowling centers, searchable by state or province.

323. **USA Bowling.** http://www.bowl.com/bowl/usa (accessed March 31, 2004).

USA Bowling is the national governing body for bowling competition, as recognized by the United States Olympic Committee. The site provides news, an events calendar, tournament results, records and statistics, the rules of bowling, and profiles of the men's and women's Olympic bowling team members.

Curling

Reference Source

324. Hansen, Warren. **Curling: The History, the Players, the Game.** Toronto, ON: Key Porter Books, 1999. 176 pp. $29.95. ISBN 1-55263-083-8.

This fascinating account of curling history also contains significant reference material; detailed information on rules and etiquette; fundamentals of play such as equipment, game objectives, and scoring; and well-illustrated technique and strategy of play. Appendices provide contact information for major associations, a list of WCF member nations, and lists of Olympic winners and hall of fame members. Includes a glossary of terms. Indexed.

Instructional Sources

325. Bolton, Rod, and Ann Douglas. **The Complete Idiot's Guide to Curling.** Scarborough, ON: Prentice Hall Canada, 1998. 227 pp. $21.95. ISBN 0-13-081815-1.

This interesting guide to curling contains a full chapter on the history of the game, followed by chapters on equipment, team composition, and the rules of the game. Also included is information on the physics of curling, as well as basic skills, advanced techniques, and training for the game. Illustrated with black-and-white diagrams. Appendices contain official Canadian and U.S. rules of play; other sources for information; contact information for major associations; lists of championship results; and hall of fame members. Includes an extensive glossary of curling terms. Indexed.

326. Weeks, Bob. **Curling for Dummies.** Toronto, ON: CDG Books Canada, 2001. 342 pp. $21.99. ISBN 1-894413-30-X.

This guide to the sport of curling contains information on history, equipment, the rules, techniques and strategy, and much more. Includes details of competition, as well as coverage of coaching and curling for kids. Illustrated with diagrams and black-and-white photographs. Contains a brief glossary and an extensive index.

Web Sites

327. **Canadian Curling Association.** http://www.curling.ca/ (accessed December 2, 2004).

Canada's curling Web site provides news, information on championships, a history of curling, instructions for how to play, a glossary of terms, rules of the game, and in-depth coverage of the business aspects of the sport. The site also allows interactive access to member curling clubs in Canada and a look at members of the Canadian Curling Hall of Fame.

328. **United States Curling Association.** http://www.usacurl.org (accessed March 26, 2004).

The national governing body for curling maintains a comprehensive and informative Web site containing news; results; a bonspiel schedule; the World Curling Federation rules; a thorough description of technique, strategy, scoring; a glossary of terms; information on clubs, and much more.

329. **World Curling Federation (WCF).** http://www.worldcurlingfederation. org/ (accessed March 27, 2004).

As the international governing body for curling competition, the WCF maintains a comprehensive Web site with news, results, statistics, information about curling, a history of the federation, and information on wheelchair curling.

Golf

Reference Sources

330. Campbell, Malcolm. **The New Encyclopedia of Golf.** 3rd American ed. New York: Dorling Kindersley, 2001. 384 pp. $40.00. ISBN 0-7894-8036-0.

This visually stunning encyclopedia of golf begins with chapters that detail the history of the early game and its equipment, and then the modern game and its equipment and course architects. It features 100 golf courses, with a descriptive essay for each, along with course statistics, color photographs, and a map of each course. The location of each course is marked on a world map. An additional fifty world courses are described more briefly but also include maps and statistics. Another section profiles 100 men and women who have been instrumental in golf. Records from all the important championships are listed in a final section. Contains a glossary of terms and an index.

331. Davies, Peter. **The Historical Dictionary of Golfing Terms: From 1500 to the Present.** New York: Michael Kesend Publishing, 1992. 188 pp. $16.95. ISBN 0-935576-44-4.

A serious golf dictionary, this one traces the historical development and continuity of the terminology's meaning and provides dated citations that illustrate the terminology's use. The author provides his primary source in the foreword. Illustrated with finely detailed drawings of golf bags and clubs.

332. Galyean, Gary A. **Golf Rules Illustrated.** New and rev. ed. New York: Hamlyn; Distributed by Sterling Publishing, 2001. 151 pp. $19.95. ISBN 0-600-60219-2.

In this official publication of the United States Golf Association, the current rules are explained in detail and presented clearly through more than 100 color photographs and drawings. Particular attention is paid to the difficult incidents for which rules are needed in order to interpret the proper course of action. Intended for golfers of all playing levels. Topics include etiquette, equipment, the green, and play itself and various forms of play. The official USGA rules book does not contain illustrations, so this volume complements it nicely. This edition contains the USGA rules as revised in January, 2000 and is effective through 2003.

333. *Golf* **Magazine's Encyclopedia of Golf: The Complete Reference.** 2nd ed. New York: HarperCollins, 1993. 517 pp. $40.00. ISBN 0-06-270019-7.

An excellent source of many different types of information about golf, this encyclopedia provides good historical coverage. It begins with a chapter of general history, then moves on to major championships and other significant tournaments, with year-by-year lists of winners and scores for each. The next section profiles golf's greatest players; entries are arranged alphabetically by name and include career highlights and tournament records for each golfer. Award winners and hall of famers are listed, as are leading money winners. Other sections focus on equipment, the principles of golf, the rules, and golf architecture. Illustrated with black-and-white photographs and drawings. Contains a glossary of terms and an index.

334. Lawrenson, Derek. **The Complete Encyclopedia of Golf: Definitive World Golf Reference.** London: Carlton Books, 1999. 648 pp. $45.00. ISBN 1-85868-752-7.

This impressive encyclopedia traces the history of golf from its early years to the present. Describes the four major tournaments and many of the others with substantial, informative essays and complete statistics for each year. This source also ranks the top 200 male golfers and the top 50 women, providing biographical information on their lives and golf careers. The top 100 golf courses in the world also are ranked and described. A final chapter in the work contains records such as for persons with the most wins in major championships, individual records for major championships, and the leading money winners. Illustrated with many excellent photographs, in both black-and-white and color. Indexed.

335. Marrandette, David G. **Golf Playoffs: A Sourcebook of Major Championship Men's and Women's Amateur and Professional Playoffs, 1876–1990.** Jefferson, N.C.: McFarland, 1991. 157 pp. $28.50. ISBN 0-89950-552-X.

Focused on the tie-breaking golf playoff, this sourcebook provides the context and outcome of every such instance that occurred between 1876 and 1990. For each men's and women's championship, the playoff circumstances are described in a brief essay. Illustrated with black-and-white photographs. Appendices for men and women provide a chronological playoff list, a list by tournament, an alphabetical list by winner, and numerous other lists and little-known facts. Contains a bibliography and an index.

336. McCallen, Brian. *Golf Magazine*'s **Top 100 Courses You Can Play.** New York: Harry N. Abrams, 1999. 304 pp. $45.00. ISBN 0-8109-4134-1.

A beautifully illustrated guide based on a biennial survey in *Golf Magazine*, this work shows exactly what to expect at each of the 100 top U.S. courses that admit nonmembers. Located in all parts of the country, some courses are municipal, some require only a daily green fee, some are at resorts, and all are high-quality experiences. This book also provides dining and lodging listings and indicates the availability of spas, other recreation and entertainment activities, and side trips. The courses are arranged by geographic region. Includes a list of the Audubon certified sanctuaries and a ranked list of the top 100.

337. Pedroli, Hubert and Mary Tiegreen. **The American Golfer's Guide: Over 500 of the Best American Golf Courses Open to the Public.** Atlanta, Ga.: Turner Publishing, 1992. 304 pp. $19.95. ISBN 1-878685-10-4.

Divided into ten regional chapters then arranged by state within each region, this guide shows a map of each region with the courses identified on it. For each of the courses the following information is provided: phone numbers, accommodations, number of holes, par, yardage, USGA and slope ratings, style, access, season, high, green fees, availability of reduced fees, reservation period, and whether a driving range is available. Well illustrated with beautiful color photographs, maps, and course diagrams.

338. Pedroli, Hubert, ed. **Let the Big Dog Eat! A Dictionary of the Secret Language of Golf.** New York: William Morrow, 2000. 94 pp. $18.00. ISBN 0-688-17576-7.

A humorous dictionary of golf slang, this one defines the terms that may be used frequently but that don't make it into the other reference works. More a popular source, it will be most appropriate in public libraries.

339. Rutter, Hadyn. **The Illustrated Golf Rules Dictionary.** Rev. and updated ed. Chicago, Ill.: Triumph Books, 2004. 384 pp. $19.95. ISBN 1-57243-623-9.

The first edition (1998) and the second edition (2000) of this work were published as *The Golf Rules Dictionary*. This third edition reflects the USGA rules, as amended for 2004. The format of the dictionary is intended to be less formal than the official rules, helping golfers easily locate a rule in common language. Arranged alphabetically by the name or topic of the rule and collated by relevancy; for example, all rules related to the club are found together under "Club." Illustrated with many color photographs. Although there is no index, it is easy to navigate because of the color headings at the top of every page.

340. Sandler, Corey. **Golf U.S.A.: A Guide to the Best Golf Courses and Resorts.** Chicago: Contemporary Books, 2000. 328 pp. $16.95. ISBN 0-8092-2644-8.

A directory of golf courses and resorts, this source provides information on 2500 public, resort, and semiprivate courses in the United States. It contains four introductory chapters that explain and advise on how to save money on air and travel packages and at hotels. The directory is arranged by region and then by state. It offers ratings of the best courses in each state, as well as the best deals for golfers. Discount rates are noted, as is the range of greens fees for each course. The city and phone number for each course is provided, and other features are noted along with the numerical rating. Includes a quick-find index.

341. Swift, Duncan. **The Golfers Reference Dictionary Illustrated.** Classic Golf Collection. Dearborn, Mich.: Schaefer's Publishing, 1999. 255 pp. $16.95. ISBN 0-9658132-1-5.

The author of this golf dictionary states in the introduction that the purpose of the volume is to teach readers about the game of golf through its rich collection of terms and phrases. Arranged alphabetically, 2000 words and expressions are defined and illustrated with over 330 black-and-white drawings and photographs. A lengthy appendix contains many additional resources, such as contact information for U.S. and international golf associations, including separate listings for women's and junior associations. Also lists contact information for nearly thirty golf periodicals.

342. United States Golf Association. **The Rules of Golf.** Larger type, 2002–2003 ed. Far Hills, N.J.: United States Golf Association, 2002. 225 pp. $9.50. ISBN 0-9714881-1-8.

Also published under the title *The Official Rules of Golf*, these rules are approved by the United States Golf Association and the Royal and Ancient Golf Club of St. Andrews, Scotland; they are reviewed every four years by these and other official bodies of the sport. Each version prominently lists the changes since the previous revision. Covers etiquette, definitions, and the detailed rules of play. Appendices contain local rules, specifications for the design of clubs and the ball, and the rules of amateur status. This version also includes the USGA policy on gambling, lightning safety tips, and USGA contact info. Illustrated with only a few drawings that show the design of clubs; the cover is illustrated with a photograph of a woman playing golf. Indexed.

Instructional Sources

343. Adams, Mike, and T. J. Tomasi. **Total Golf.** With Kathryn Maloney of the Academy of Golf at PGA National. Chicago: Triumph Books, 2002. 256 pp. $29.95. ISBN 1-57243-458-9.

Primarily an instructional source and guide to technique, this encyclopedia offers abundant information for the beginner as well as for the experienced golfer in need of tips from the pros. Each chapter analyzes a different aspect of the game, using photographs of professional and amateur players to illustrate the differences between correct and incorrect technique. According to the cover of the book, it is "the most comprehensive guide to golf and golf instruction." Illustrated with sequential color photographs of golf's most famous stars. Indexed.

344. Curtis, Bruce and Jay Morelli. **Beginning Golf.** New York: Sterling Publishing, 2000. 96 pp. $19.95. ISBN 0-8069-4970-8.

A great start for kids or adults, this guide to golf provides all the fundamentals in a clear and concise format. Also includes good information for the golfer who wants to improve skills or technique. The instructions flow in a step-by-step approach, beginning with equipment that fits. Illustrated with many color photographs.

345. Folio, M. Rhonda, and Robert W. Nichols. **Skill Building for Beginning Golf.** Boston: Allyn & Bacon, 1997. 189 pp. $26.00. ISBN 0-205-16006-9.

Intended to benefit all golfers, from beginners to the more advanced golfers who wish to fine-tune their skills, this instructional source places emphasis on the fundamental skills, featuring both simple and complex drills. Readers learn how to practice successfully in both indoor and outdoor environments.

346. Gensemer, Robert. **Beginning Golf.** 2nd ed. Morton Activity Series. Englewood, Colo.: Morton Publishing, 1995. 122 pp. $21.95. ISBN 0-89582-264-4.

This how-to book for beginners provides a basic guide to the game and clear information on technique, strokes, strategy, and the mental aspects of the game of golf. Includes exercises for strength and flexibility. Illustrated with black-and-white photographs and drawings. Appendices provide a simplified version of the rules and basic information on equipment. Contains a glossary of terms. Indexed.

347. Levy, Allan M., and Mark L. Fuerst. **Golf Injury Handbook: Professional Advice for Amateur Athletes.** New York: John Wiley, 1999. 171 pp. $14.95. ISBN 0-471-24853-3.

Intended to encourage amateur golfers to utilize conditioning techniques to build flexibility and strength so they will prevent injuries but also take care of themselves properly after injuries occur. Includes detailed explanation of proper warm-up, conditioning, and strength training, as well as specific exercises that strengthen every part of the body. Treats the body from head to toe, with coverage of typical injury-prone areas. The many exercises are illustrated with drawings. Includes special sections for seniors, women, and people with disabilities. Indexed.

348. Metzler, Michael W. **Golf: Mastering the Basics with the Personalized Sport Instruction System.** Personalized Sport Instruction. Boston: Allyn & Bacon, 2001. 121 pp. $17.00. ISBN 0-205-32386-3.

This workbook teaches the fundamentals of golf and can be used in a formal course setting or by individuals who want to work at their own pace outside a course and chart their own progress. Each chapter presents a module of information about performance skills, shots, or the game itself and concludes with tasks that test what was learned. Includes the rules of golf. Illustrated with photographs and diagrams.

349. Nance, Virginia Lindblad, Elwood Craig Davis, and Kay E. McMahon. **Golf.** Sports and Fitness. 8th ed. Boston: McGraw-Hill, 1998. 128 pp. $9.60. ISBN 0-697-34538-6.

This is an informative source not only for the beginner but also for experienced golfers who want to improve their performance. It imparts knowledge on many aspects of the game, from the basic techniques to the mental strategy used on the course. Chapters provide detailed coverage of the game, safety, basic golf concepts, grip and stance, short approach shots, the full strokes, the putting stroke, other shots, and strategies. Illustrated with black-and-white photographs, drawings and diagrams. Contains a rules test, a glossary of golf terms, and an index.

350. Owens, DeDe, and Linda K. Bunker. **Advanced Golf: Steps to Success.** Steps to Success Activity Series. Champaign, Ill.: Leisure Press, 1992. 170 pp. $15.95. ISBN 0-88011-464-9.

In fourteen sequential steps, this second-level guide to advanced golf explains proper technique. Accompanying drills reinforce the skills being taught and assist with correcting typical errors. At each step, a checklist for evaluating technique is offered so users can proceed at their own pace. Includes in-depth chapters on swing fundamentals, controlling ball flight and distance, variations in shots, advanced putting, and other challenges of play. Illustrated with drawings at every step. Includes a list of suggested readings.

351. Owens, DeDe, and Linda K. Bunker. **Golf: Steps to Success.** Steps to Success Activity Series. 2nd ed. Champaign, Ill.: Human Kinetics, 1995. 161 pp. $17.95. ISBN 0-87322-578-3.

A sequential set of learning tools is presented in this beginning guide to golf. Each step builds on the previous one and is illustrated with drawings that will assist the reader in visualizing the goals. The skills are complemented by over eighty drills and practice techniques that reinforce what is being taught. Self-evaluation tools are included, as is information about the history of the game, scorekeeping, and mental strategies.

352. Saunders, Vivien. **The Golf Handbook for Women: The Complete Guide to Improving Your Game.** New York: Three Rivers Press, 2000. 224 pp. $18.00. ISBN 0-609-80511-8.

Illustrated with beautiful color photographs and diagrams, this excellent handbook takes the novice through the basics and the experienced golfer through additional points of advanced technique. Begins with discussion of proper equipment and moves into first lessons, techniques, and further strategies, all carefully described and illustrated. Provides information on etiquette, competition, and rules. Includes a glossary and an index.

353. Saunders, Vivien. **The Golf Handbook: The Complete Guide to the Greatest Game.** A Marshall, ed.; 1st American ed. New York: Crown Trade Paperbacks, 1997. 224 pp. $15.00. ISBN 0-609-80066-3.

Intended for everyone, from the beginner to the seasoned golfer, this handbook covers all aspects of the game, from technique, tactics, and practice to history, language, and etiquette of the game. Includes information on reading the course and a program of exercises to increase strength and flexibility. Well illustrated with color and black-and-white photographs and many drawings that support the text. Contains a glossary of terms and an index.

Web Sites

354. **International Golf Federation (IGF).** http://www.internationalgolf federation.org/ (accessed April 4, 2004).

The mission of the IGF is to promote golf as an Olympic sport and, once that is approved, act as the federation for golf in the Olympic Games. The Web site contains history, a list of notable past players, records, and a directory of member nations.

355. **Ladies Professional Golf Association (LPGA).** http://www.lpga.com/ (accessed April 4, 2004).

Features LPGA tournament results, player interviews, golf tournament directory and schedule, youth golf programs, a database listing more than 1100 teaching professionals worldwide, and much more.

356. **Professional Golfer's Association of America (PGA).** http://www.pga .com (accessed December 2, 2004).

The PGA maintains an informative Web site with news, tournament schedules, results, a learning center, and much more.

357. **United States Golf Association (USGA).** http://www.usga.org (accessed April 4, 2004).

The national governing body for golf competition in the United States, the USGA maintains a very informative Web site. Includes rules, handicap, equipment, etiquette, guidelines for amateur status, USGA history, complete list of championships and other events, information on turf management, and much more.

Shooting

Reference Source

358. Biscotti, M. L. **A Bibliography of American Sporting Books, 1926–1985.** Far Hills, N.J.: Meadow Run Press, 1997. 573 pp. ISBN 188696-706-7.

This scholarly bibliography describes books and pamphlets published about American game mammals and birds between 1926 and 1985. It also includes a significant number of books about hunting, firearms used for sporting purposes, bow hunting, hunting dogs, and foxhunting. The arrangement is alphabetical by author, and many entries are briefly annotated. Notes indicating scarcity are also provided. The title page indicates that this book has been "approved by the Boone and Crockett Club."

Instructional Source

359. Painter, Doug. **The Complete Hunter.** Guilford, Conn.: Lyons Press, 2004. 512 pp. $16.95. ISBN 1-59228-427-2.

Written by the editors of *Field & Stream* magazine, this practical book is intended for hunters with any level of experience. It covers topics such as the best way to hunt white-tailed deer; how to choose appropriate bow-hunting gear; taking care of firearms and using safety measures; the best methods for hunting specific game birds such as turkeys, pheasants, grouse, doves, quail, and other upland birds; and how to develop accuracy in all shooting sports, including trap, skeet, and sporting clays. Illustrated with photographs and drawings.

Web Sites

360. **International Shooting Sport Federation (ISSF).** http://www.issf-shooting.org (accessed March 4, 2004).

The ISSF, world governing body for the sport of shooting, maintains an informative Web site. It offers in-depth information on the structure of the organization, official rules and regulations, results for men and women, world ranking, championships, the Olympic Games, a calendar of events, news, links to other sites, and much more. Formerly called the Union Internationale de Tir (UIT).

361. **USA Shooting.** http://www.usashooting.com (accessed March 27, 2004).

This organization is the national governing body for the Olympic shooting sports, and their Web site is a good source of news, information about upcoming competitions, results, records, and biographies of athletes, shooting clubs, and much more.

Ice and Snow Sports

6

This chapter on ice and snow sports lists information sources on biathlons, bobsledding, hockey, luge, skating, and skiing. Of these, hockey is the most prominent spectator sport by far, so many more print sources are published on hockey than on the other sports. For some ice and snow sports, the information available at the governing body's Web site was the best available, so no print sources were included.

Biathlon

Web Sites

362. **International Biathlon Union (IBU).** http://www.biathlonworld.com (accessed January 9, 2004).

The international governing body for biathlon competition, the IBU has developed a comprehensive Web site containing information about the organization, a directory of member nations, history of the sport, an international directory of training centers, and the *IBU Handbook*, which is available as a PDF. The site also offers news, an events calendar, and a time line of important events in biathlon history, a data archive, and a database of athlete profiles.

363. **United States Biathlon Association.** http://www.usbiathlon.com (accessed March 20, 2004).

The national governing body for biathlons maintains a Web site that contains news, rankings, a calendar of events, and much more.

Bobsledding

Instructional Source

364. Kummer, Hans, and United States Olympic Committee. **A Basic Guide to Bobsledding.** An Official United States Olympic Committee Sports Series.

Torrance, Calif.: Griffin Publishing Group / Gareth Stevens Publishing, 2002. 160 pp. $22.60. ISBN 0-8368-3101-2.

This guide provides basic information intended to help the novice user get started with the sport. Covers history and fundamentals of bobsledding, as well as information on the Olympics and other competitions, sleds, clothing, other equipment, safety, and nutrition and training. Describes the preparation necessary to participate in bobsledding. Illustrated with drawings and black-and-white photographs. Includes a glossary of terms and identifies famous competitors.

Web Sites

365. **Federation Internationale de Bobsleigh et de Tobogganing (FIBT).** http://www.bobsleigh.com (accessed January 19, 2004).

As the international governing body for bobsleigh and skeleton, the FIBT maintains an informative Web site that includes a history of the organization and of the sport, rules in PDF format, and a description of the sled, the race, and the track. It also includes news, a calendar of events, results of competition, athlete biographies, links to national federations, and links to tracks worldwide.

366. **United States Bobsled and Skeleton Federation.** http://www.usabob sledandskeleton.org (accessed March 26, 2004).

The national governing body for the sports of bobsledding and skeleton provides an informative Web site with profiles of athletes, news, results, a calendar of events, and much more.

Hockey

Reference Sources

367. Brown, Michael. **Hockey Rules in Pictures.** New, rev. ed. New York: Putnam Publishing Group, 1992. 95 pp. $10.75. ISBN 0399517723.

This official rule book of the National Hockey League is illustrated with over eighty line drawings that may be useful to young players who are learning the rules for the first time or anyone who appreciates a visual presentation in addition to text.

368. Carroll, M. R. **The Concise Encyclopedia of Hockey.** Vancouver, BC: Greystone Books, 2001. 244 pp. $19.95. ISBN 1-55054-845-X.

The diverse entries in this encyclopedia, from All-Star Game to Zamboni, cover all the major events that characterize hockey, terminology, rules and unique features of the game, as well as biographies of the major athletes and promoters. Also contains coverage of women's hockey. Appendices list major NHL, minor-league, college, junior, and international award and trophy winners. Lists Stanley Cup winners and finalists from 1893 to 2001. Illustrated with black-and-white photographs. Indexed.

369. Carter, Craig, ed. *The Sporting News* **Hockey Guide.** 2002–2003 ed. St. Louis, Mo.: Sporting News Publishing, 2002. 420 pp. $16.95. ISBN 0-89204-679-1.

This standard hockey reference annual contains the complete team-by-team schedules for the current season, as well as team-by-team histories and club directories, all-time NHL records and award-winners, and complete minor-league and college statistics. It also contains a day-by-day season schedule for the current season and an in-depth review of the previous season. Provides a listing of Stanley Cup champions, year-by-year standings, records, and a hall of fame member list. At the end of the book is an index of teams from all leagues.

370. Diamond, Dan. **Total Hockey: The Official Encyclopedia of the National Hockey League.** 2nd ed. Kingston, N.Y.: Total Sports Publishing, 2000. 1974 pp. $54.95. ISBN 1-892129-85-X.

In this tome of hockey history and statistics, complete career data is presented for over 5000 athletes, covering their NHL careers and also statistics from junior, collegiate, senior, minor pro, European, Olympics, and World Championship play. Sections of the book cover the origins and history of hockey; the current state of the game for Canada, the United States, Europe, and women; the NHL; junior and other pro hockey; the international game; other aspects of the game; and the statistical and biographical player registers. Includes team histories, year-by-year histories, demographics, and detailed essays on other aspects of hockey. Recommended for all libraries that serve hockey fans.

371. Diamond, Dan. **Total Stanley Cup: An Official Publication of the National Hockey League.** Kingston, N.Y.: Total Sports Publishing, 2000. 218 pp. $12.95. ISBN 1-892129-07-8.

This history and statistical compendium of hockey's major championship is divided into four sections. The first section contains five essays on the history and origins of the Stanley Cup, with good coverage of the trophy itself. The second section contains playoff history and records, and the third covers the final-series history, records, scoring, and players. The last section contains the NHL playoff registers for players and goaltenders. Illustrated with color photographs.

372. Diamond, Dan, Paul Bontje, Ralph Dinger, and Eric Zweig, eds. **Total NHL: The Ultimate Source on the NHL.** Chicago: Triumph Books, 2003. 928 pp. $45.00. ISBN 1-57243-604-2.

This comprehensive encyclopedia of history and statistics contains team-by-team and season-by-season coverage from 1917 to the present. It includes playoff game scores, statistics for every player and goaltender, draft picks since 1963, all-stars, and award winners. Also covers hall of fame inductees and milestones in hockey. Illustrated with over 250 black-and-white photographs.

373. Dryden, Steve. **Century of Hockey: A Season-by-Season Celebration.** Toronto, ON: McClelland & Stewart, 2000. 160 pp. $24.95. ISBN 0-7710-4179-9.

Produced by the *Hockey News*, this source gives a year-by-year review of eighty-three seasons in the National Hockey League, from 1900 through the 1999–2000 season. Contains much historical information on players, teams, and important events. Illustrated with both black-and-white and color photographs, as well as tables and graphs. Arranged chronologically, with an index of names at the end.

374. Duplacey, James, and Dan Diamond. **The Annotated Rules of Hockey.** New York: Lyons & Burford, 1996. 199 pp. $17.95. ISBN 1-55821-466-6.

This National Hockey League official publication looks at the history and evolution of each rule of the game, describing how, why, and when the rule was defined. Arranged numerically, from rule 1, "Describing the rink," to rule 87, "Describing the role of the 'video goal judge.'" Illustrated with black-and-white diagrams and photographs. An appendix contains the full NHL official rules. Indexed.

375. Fischler, Stan. **The Ultimate Bad Boys.** Los Angeles: Warwick Publishing, 1999. 260 pp. $15.95. ISBN 1-894020-35-9.

In this unusual volume of biographical information about hockey players, the author limits the scope to the fighters of hockey: players whose claim to fame was being the team tough guy. A comprehensive list of thirty-seven fighters is profiled briefly, while twenty-three fighters are given more extensive attention, including lively quotes, oral histories, and interviews. Sparsely illustrated with black-and-white photographs. Not indexed.

376. Fischler, Stan, and Shirley Fischler. **Who's Who in Hockey.** Kansas City, Mo.: Andrews McMeel Universal, 2003. 459 pp. $19.95. ISBN 0-7407-1904-1.

This biographical source profiles over 700 hockey players and coaches who have been important in the game's development. Entries vary in length from half a page to three pages and include basic biographical information, career history, and an essay that describes the person's career statistics and highlights. Some entries contain a black-and-white photograph. The complete list of persons profiled is listed in the front of the book. The arrangement is alphabetical by name.

377. Hollander, Zander. **The *Hockey News* Hockey Almanac 2000: The Complete Guide.** Detroit, Mich.: Visible Ink Press, 2000. 902 pp. $19.95. ISBN 1-57859-084-1.

This bible of hockey presents the history of the game, beginning with 1917. For each year thereafter, the important events are described, and final standings and results are listed. Contains additional chapters on the top 100 NHL players of all time; NHL records; championships; hockey hall of fame; other leagues besides the NHL (women, juniors, college, minor leagues, and Olympic competition); and NHL player and coach registers. Illustrated with black-and-white photographs and many tables of data. Includes a glossary and an index.

378. Hollander, Zander, ed. *Inside Sports Magazine* **Hockey.** Updated and expanded ed. Detroit, Mich.: Visible Ink Press, 1998. 714 pp. $19.95. ISBN 1-57859-019-1.

This encyclopedia of hockey history and statistics provides a review of each season, with the final standings and leading scorers and goalies. It also provides Stanley Cup highlights and in-depth profiles of thirty-five selected star players, as well as an all-time player register and brief info on hall of fame members. It also provides coverage of the International Hockey League, the Canadian junior leagues, and the most famous hockey announcers. Illustrated with 300 black-and-white photographs. This is a revised edition of *The Complete Encyclopedia of Hockey* (1993) by the same author.

379. Klein, Jeff Z., and Karl-Eric Reif. **The Hockey Compendium: NHL Facts, Stats and Stories.** Toronto, ON: McClelland & Stewart, 2001. 235 pp. $19.95. ISBN 0-7710-9575-9.

In this collection of statistics that serves to a settle the debates in which hockey fans become embroiled, the authors provide full coverage of the individuals, teams, best and worst seasons, scoring dominance, goaltending perseverance, and playoff performance. Offers a complete listing of stats for every player and team in the NHL. An appendix provides major league final standings from 1908–1909 to 2000–2001.

380. National Collegiate Athletic Association. **NCAA Men's and Women's Ice Hockey Rules and Interpretations.** 2002 ed. Indianapolis, Ind.: National Collegiate Athletic Association, 2001. 148 pp. $7.50. ISSN 0735-9195.

Contains the official NCAA rules, including modifications for women's ice hockey. The current year's changes are pulled out for emphasis. Includes rink diagrams and illustrated officials' signals, as well as an illustrated section on officials' mechanics. The rules and interpretations are indexed separately.

381. National Hockey League. **National Hockey League Official Guide and Record Book, 2004.** 72nd (2004) ed. Chicago: Triumph Books, 2003. 640 pp. $24.95. ISBN 1-57243-603-4.

This annual official guide and record book is a standard hockey reference. It contains a brief chronological review of NHL history, attendance figures for the regular season and playoffs, rink dimensions, an Olympic hockey review of the 2002 games, statistics from previous Olympic games, and records and a directory for each NHL team. Includes Stanley Cup records, the player register, with prospects and goaltenders listed separately, and a retired NHL player index. Provides detailed statistics for the 2002–2003 season and contains the 2003–2004 NHL schedule.

382. National Hockey League. **Official Rules of the NHL.** 2003 ed. Chicago: Triumph Books, 2002. 192 pp. $9.95. ISBN 1-57243-510-0.

The official rules are also available on the NHL's Web site, but for those who prefer the printed page or want to carry it along to a game, this annual pocket-sized volume serves the purpose. Contains all the rules, plus rink diagrams, illustrations of officials' signals, and the current year's schedule of games.

383. Pincus, Arthur. **NHL: The Official Illustrated History.** Rev. and updated ed. Chicago: Triumph Books, 2001. 224 pp. $24.95. ISBN 1-57243-445-7.

This historical encyclopedia of the NHL is arranged chronologically by decade, starting with the origins of hockey and the beginning of the NHL in 1917, and continuing to the 1990s and beyond. For each decade, the significant events are described and personalities and players are profiled in detail. There is an additional chapter on the Stanley Cup. Well illustrated with many black-and-white and color photographs. Appendices include a chronology of NHL events from 1917 to 2001, a list of hall of fame members, and a records section. Contains a glossary of terms. Indexed.

384. Poteet, Lewis J., and Aaron C. Poteet. **The Hockey Phrase Book.** Hantsport, NS: Lancelot Press, 1991. 144 pp. $7.95. ISBN 0-88999-461-7.

In this fascinating book of definitions, the language of hockey is documented. The work contains names, nostalgia, facts, technical terms, history, and insults, all described for the otherwise uninformed reader. The terms and phrases are arranged by topic. Includes a reading and source list. Indexed by phrase.

385. USA Hockey Inline. **Official Rules of Inline Hockey.** 2003–2005 ed. Chicago: Triumph Books, 2003. 152 pp. $9.95. ISBN 1-57243-586-0.

Contains USA Hockey Inline's official playing rules and interpretations, referee signals, and rink diagrams, with dimensions. Covers teams, penalties, and equipment and includes a glossary of terms. Indexed.

386. Walton, David and Jeff Paur. **The *Sporting News* Hockey Register: Every Player, Every Stat.** 2002–2003 ed. St. Louis, Mo.: Sporting News Publishing, 2002. 464 pp. $16.95. ISBN 0-89204-678-3.

This alphabetical list of hockey players contains every player's complete career statistics. It also contains a list of the top draft picks for the season, as well as the head coaches. The information on each player includes statistics from every season played, a history of trades, injuries, and awards. The coach's entries include the team's season win/loss records. An annual publication appropriate for every library that serves sports fans.

387. Weber, Dan. **The Best Book of Hockey Facts and Stats.** Buffalo, N.Y.: Firefly Books, 2002. 304 pp. $14.95. ISBN 1-55297-660-2.

With statistics through the 2001–2002 season, this guide details the facts on the history of hockey. Describes notable NHL games and events, provides brief biographies of all the players, and profiles each NHL franchise team. Franchise histories are arranged by conference. Lists hall of fame inductees from 1945 to 2001, winners of all the major awards, and the Stanley Cup results from 1927 through 2002. Includes a brief glossary. Produced in association with Stats Inc.

Instructional Sources

388. Stewart, Barbara. **She Shoots . . . She Scores: A Complete Guide to Girls' and Women's Hockey.** Rev. and updated ed. Buffalo, N.Y.: Firefly Books, 1998. 204 pp. $17.95. ISBN 1-55209-288-7.

This comprehensive guide to hockey presents all the information that a beginning player, fan, parent, or coach might need to get started in the game. Contains chapters on the history of the game and of women's participation, the rules for women's hockey, the equipment required, the techniques of moving, passing, shooting, and the players' positions. Also includes special coverage of goaltending. Additional chapters provide coverage of women's hockey programs and associations, coaching, officiating, and national teams around the world and in the Olympic Games. Includes a list of important addresses, a glossary, and a brief list of books for further reading.

389. United States Olympic Committee. **A Basic Guide to Ice Hockey.** An Official U.S. Olympic Committee Sports Series. Torrance, Calif.: Griffin Publishing, 2001. 152 pp. $9.95. ISBN 0-8368-3103-9.

This guide provides basic information intended to help the novice user get started with the sport. Covers history, fundamentals of the sport, and information on the Olympics and other competitions, equipment, safety, and nutrition and training. Includes rules for hockey and member biographies for the U.S. men's and women's ice hockey teams at the 2002 Olympics. Illustrated with drawings and black-and-white photographs. Includes contact information for important hockey organizations and a glossary.

Web Sites

390. **Hockey Hall of Fame (HHOF).** http://www.hhof.com (accessed April 2, 2004).

The HHOF Web site provides a comprehensive history of Canada's national game. Contains detailed biographical information on hall of fame inductees (players, broadcasters, writers, and others), plus statistics and many other facts. Includes a guide to their exhibits, resource collection, and education program.

391. **International Ice Hockey Federation (IIHF).** http://www.iihf.com (accessed December 2, 2004).

As the international governing body for ice hockey competition, the IIHF maintains an informative and well-organized Web site. It includes history of the organization and its activities and a directory of member nations with links to their sites, plus IIHF Hall of Fame inductee profiles and rules, and international championship results.

392. **National Hockey League.** http://www.nhl.com (accessed December 2, 2004).

The NHL's Web site is a full-service site, with all the news, scores, schedules, statistics, and standings that a fan would expect. Contains the current NHL rule book, detailed information on the Stanley Cup, the World Cup, the entry draft, and much more.

393. **United States Hockey Hall of Fame.** http://www.ushockeyhall.com/ (accessed December 2, 2004).

Supporting the game of hockey in the United States, the hall of fame provides exhibits that inform readers or visitors about the historical record of hockey in the United States. Contains biographical profiles of the inductees, with photographs. Provides U.S. Olympic team history.

394. **USA Hockey.** http://www.usahockey.com (accessed March 26, 2004).

As the national governing body for hockey in the United States, USA Hockey maintains an informative Web site. It includes news, dates of tournaments and other events, information on safety, terminology, and much more. Contains a link to USA Hockey Inline, USA Hockey's official inline-hockey program.

Luge

Web Sites

395. **International Luge Federation (FIL).** http://www.fil-luge.org (accessed March 3, 2004).

This international governing body's Web site contains news, a calendar of events, rules and regulations, results, a directory of athletes, and a directory of member federations.

396. **United States Luge Association.** http://www.usaluge.org (accessed January 2, 2004).

Headquartered in Lake Placid, New York, the mission of this national association is to support luge-sledding athletes. The site provides information on the history of the sport and describes programs and events. Includes news, race schedules and results, team rosters with biographical information, and detailed coverage of Olympic competition.

Skating

Reference Sources

397. Berman, Alice. **Skater's Edge Sourcebook: Ice Skating Resource Guide.** 3rd ed. Kensington, Md.: Skater's Edge, 2003. 552 pp. $35.00. ISBN 0-9643027-2-1.

In this directory of ice skating resources, a wealth of practical information is provided. It contains an annotated directory of skating rinks, arranged by U.S. state, plus help with finding rinks in Canada; and it provides another list of rinks that are affiliated with colleges and universities. It offers lists of books and videos, sources for purchasing boots, blades and other equipment, clothing, catalogues, and other publications. It also lists results of U.S., World, and Olympic competition.

398. Malone, John Williams. **The Encyclopedia of Figure Skating.** New York: Facts On File, 1998. 264 pp. $37.00; $18.95 (pbk.). ISBN 0-8160-3226-2; 0-8160-3796-5 (pbk.).

This engaging reference contains biographies of all the major ice skating champions worldwide. The biographies vary in length and contain interesting personal details as well as highlights of each individual's skating career. In addition, the work contains histories of the major branches of competition, descriptions of figure skating forms, and detailed information about competition, including referees, scoring, judges, music, and costumes. Appendices provide lists of U.S., World, and Olympic medalists through 1997, and illustrated with black-and-white photographs of notable figures. Indexed.

399. Milton, Steve. **Skate: 100 Years of Figure Skating.** With principal photography by Barbara McCutcheon. North Pomfret, Vt.: Trafalgar Square Publishing, 1996. 200 pp. $29.95. ISBN 1-57076-056-X.

Beautifully illustrated with color photographs, this volume contains eleven chapters of essays on topics as varied as athleticism and skating and the movies. The appendices hold lists of hall of fame members and title holders. A skating chronology is included through 1995. A glossary and an index are also provided. A paperback edition of this title was published in 2000 by Key Porter Books.

400. U.S. Figure Skating Association. **The Official Book of Figure Skating: History, Competition, Technique.** New York: Simon & Schuster, 1998. 266 pp. $30.00. ISBN 0-684-84673-X.

This beautifully illustrated volume offers a history of figure skating in photographs as well as text, and profiles of major champions, both past and present. It also provides a primer on skating techniques, skating fashion, fitness advice, tips on creating routines, and an overview of the judging system. The different types of competition are discussed and a list of championship winners is given. Includes a list of skating clubs in the U.S., a glossary, and an index.

Instructional Sources

401. Kunzle-Watson, Karin, and Stephen J. DeArmond. **Ice Skating: Steps to Success.** Steps to Success Activity Series. Champaign, Ill.: Human Kinetics, 1996. 157 pp. $17.95. ISBN 0-87322-669-0.

This source offers a sequential approach to learning the form and technique of ice skating. Includes fifty drills to actively reinforce the skills being learned. Appropriate for beginners or those who want to increase their level of performance. Illustrated with over 300 detailed drawings to accompany the step-by-step instruction. Also contains a brief glossary of skating terms.

402. Shulman, Carole. **The Complete Book of Figure Skating.** Champaign, Ill.: Human Kinetics, 2002. 225 pp. $21.95. ISBN 0-7360-3548-6.
    Covers the basics of skating such as equipment, apparel, and fitness, as well as detailed information on technique and elements of performance and competition. Presents over 100 skills in progressive order of difficulty. An appendix contains a code of ethics for coaches. Well illustrated with many sequential black-and-white photographs that demonstrate proper form. Includes contact information for the Professional Skaters Association and a brief glossary. Indexed.

Web Sites

403. **International Skating Union (ISU).** http://www.isu.org (accessed December 2, 2004).
    The ISU is the international governing body for ice skating competition, including figure skating/ice dancing, synchronized skating, speed skating, and short track skating. Its Web site provides comprehensive information for the skating world, including links to member federations' Web sites. Provides news, championships results, rules, publications, a calendar of events, and much more.

404. **United States Figure Skating Association.** http://www.usfsa.org (accessed March 21, 2004).
    The USFSA, the national governing body for figure skating in the United States, maintains a comprehensive Web site with news, athlete biographies, a calendar of events, results of competition, a directory of clubs, and much more.

405. **United States Speedskating.** http://www.usspeedskating.org (accessed March 21, 2004).
    The national governing body for speed skating, this organization's Web site provides news, a schedule of events, results of competition, records, a press release archive, and much more.

Skiing

Reference Sources

406. Hardy, Peter, and Felice Hardy. **The Good Skiing and Snowboarding Guide 2004.** London: Which? Books, 2003. 592 pp. $28.95. ISBN 0-85202-943-8.
    The title says it all. This evaluative directory of over 600 ski resorts across five continents will be very helpful in planning a skiing or snowboarding vacation. Detailed, practical information is provided on ski schools, facilities, ac-

commodation, nightlife, food, prices, suitability for children, transportation, surrounding area, and much more. Also includes a directory of tour operators and full contact information.

407. Leach, Robert E., ed. **Alpine Skiing.** Handbook of Sports Medicine and Science. Malden, Mass.: Blackwell Science, 1994. 144 pp. $34.95. ISBN 0-632-03033-X.

This series is published under the auspices of the International Olympic Committee Medical Commission. This volume on alpine skiing covers the epidemiology of injury in the sport; physiological and nutritional aspects; preventive medicine; and information on environmental conditions that can cause injury. The articles in the handbook are intended for use by physicians, trainers, and coaches but would also be useful references for athletes or for parents of children who are participating in athletics. Illustrated with diagrams, tables, and black-and-white photographs. Each chapter contains a list of references for further reading. Indexed. This series is most appropriate for college and university collections in sports medicine.

408. Leocha, Charles A. **Ski Snowboard American and Canada.** 16th (2004) ed. Hampstead, N.H.: World Leisure Corporation, 2004. 560 pp. $24.95. ISBN 0-915009-81-1.

This directory of ski resorts is informative and unbiased, with current, detailed entries on over 100 resorts in the United States and Canada. Contact information is provided for each one, including a Web site address when available. Entries also include rates, snow activities and facilities, a rating of the ski terrain, accommodations, dining, nightlife, other activities, and the overall ambience of the resort. Lift-ticket prices are given, as is information about the availability of ski-school programs and child care. A great source for anyone planning a ski vacation, this will be a popular source in public libraries.

409. **NCAA Men's and Women's Skiing Rules.** 2004 ed. Indianapolis, Ind.: National Collegiate Athletic Association, 2003. 90 pp. $7.50. ISSN 0736-5160.

In this annual official rule book, the major rule changes for the year are noted. It also covers the various skiing events in alpine and cross-country, as well as procedures for establishing the course, seeding, results, timing, scoring specifications, fouls, and penalties. Also includes scoring tables and an explanation of the process for protests and appeals. Indexed.

410. Rusko, Heikki, ed. **Cross Country Skiing.** Handbook of Sports Medicine and Science. Malden, Mass.: Blackwell Science, 2003. 208 pp. $39.95.

This series is published under the auspices of the International Olympic Committee Medical Commission. The volume on cross-country skiing covers the epidemiology of injury in the sport; physiological and nutritional aspects; preventive medicine; and information on the biomechanics cross-country skiing. The articles in the handbook are intended for use by physicians, trainers, and coaches but would also be useful for athletes or for parents of children who are participating in athletics. Illustrated with diagrams, tables, and black-and-white photographs. Each chapter contains a list of references for further reading. Indexed. This series is most appropriate for college and university collections in sports medicine.

411. **Skiing USA: The Top 31 U.S. Resorts for Skiers and Snowboarders.** 4th ed. New York: Fodor's Travel Publications / Random House, 2002. 386 pp. $18.95. ISBN 1-4000-1230-9.

This updated guide to skiing and snowboarding destinations provides in-depth information on a selection of the thirty-one best ski resorts in the United States. Entries describe the skiing and snowboarding facilities, transportation options (with maps), prices, accommodations and restaurants in a variety of price ranges, and other entertainment options.

Instructional Sources

412. Cook, Charles. **The Essential Guide to Cross-Country Skiing and Snowshoeing in the United States.** New York: Henry Holt, 1997. 258 pp. $17.95. ISBN 0-8050-4113-3.

This guide contains excellent general information on preparing for outdoor activities in the winter: what to wear, other necessary gear, safety and comfort in winter conditions. It describes in detail the fundamentals, equipment, and technique for Nordic skiing and snowshoeing. Also contains a state-by-state directory of over 500 U.S. cross-country skiing and snowshoeing sites, with contact information and a good description of each, as well as a state map showing the sites' locations. Indexed.

413. Gullion, Laurie. **Nordic Skiing: Steps to Success.** Steps to Success Activity Series. Champaign, Ill.: Human Kinetics, 1993. 152 pp. $14.95. ISBN 0-87322-394-2.

This popular step-by-step approach to learning cross country skiing presents all the basic skills in a series of 13 steps, all illustrated with sequential drawings. Includes information on equipment and conditioning, as well as drills to reinforce the skills being introduced. Includes a glossary of terms.

414. Heckelman, Martin. **The New Guide to Skiing.** Rev. ed. New York: Norton, 2001. 138 pp. $21.95. ISBN 0-393-31966-0.

In this guide to mastering alpine skiing the author defines the new language and also offers a new method of learning the sport. All the beginning techniques are here, including navigating turns and bump skiing. Advanced techniques are also presented, and there is a separate section on powder skiing. Illustrated with over eighty color photograph sequences and a total of over 350 photos.

415. Kleh, Cindy. **Snowboarding Skills: The Back-to-Basics Essentials for All Levels.** Buffalo, N.Y.: Firefly Books, 2002. 128 pp. $16.95. ISBN 1-55297-626-2.

This guide to snowboarding is intended for either the beginner or the seasoned athlete because of its easy-to-understand format. Includes information on training, technique, choosing equipment, and staying safe, as well as tips from the pros. Step-by-step color photographs and diagrams illustrate the instructions that are given. Includes a glossary of terms and an index.

416. Reichenfeld, Rob, and Anna Bruechert. **Snow-Boarding.** Outdoor Pursuits. Champaign, Ill.: Human Kinetics, 1995. $13.95. ISBN 0-87322-677-1.

This guide to snowboarding covers the basics of getting started, choosing equipment, dressing appropriately, and learning the skills and techniques of the sport in a safe manner. Includes information on finding the best places to snowboard and on variations of the sport (backcountry, racing, etc.). Illustrated with color photographs and drawings. Includes a glossary of terms and an index.

417. Yacenda, John. **Alpine Skiing: Steps to Success.** Steps to Success Activity Series. Champaign, Ill.: Leisure Press, 1992. 168 pp. $13.95. ISBN 0-88011-455-X.

This guide to alpine skiing takes a sequential approach to teaching the basic concepts and skills, building on each step to progress to the next. It includes drills to reinforce the skills that are presented. Coverage includes equipment and clothing, conditioning, safety, and all the essential techniques of skiing. Illustrated with drawings. Includes a glossary.

Web Sites

418. **International Ski Federation / Federation Internationale de Ski (FIS).** http://www.fis-ski.com (accessed March 19, 2004).

FIS is the international governing body for skiing competition at the Olympic Games, and it maintains an informative Web site. It includes a calendar of upcoming events and lists the results and standings from recent competition. Provides news, rules, competitor biographies, and information on championships and the Olympics. Contains a list of member national organizations and a history of skiing and of the FIS.

419. **U.S. Skiing.** http://www.usskiing.com (accessed March 22, 2004).

A comprehensive directory of ski and snowboard areas in the United States, arranged by state, with a map of each state showing the location of the areas. For each area, the resorts are described briefly. Information on type of skiing facilities, lodging, and cost of lift tickets, transportation, and other amenities is given. Weather and snow conditions are also reported.

420. **United States Collegiate Ski and Snowboard Association.** http://www.uscsa.com/ (accessed March 12, 2004).

USCSA is the sports federation for collegiate team ski racing and snowboard competition in America. Provides support for alpine and cross-country skiing and snowboarding.

421. **United States Ski and Snowboard Association.** http://www.ussa.org/ (accessed March 21, 2004).

The USSA is the national governing body for Olympic skiing and snowboarding. Its Web site contains news, competition guides, rule books, an event schedule, results, standings, athlete rankings and history, a competition club directory, and much more.

Racquet Sports

Popular for recreation and fitness, as well as for serious international competition, the racquet sports offer opportunity for play either indoors or outdoors. Included in this chapter are information sources on badminton, racquetball, squash, table tennis, and tennis.

Badminton

Instructional Sources

422. Bloss, Margaret Varner, and R. Stanton Hales. **Badminton.** Winning Edge. 8th ed. Boston: McGraw-Hill, 2001. 150 pp. $10.00. ISBN 0-697-34534-3.

Intended for badminton players at all skill levels, this guide is a well-organized reference. It includes a short history of badminton, the fundamentals of the game, rules of play, skills for beginners and more advanced players, strategies and techniques for success, and information on physical conditioning and on competition. Each chapter concludes with a summary of important points. Illustrated with black-and-white photographs and diagrams. Appendices provide the official laws of badminton and guidelines for players with disabilities. Includes a glossary, a list of references, and an index.

423. Grice, Tony. **Badminton: Steps to Success.** Steps to Success Activity Series. Champaign, Ill.: Human Kinetics, 1996. 141 pp. $15.95. ISBN 0-87322-613-5.

Using a step-by-step approach, this book moves the reader from basic skills to the more advanced techniques required for play. Introduces the game, its history, and its equipment and then begins the ten steps to success at badminton. Provides coverage of singles and doubles play. Includes a glossary of terms and a list of suggested readings. Illustrated with drawings and diagrams.

424. Kim, Sunny, Mike Walker, and Tariq Wadood. **Badminton Today.** 2nd ed. Belmont, Calif.: Thomson / Wadsworth, 2001. 104 pp. $23.95. ISBN 0-534-55233-1.

Covers all aspects of badminton, from the rules and etiquette to the strokes and tactics for competitive play. Includes information appropriate for beginners as well as advanced players. Provides techniques for strength training and conditioning and preparing for the mental aspects of the game. Includes the official International Badminton Federation (IBF) rules. Illustrations provide enhanced step-by-step instructions.

425. Metzler, Michael W. **Badminton: Mastering the Basics with the Personalized Sports Instruction System.** Personalized Sport Instruction. Boston: Allyn & Bacon, 2001. 129 pp. $14.00. ISBN 0-205-32369-3.

This workbook teaches the fundamentals of badminton and can be used either in a formal course setting or by individuals who want to work at their own pace outside a course and chart their own progress. Each chapter presents a module of information about performance skills, shots, or the game itself and concludes with tasks that test what was learned. Includes the laws of badminton.

426. Sweeting, Roger, and Janet S. Wilson. **Badminton: Basic Skills and Drills.** Mountain View, Calif.: Mayfield Publishing, 1992. 179 pp. $16.95. ISBN 0-87484-985-3.

This practical guide to badminton provides an introduction to the game and a short history. Other topics covered include equipment and facilities, terminology, rules and etiquette of the game, basic skills, and more advanced skills and drills. Tactics are discussed for both singles and doubles play, and a chapter on learning theory is included for teachers, as is a sample lesson plan. Includes official USBA rules, a glossary, references, and an index. Illustrated with diagrams and drawings.

427. United States Olympic Committee. **A Basic Guide to Badminton.** Updated Olympic ed. An Official United States Olympic Committee Sports Series. Glendale, Calif.: Griffin Publishing, 1998. 117 pp. $7.95. ISBN 1-882180-76-3.

Intended for the spectator or the player, this concise guide to badminton provides the information needed to get started. It begins with a brief history of the sport and then covers rules and fundamental skills, etiquette, equipment, and clothing. Contains brief biographies and black-and-white photographs of 1996 Olympic medalists. It includes a list of places to play in the United States; contact information for USA Badminton, the national governing body; a glossary of badminton terms.

Web Sites

428. **International Badminton Federation (IBF).** http://www.intbadfed.org/ (accessed December 2, 2004).

The IBF is the international governing body for badminton. Their Web site contains international badminton news, world rankings, a calendar of events, competition results and draws, Olympic facts and figures, results of Olympic Games, rules and laws of badminton, equipment standards, and contact information for member associations.

429. United States Badminton Association. http://www.usabadminton.org (accessed March 26, 2004).

The national governing body for badminton competition maintains a comprehensive Web site that includes information on teams, rankings, results, rules, news, and events. The site offers a "Where to Play" guide for the United States.

Racquetball

Instructional Sources

430. Allsen, Philip E., and Pete Witbeck. **Racquetball.** 6th ed. Sports and Fitness. Madison, Wisc.: Brown and Benchmark, 1996. 116 pp. $18.43. ISBN 0-697-25627-8.

This basic guide to racquetball provides a brief history of the game, discusses the court, equipment, and safety, and covers all the essential skills, shots, and patterns of play. Provides drills to enhance progress and includes a chapter on the language and rules of racquetball. Illustrated with black-and-white photographs, diagrams, and drawings. Contains a bibliography and an index.

431. Kittleson, Stan. **Racquetball: Steps to Success.** Steps to Success Activity Series. Champaign, Ill.: Human Kinetics, 1992. 149 pp. $17.95. ISBN 0-88011-440-1.

In this basic guide to racquetball, students learn essential skills and valuable strategies by playing the game. The author presents a sequential progression of eighteen steps that gradually teach the skills, concepts, and techniques required for play. Covers the grips, strokes, serves, and shots. Illustrated with drawings and diagrams that show every step. Includes a glossary of terms and list of further readings.

432. Metzler, Michael W. **Racquetball: Mastering the Basics with the Personalized Sport Instruction System.** Personalized Sport Instruction. Boston: Allyn & Bacon, 2001. 136 pp. $17.00. ISBN 0-205-32372-3.

This workbook teaches the fundamentals of racquetball and can be used either in a formal course setting or by individuals who want to work at their own pace outside a course and chart their own progress. Each chapter presents a module of information about performance skills, shots, or the game itself and concludes with tasks that test what was learned. Includes the rules of racquetball. Illustrated with photographs and diagrams.

433. Norton, Cheryl, and James E. Bryant. **Beginning Racquetball.** 6th ed. Belmont, Calif.: Thomson / Wadsworth, 2004. 144 pp. $21.95. ISBN 0-534-56896-3.

The basic information presented in this volume is appropriate for beginners, those taking a course in racquetball, or for those who want to review and improve skills. Includes discussion of the court, equipment, and safety; preparing for strokes; offensive and defensive strokes; serves; strategy; drills; etiquette; and rule interpretation. Helpful hints and study questions are included for each chapter. Illustrated with over 180 color photographs, diagrams, and drawings. An appendix contains the 2000 *Official Rules of Racquetball* from the U.S. Racquetball Association. Contains a glossary of terms and an index.

Web Site

434. **USA Racquetball Association.** http://www.usra.org (accessed December 2, 2004).

The Web site offers an events calendar, history of events, official rules and records, rankings, a hall of fame, links to state associations, and more.

Squash

Instructional Sources

435. Francis, Austin M. **Smart Squash: How to Win at Soft Ball.** New York: Lyons & Burford / Lyons Press, 1995. 160 pp. $26.95; $16.95 (pbk.). ISBN 1-55821-384-8; 1-55821-341-4 (pbk.).

This handbook of soft-ball squash, or squash rackets, is written for the novice player or the experienced one who is moving from North American, or hard-ball, squash to international soft-ball squash. Covers the fundamentals of the game, such as grip, stroke, and footwork, as well as the basic shots. Includes drills and outlines a program for further training. Also covers match play. Illustrated with black-and-white photographs and drawings. Contains a glossary of squash terms and an index.

436. Hawkey, Dick. **Play the Game: Squash.** Updated and rev. ed. London: Blandford, 1994. 80 pp. $7.95. ISBN 0-7137-2443-9.

Intended for the beginner, this brief volume describes the history and development of the game of squash and identifies the equipment and terminology of the game. A major focus is on the rules of the game, and included is a "rules clinic," with its own index. A well-illustrated chapter on technique is provided. Includes contact information for major associations in the United Kingdom. Illustrated with black-and-white photographs, drawings, and diagrams. Indexed.

437. Khan, Jahangir. **Learn Squash and Racquetball in a Weekend.** New York: Knopf / Dorling Kindersley, 1993. 96 pp. $16.00. ISBN 0679-42753-8.

In this brief but well-organized and complete guide to learning squash and racquetball, this noted author describes the equipment, dress, court dimensions, rules, grips, and strokes of these similar racquet sports. Serving the ball, more advanced shots, rallying, and improving through competition are also covered. A very well-illustrated volume, with abundant color photographs throughout. Includes a glossary and an index.

438. McKenzie, Ian. **Ian McKenzie's Squash Skills.** Marlborough, Wiltshire, U.K.: Crowood Press, 2002. 143 pp. $19.95. ISBN 1-86126-495-X.

A previous edition of this book was published as *Squash: The Skills of the Game,* (1996). This new version offers an additional chapter on fitness for squash, including training activities and nutrition considerations. A classic guide to the game, the author provides in-depth coverage of technique, skills and practice strategy, and tactics of the game. Includes a sample training-program outline. Illustrated with black-and-white photographs and useful diagrams and drawings. Indexed.

439. Sales, Pippa. **Improve Your Squash Game: 101 Drills, Coaching Tips and Resources.** Honolulu, Hawaii: Disa Publications, 1996. 94 pp. $13.95. ISBN 1-884633-03-X.

This squash guide includes 101 specific drills that, if practiced, are intended to improve a player's performance; 101 drills are included, as well as more general tips on improving one's play. Appendices cover stretching exercises, a listing of contact information for World Squash Federation member organizations, and a glossary. There is also a list of suggested reading to gain knowledge of other aspects of the game.

440. Sommers, Eric. **Squash: Technique, Tactics, Training.** Crowood Sports Guides. Ramsbury, Marlborough, Wiltshire, U.K.: Crowood Press, 1991. 127 pp. $10.00. ISBN 1-85223-543-8.

Useful to the beginner or the advanced player, this guide to the sport of squash is clearly written and well-illustrated with plenty of color photographs to show a step-by-step view of the instructions described. It also includes many color drawings of the court showing how shots can be made to accomplish a certain goal. In-depth information is given on the rules and equipment, strokes and the tactics of play, as well as on fitness in general. Indexed.

441. **Squash.** With the Squash Rackets Association. Know the Sport. Mechanicsburg, Pa.: Stackpole Books, 1997. 48 pp. $5.95. ISBN 0-8117-2839-0.

This brief but efficient guide to the sport of squash utilizes the international scoring system, which may be different from that used in North America. Dimensions of the court are shown by illustration; equipment, scoring, and basic techniques as well as more complex tactics of play are explained and illustrated with color diagrams and photographs. Indexed.

442. Yarrow, Philip. **Squash: Steps to Success.** Steps to Success Activity Series. Champaign, Ill.: Human Kinetics, 1997. 149 pp. $16.95. ISBN 0-88011-541-6.

This guide to playing squash presents a sequence of steps that are designed to identify correct technique and practice each skill in a real playing situation.

The steps take the learner from basic strokes and court movements to more specific shots and strategies.

Web Sites

443. **United States Squash Racquets Association (USSRA).** http://www.ussquash.org (accessed April 24, 2004).

The national governing body for squash competition, the USSRA, maintains an informative Web site that contains news, ratings, rankings, tournament information, links to regional squash associations and clubs, lessons, history, a glossary of terms, and much more.

444. **World Squash Federation (WSF).** http://www.squash.org (accessed April 24, 2004).

The WSF is the international governing body for competitive squash. Their Web site provides a history of squash and of the organization. It also includes tournament results, world rankings, player profiles, information on courts and equipment, a calendar of events, and a directory of World Squash Federation member nations.

Table Tennis

Reference Source

445. Uzorinac, Zdenko. **ITTF 1926-2001: Table Tennis Legends.** Lausanne, Switzerland: The International Table Tennis Federation, 2001. 495 pp. $90.00. ISBN 2-940312-00-1.

Created to celebrate the 75th anniversary of the ITTF, this volume documents the history of the organization and of the sport of table tennis and its champions. It provides essays on the origin and history of table tennis, the evolution of the racquet, profiles of all the important players and personalities of the international game, and further essays on Olympic medalists, the regional federations, hall of fame members, championships, and many other fascinating aspects of the sport. It is illustrated with many black-and-white and color photographs of the persons and events that are featured.

Instructional Sources

446. Hodges, Larry. **Table Tennis: Steps to Success.** With the United States Table Tennis Association. Steps to Success Activity Series. Champaign, Ill.: Human Kinetics, 1993. 151 pp. $17.95. ISBN 0-87322-403-5.

This instruction manual presents a sequence of fifteen steps that transition from one skill to the next. The fundamental skills and concepts are defined and presented clearly, followed by more complex skills such as blocking, looping, flipping, and advanced serves. Playing styles, rallying tactics, and advanced strategy are also covered. Includes information on tournament play and the mental aspects of the game. Includes a glossary of terms. Illustrated with drawings.

447. Parker, Donald, and David Hewitt. **Table Tennis.** Rev. ed. Play the Game. London: Blandford, 1993. 80 pp. $10.00 est. ISBN 0-7137-2412-9.

This guide to the game of table tennis is endorsed by the English Table Tennis Association. It includes a chapter on the history and development of the game, in-depth specifications for equipment, and definitions of terminology. The game is explained briefly, followed by detailed description of the playing technique. It is illustrated with many step-by-step drawings, diagrams, and black-and-white photographs. Indexed.

448. Preiss, Scott M. **Table Tennis: The Sport.** Dubuque, Iowa: William C. Brown, 1992. 67 pp. $15.00. ISBN 0-697-13635-3.

This guide to table tennis describes the history of table tennis in Olympic competition, explains the equipment needed and its use, and provides in-depth information on the technique of play. It is illustrated with black-and-white photographs, diagrams, and drawings. Contains the USTTA's rules and regulations, a list of equipment manufacturers, and a glossary of terms.

449. Seemiller, Dan, and Mark Holowchak. **Winning Table Tennis: Skills, Drills, and Strategies.** Champaign, Ill.: Human Kinetics, 1997. 184 pp. $17.95. ISBN 0-88011-520-3.

Intended to help players at any level improve their game, this instructional source features techniques and strategies but also includes information on equipment, effective practice, preparation for competition, and conditioning for best performance. Illustrated with black-and-white photographs. Indexed.

450. **Table Tennis.** 3rd ed. With the English Table Tennis Association. Know the Game. London: A & C Black, 2002. 48 pp. $9.98. ISBN 0-7136-6005-8.

This brief guide to the sport provides concise information on table tennis. It covers the equipment used, as well as the techniques and tactics that are employed in play. Contains a description of scoring, coaching, and competitive play, and a plan for practice. Describes and lists the tests for the English Table Tennis Association skills awards scheme. Illustrated with color photographs and drawings. Indexed.

Web Sites

451. **International Table Tennis Federation.** http://www.ittf.com (accessed March 4, 2004).

The ITTF is the international governing body for table tennis competition. Their Web site contains statistics, world ranking, team ranking, a photo gallery, news, publications, a directory of national federations, and an electronic table tennis museum. Rules and regulations are also included, as is the downloadable

ITTF Handbook. There is detailed information about equipment and the Olympic Games.

452. **USA Table Tennis (USATT).** http://www.usatt.org (accessed March 4, 2004).

The national governing body for table tennis, USATT maintains a comprehensive Web site. With information on the organization, membership, clubs, player categories, tournaments and rules, this is the place to go for more on competitive table tennis play. Also includes profiles of athletes from the USATT hall of fame and a link to information about leagues.

Tennis

Reference Sources

453. Barrett, John, ed. **World of Tennis, 2001.** 33rd ed. London: HarperCollins, 2001. 544 pp. $22.95. ISBN 0-00-711129-0.

Published in association with the International Tennis Federation, this comprehensive world yearbook includes the results of major ITF events, as well as other international championships and tours. Each annual volume details "the year in review" and "players of the year." Includes world rankings and a reference section with detailed biographical information on the top singles and doubles players in the world. Also includes organizational information on the ITF, regional reports, a review of wheelchair tennis, and a directory of national associations. Contains black-and-white and color photographs, both current and historic. Indexed.

454. Brown, Joanie Stearns, and Bill Brown. **Tennis Camps, Clinics, and Resorts.** Wakefield, R.I.: Moyer Bell, 1998. 230 pp. $14.95. ISBN 1-55921-217-9.

Arranged geographically, this guide to tennis camps, clinics, and resorts provides information on each site's location, instructors, philosophy of instruction, and type of programs, facilities, accommodations, special features, and costs. For ease of use, includes separate indexes for different player groups. The book is endorsed by Vic Braden and has a forward by John Austin. This title was previously published as *Peterson's Tennis Camps & Clinics* (1995).

455. Collins, Bud, ed. **Total Tennis: The Ultimate Tennis Encyclopedia.** Rev. ed. Toronto, ON: Sports Media Publishing, 2003. 938 pp. $34.95. ISBN 0-9731443-4-3.

This comprehensive tennis reference builds on the earlier work of the author. The first half of the encyclopedia contains a year-by-year chronology of tennis highlights from 1919 to 2002. Statistics from all the major championships are included, as are historical essays on the tournaments. Top stars are covered in depth, but the source also contains biographical profiles of other significant players, including statistics. Provides world rankings back to 1913 and detailed historical player registers. Illustrated with color photographs. A must-have tennis reference, appropriate for every library.

456. Collins, Bud, and Zander Hollander. **Bud Collins' Tennis Encyclopedia.** 3rd ed. Detroit, Mich.: Visible Ink Press, 1997. 698 pp. $19.95. ISBN 1-57859-000-0.

This comprehensive encyclopedia provides year-by-year highlights of every season in tennis from 1874 through 1996. A great source for biographies of the world's greatest players, complete with black-and-white photographs, this work also includes historical description of major international championships and yearly records. There is a chapter on the International Tennis Hall of Fame, including history and detailed information on members. Appendices contain the 1996 USTA rules and a glossary of tennis terminology and lingo. This is a revised version of *Bud Collins' Modern Encyclopedia of Tennis* (1994).

457. Parsons, John. **The Ultimate Encyclopedia of Tennis: The Definitive Illustrated Guide to World Tennis.** London: Carlton / Hodder & Stoughton, 1998. 224 pp. $29.95. ISBN 0-34073-886-3.

Attractively illustrated with many wonderful color photographs, this encyclopedia traces the early history of tennis, and provides a country-by-country overview of the role of tennis throughout the world, including the founding of the national association, as well as number of players, and clubs and courts in each country. Additional chapters provide detailed coverage of major tournaments, players, arenas, and the greatest matches. Includes brief information on rules, a section on equipment, and unique information on politics, scandals, and oddities in tennis, such as flooded tournaments. Also includes a chronology of major events. Indexed.

458. Phillips, Dennis J. **The Tennis Sourcebook.** Lanham, Md.: Scarecrow Press, 1995. 530 pp. $84.00. ISBN 0-8108-3001-9.

This extensive bibliography provides annotations for the standard reference sources, a list of serials, and references to the literature on subjects such as administration, camps and resorts, conditioning, equipment, history, psychology, teaching and coaching and women's tennis. A lengthy biography section provides an index to the literature on players, coaches, officials, and other tennis personalities. This source also provides an annotated list of videos on tennis. Includes indexes of persons in the biography section and of international associations, by country. Phillips' earlier, more limited, bibliography was called *Teaching, Coaching, and Learning Tennis: An Annotated Bibliography* (1989).

459. Renstrom, Per A. F., ed. **Tennis.** Handbook of Sports Medicine and Science. Malden, Mass.: Blackwell Science, 2002. 320 pp. $33.95. ISBN 0-632-05034-9.

This series is published under the auspices of the International Olympic Committee Medical Commission. The volume on tennis covers the epidemiology of injury in the sport; physiological and nutritional aspects; preventive medicine; and information on the biomechanics of tennis. The articles in the handbook are intended for use by physicians, trainers, and coaches but would also be useful for athletes or for parents of children who are participating in athletics. Illustrated with diagrams, tables, and black-and-white photographs. Each chapter contains a list of references for further reading. Indexed. This series is most appropriate for college and university collections in sports medicine.

459a.   Shine, Ossian. **The Language of Tennis.** The Language of Series. Chicago, Ill.: Shelfmark, 2004. 245 pp. $35.00. ISBN 0-9743318-0-5.

This unique reference source explains the origins, as well as current definitions, of approximately 300 terms from the sport of tennis. The definitions are enhanced with lively quotations from popular sources, to show how they are used in the media.

460.   United States Tennis Association. **Official Rules of Tennis.** 2005 ed. Chicago, Ill.: Triumph Books. United States Tennis Association, 2004. 112 pp. $9.95. ISBN 1-57243-686-7.

This tennis rules book contains everything that a beginning player needs to get started. Written in an easy-to-understand format, it is intended for kids and for beginners of all ages. Includes the official rules and the code, as well as information on scoring and court etiquette.

461.   United States Tennis Association. **USTA Yearbook.** 2003 ed. Lynn, Mass.: H. O. Zimman, 2003. 568 pp. $9.95.

This annual yearbook was previously called the *USTA Tennis Yearbook.* It contains every important statistic for the current year, the year in review, national and sectional rankings, amateur and professional results for the year, and detailed information about the USTA as an organization. In addition, it provides comprehensive historical records, rankings, and results for U.S. and international competition. Also includes the USTA constitution and bylaws, the official rules, International Tennis Hall of Fame inductees, the current year's tournament schedule, a list of tennis periodicals, contact information for the world's major tennis organizations and related sport and recreation organizations.

Instructional Sources

462. American Sport Education Program. **Coaching Youth Tennis.** 2nd ed. Champaign, Ill.: Human Kinetics, 1998. 142 pp. $12.95. ISBN 0-87322-966-5.

Designed specifically for novice coaches, this book is written by staff of the American Sport Education Program in cooperation with the United States Tennis Association. The first edition was called *Rookie Coaches Tennis Guide* (1991). Contains all the basic information coaches will need to get started: tips on communicating effectively, safety, what skills and drills to teach, and how to motivate players. Each chapter ends with a summary checklist or test. Also includes a glossary of terms.

463. Braden, Vic, and William Bruns. **Tennis 2000: Strokes, Strategy, and Psychology for a Lifetime.** Rev. ed. Boston: Little, Brown, 1998. 284 pp. $19.00. ISBN 0-316-10503-1.

A revised edition of the classic 1977 work *Vic Braden's Tennis for the Future*. This updated version carries the same primary message as the original: work for consistent shots under pressure. Illustrated with many black-and-white photographs and diagrams, each chapter of this work includes numerous practice drills for the stroke being discussed and detailed description of both mechanical and psychological strategies, tips, and checkpoints. A substantial handbook for tennis.

464. Brown, Jim. **Tennis: Steps to Success.** 3rd ed. Steps to Success Activity Series. Champaign, Ill.: Human Kinetics, 2004. 151 pp. $17.95. ISBN 0-7360-5363-8.

Organized into eleven sequenced steps, this book helps the beginner learn basic skills of the game and then move toward the more complex strategies of play. For each step, goals are clearly outlined and instructions are illustrated with drawings and court diagrams. A number of appropriate practice drills are included for each step, and suggestions are given for correcting typical errors. Includes a glossary of terms.

465. Bryant, James E. **Game, Set, Match: A Tennis Guide.** 5th ed. Wadsworth Physical Activity Series. Belmont, Calif.: Thomson / Wadsworth, 2001. 152 pp. $20.95. ISBN 0-534-57146-8.

Intended for the beginning or intermediate player who is currently receiving instruction and wants to learn more about technique and strategy. Abundant color photographs and illustrations aid the user in developing a mental image of how skills are executed. In addition, skills are described thoroughly, and charts are used to illustrate important tips on technique and ways to eliminate errors in play. Includes chapters on mental aspects of competition, the physical-fitness aspect, etiquette and interpretation of rules, singles and doubles strategies, tennis-court and equipment design, tournament competition, and other resources. At the end of each chapter are study questions. Includes USTA's "The Code: The Player's Guide for Unofficiated Matches," a glossary of terms, and an index.

466. Douglas, Paul. **The Handbook of Tennis.** Rev. ed. New York: Knopf, 1992. 288 pp. $24.00. ISBN 0-679-74062-7.

This comprehensive handbook contains 1500 drawings, photographs, and diagrams that illustrate the basic strokes, styles, and strategies of tennis. The book begins with a historical overview of the game, complete with photographs of early stars. Contains full coverage of the individual strokes and also covers strategy, how to develop a winning attitude, fitness, training, injuries, and treatments. Appendices include information on equipment, tournament procedure, and rules. Indexed.

467. **International Book of Tennis Drills: Over 100 Skill-Specific Drills Adopted by Tennis Professionals Worldwide.** Chicago: Triumph Books, 1998. 289 pp. $14.95. ISBN 1-57243-283-7.

Created by the United States Professional Tennis Registry, this book of drills is intended for both the tennis coach and the tennis teaching professional. Well organized and consistently presented, the drills are arranged by specific stroke or court situation (service, lob, doubles play, etc.). Each drill is described in outline format and illustrated with a full-page black-and-white drawing of the court and playing positions. The book begins with drills that support fundamental skills, then advances to more complex drills for advanced players. Updated from the 1993 edition.

468. Johnson, Joan D., Paul J. Xanthos, and Ann V. Lebedeff. **Tennis.** 8th ed. Winning Edge. Boston: WCB/McGraw-Hill, 2003. 231 pp. $12.80. ISBN 0-072-35385-6.

Designed as a complete guide for the student, this book presents material appropriate for the beginner or the advanced player who wishes to learn more about the game. Covers basic information on topics such as values, types of courts, dress, and equipment, as well as all the fundamental skills of the game. Includes sections on advanced skills and strategies and on rules and etiquette, a list of selected resources and publications, and information on the National Tennis Rating Program. Each chapter contains a tennis knowledge assessment. Illustrated with court and footwork diagrams and black-and-white photos. Indexed.

469. Levy, Allan M., and Mark L. Fuerst. **Tennis Injury Handbook: Professional Advice for Amateur Athletes.** New York: John Wiley, 1999. 184 pp. $14.95. ISBN 0-471-24854-1.

This illustrated guide to tennis injuries not only describes the injuries but also gives easy-to-follow instructions for stretching, conditioning, and exercising to prevent injuries. Includes information on nutrition, first aid, and health fads. Specific injuries are organized by area of the body. Also includes information that may be relevant for seniors, juniors, and women.

470. MacCurdy, Doug, and Shawn Tully. **Sports Illustrated Tennis: Strokes for Success.** 2nd ed. *Sports Illustrated* Winner's Circle Books. Lanham, Md.: Sports Illustrated Books, 1994. 158 pp. $12.95. ISBN 1-56800-006-5.

A basic guide to developing solid technique for tennis, this book describes the skills and drills necessary to develop the primary strokes and strategies involved in the game. Illustrated with black-and-white photographs and court diagrams.

471. Metzler, Michael W. **Tennis: Mastering the Basics with the Personalized Sports Instruction System.** Personalized Sport Instruction. Boston: Allyn & Bacon, 2001. 129 pp. $17.00. ISBN 0-205-32257-3.

This workbook teaches the fundamentals of tennis and can be used in a formal course setting or by individuals who want to work at their own pace outside a course and chart their own progress. Each chapter presents a module of information about performance skills, shots, or the game itself and concludes with tasks that test what was learned. Includes the rules of tennis. Illustrated with photographs and diagrams.

472. Sadzeck, Tom. **Tennis Skills: The Player's Guide.** Buffalo, N.Y.: Firefly Books, 2001. 128 pp. $14.95. ISBN 1-55209-494-4.

This beautifully illustrated training guide begins with a brief glossary of terms and basic instruction on stretching, equipment, and the variety of tennis grips. The bulk of the text covers skills, drills, and footwork, all presented in a visually interesting, step-by-step format. Also contains many colorful drawings and court diagrams that illustrate the skill being discussed.

473. Schwartz, Brett C., and Chris A. Dazet. **Competitive Tennis: Climbing the NTRP Ladder.** Champaign, Ill.: Human Kinetics, 1998. 255 pp. $17.95. ISBN 0-88011-755-9.

Organized according to the USTA's National Tennis Rating Program (NTRP) Classification System. For each level, identifies strengths and weaknesses and offers specific objective and instructive drills to improve. Valuable for coaches as well as players at all competitive levels. Includes many photos and figures to illustrate points of play.

474. Slaikeu, Karl, and Robert Trogolo. **Focused for Tennis.** Champaign, Ill.: Human Kinetics, 1998. 135 pp. $15.95. ISBN 0-88011-722-2.

This tennis source utilizes sport psychology, as well as techniques from clinical psychology, to help players improve their game. Promotes a system called the Three Rs—Release, Review, and Reset for mental training in the time between points. Includes practical exercises and profiles of elite players. Illustrated with black-and-white photographs. Includes a short list of references and an index.

475. United States Tennis Association. **Coaching Tennis Successfully.** 2nd ed. Champaign, Ill.: Human Kinetics, 2004. 199 pp. $20.95. ISBN 0-7360-4829-4.

Appropriate for public or college libraries, this coaching manual will help the coach develop a philosophy, communicate with and motivate players, build a tennis program, establish plans and a practice schedule, teach technique in an organized manner, and prepare players for competition. Illustrated with black-and-white photographs and diagrams. Indexed.

476. United States Tennis Association. **Tennis Tactics: Winning Patterns of Play.** Champaign, Ill.: Human Kinetics, 1996. 236 pp. $14.95. ISBN 0-88011-499-1.

Written by USTA staff, this tennis guide contains fifty-eight specific patterns of play and sixty-three practice drills so an individual may choose those that work best. Each pattern has an objective and is mapped to particular drills; patterns are also illustrated with court diagrams. Drills are described according to category (serve, return, etc.), purpose, and level, and a paragraph of procedure is given. At the end is a "pattern finder," a chart the player can use to easily find a pattern and drills for a unique tennis situation.

477. Zebas, Carole J., and H. Mardi Johnson. **Tennis: Back to the Basics.** 3rd ed. Dubuque, Iowa: Eddie Bowers Publishing, 1997. 136 pp. $16.95. ISBN 0-945483-66-X.

For both the player and teacher of tennis, this book places emphasis on the fundamental mechanics of basic strokes. Includes detailed information on conditioning, analysis of strokes, drills and strategy, facilities, and equipment. Illustrated with court diagrams, charts, and black-and-white photographs. Appendices include summarized USTA rules, a glossary of terms, and a sample tennis exam. There is no index, but the table of contents provides adequate detail to pinpoint specific information in the text.

Web Sites

478. **Association of Tennis Professionals (ATP).** http://www.atptennis.com (accessed December 3, 2004).

The ATP is the governing body of the men's professional tennis circuit. Their Web site provides information on the organization, its players, tournaments, records, and results. Also includes a calendar of events and a fan section with chat room.

479. **Intercollegiate Tennis Association.** http://www.itatennis.com/ (accessed December 3, 2004).

Based in Princeton, New Jersey, this nonprofit service organization is the governing body of collegiate tennis and is dedicated to the growth and promotion of college tennis. The association is made up of tennis coaches, student-athletes, and college tennis programs. Their site contains rankings for NCAA, NAIA, and junior/community college teams, as well as events, awards, rules, and links to much more information.

480. **International Tennis Federation (ITF).** http://www.itftennis.com (accessed December 3, 2004).

This very comprehensive and well-organized site provides an international player database with twenty years of records and rankings information, including rankings for wheelchair, junior, and veteran athletes. Gives the latest tennis news and an international calendar of events, as well as rules and regulations (the 2004 Rules of Tennis is available as a PDF file). Provides detailed information on the history and workings of the ITF and includes links to the national associations and major championship sites.

481. **International Tennis Hall of Fame.** http://www.tennisfame.org/ (accessed December 3, 2004).

Located in Newport, Rhode Island, in the renovated 1880 Newport Casino, the International Tennis Hall of Fame and Museum is a nonprofit organization that seeks to preserve the history of the game and honor the great tennis players, coaches, and other contributors who have been inducted into the hall of fame. This site provides a complete listing of hall of famers, along with their biographies and records and allows a virtual museum tour. It also contains information about the organization and its history, membership, and facility use, as well as contact information and a calendar of events.

482. United States Professional Tennis Registry. http://www.ptrtennis.org (accessed December 3, 2004).

A tennis teaching organization, the PTR's Web site offers schedules for both U.S. and international workshops for tennis teachers and coaches. Includes links to many related organizations and tennis publications.

483. United States Tennis Association (USTA). http://www.usta.com (accessed December 3, 2004).

In existence since 1881, the USTA is the official U.S. governing body for tennis. The nonprofit organization's goal is to promote and develop the growth of tennis in the United States. Abundant news and information sources are presented at this site, with especially strong coverage of the U.S. Open, Davis Cup, Fed Cup, and Olympic Games. Also provides information on USA League Tennis and the National Tennis Rating Program (NTRP).

Chapter 8

Small-Ball Sports

A wide range of different sports are covered in this chapter, but they all involve the use of a small-sized ball during play. Included are lists of information sources on baseball, cricket, croquet, field hockey, handball, lacrosse, and softball. Baseball's huge appeal as a spectator sport has driven the baseball reference book publishing market, so it is clearly the largest section in this chapter. Many libraries will not be able to afford all the sources listed, but a good variety is included from which to choose.

Baseball

Reference Sources

484. Aylesworth, Thomas, and Benton Minks. **The Encyclopedia of Baseball Managers: 1901 to the Present Day.** New York: Crescent Books, 1990. 224 pp. $12.99. ISBN 0-517-67909-4.

Well illustrated with nearly 400 color and black-and-white photographs, this source contains profiles and records of major league managers. Organized by league and then by team, managers are listed in chronological order. The concise profiles vary in length from one short paragraph to several pages, usually depending on the length of the manager's stay with the team. Indexed.

485. Benson, Michael. **Ballparks of North America: A Comprehensive Historical Reference to Baseball Grounds, Yards, and Stadiums, 1845 to Present.** Jefferson, N.C.: McFarland, 1989. 475 pp. $45.00. ISBN 0-89950-367-5.

Arranged by city, then chronologically under the city name, this guide to North American ballparks provides an interesting history. Each entry includes the name and any alternative name of the ballpark, the league and name of the first team to play there, when they played, and names of subsequent teams. Each entry also includes the location of the ballpark, dimensions of the playing field, seating capacity, and attendance records. Illustrated with black-and-white photographs. Other historical facts and interesting details are included when they are available. Includes a bibliography and index.

486. Bjarkman, Peter C., ed. **Encyclopedia of Major League Baseball: American League Team Histories.** First published 1991 as *Encyclopedia of Major League Baseball Team Histories*, edited by Richard Gallen. New York: Carroll & Graf, 1993. 575 pp. $14.95. ISBN 0-88184-974-x.

Each chapter covers one team's history and is presented in a substantial scholarly essay with notes, references, and an annotated bibliography. It is illustrated with black-and-white photographs of only eight of the greatest players, including Ted Williams, Ty Cobb, and Joe DiMaggio. Each chapter in the volume also contains tables of data representing career and season records through 1992. Brief biographical notes on the contributors are given at the end of the volume. There is a separate volume for the National League. Not indexed.

487. Bucek, Jeanine, editorial director. **The Baseball Encyclopedia: The Complete and Definitive Record of Major League Baseball.** 10th ed. New York: Macmillan, 1996. 3026 pp. $59.95. ISBN 0-02-860815-1; 0-02-861435-6 (with CD-ROM).

This classic baseball reference is excellent for the dates covered. It contains complete statistics for all major league players, lifetime major league team rosters, an alphabetical roster of their managers, a chronological listing of teams, inning-by-inning summaries of each World Series, and more.

488. Carter, Craig, and Dave Sloan. **Baseball Guide.** 2002 ed. St. Louis, Mo.: The Sporting News Publishing, 2002. 646 pp. $15.95. ISBN 0-89204-669-4.

This standard baseball reference has been in publication for over sixty years. Includes the current year's schedules and rosters, as well as the previous season in review, and provides complete coverage of each playoff and World Series game. Each team's front-office directory is given, along with broadcast, ticket, and ballpark information. Contains the complete major and minor league statistics and standings, plus a great deal of historical information, such as award winners, the hall of fame roster, and team-by-team yearly finishes.

489. Clark, Dick, and Larry Lester, eds. **The Negro Leagues Book.** Cleveland, Ohio: Society for American Baseball Research, 1994. 382 pp. $29.95. ISBN 0-910137-55-2.

The cover of the book indicates that it is "a monumental work from the Negro Leagues Committee of the Society for American Baseball Research." Contains historical essays on the Negro Leagues, the great teams and their cities, and eleven hall of fame players. Includes the rosters of teams by year from 1862 to 1955, with teams listed alphabetically by city, and the league standings from 1920 to 1954. Provides a Negro Baseball Register, alphabetical in arrangement through the year 1955, a list of seasonal leaders, complete box scores of East-West games from 1933 to 1950, information about players who moved to the major leagues, and records of the players. Includes a comprehensive bibliography, plus a list of reference books, theses and dissertations, and films.

490. Dewey, Donald, and Nicholas Acocella. **The New Biographical History of Baseball.** Chicago: Triumph Books, 2002. 474 pp. $28.95. ISBN 1-57243-470-8.

The first edition of this book was published as The Biographical History of Baseball (1995). The authors do not claim this is a who's who but rather that it includes those individuals who have influenced the game, for better or for worse. Includes sketches of approximately 1500 players, owners, managers, journalists and fans. Sparsely illustrated with just twenty-four black-and-white photographs. Arranged alphabetically by name.

491. Dewey, Donald, and Nicholas Acocella. **The Ball Clubs.** Rev. ed. New York: HarperCollins, 1996. 604 pp. $21.00. ISBN 0-06-273403-2.

A revised edition of the *Encyclopedia of Major League Baseball Teams*, this reference source covers clubs represented in the six officially recognized major leagues. The basic arrangement is alphabetical, by the name of the team. Essays describing the history and development of the teams are detailed and informative and vary in length from one page to over twenty pages. Illustrated with black-and-white photographs. The source provides a bibliography of sources but no index.

492. Dickson, Paul. **The New Dickson Baseball Dictionary.** Rev. ed. New York: Harcourt Brace Jovanovich, 1999. 529 pp. $20.00. ISBN 0-15-600580-8.

Written for a diverse audience, the approximately 7000 entries in this dictionary will both entertain and inform. The entries include history of the word or phrase, definition, synonyms, cited examples of a word's first use in print, and uses outside baseball. Illustrated with historic photographs and drawings. Includes a thesaurus, a bibliography, and a section on how to use the source.

493. Erickson, Hal. **The Baseball Filmography: 1915 through 2001.** 2nd ed. Jefferson, N.C.: McFarland, 2002. 552 pp. $49.95. ISBN 0-7864-1272-0.

In this updated version of Erickson's 1992 work, the author describes 111 fictional baseball films produced and released in the United States between 1915 and 2001. Twenty-nine new films are included in this edition. Each entry includes cast and production credits, year of release, a substantial summary of the film's plot, and a critique of and details on what went on behind the scenes. The films are arranged alphabetically by title. Two additional chapters contain essays on baseball short subjects and baseball in nonbaseball films. Includes an extensive bibliography and a comprehensive index.

494. Friend, Luke and Don Zminda with John Mehno, in association with STATS Inc. **The Best Book of Baseball Facts and Stats.** Rev. ed. Richmond Hill, ON: Firefly Books, 2005. 304 pp. $14.95. ISBN 1-55407-049-X.

This concise and comprehensive source brings together the players, teams, games, and statistics in an easy-to-use format. Provides profiles of over 100 great baseball players, lists award winners, follows the development of major league franchises, records the role of managers, covers the World Series from

1903 to the present, describes great stadiums, teams, games, and controversies, and includes a chapter on statistics. It's all here in one inexpensive place.

495. Holway, John B. **The Complete Book of Baseball's Negro Leagues: The Other Half of Baseball History.** Fern Park, Fla.: Hastings House, 2001. 510 pp. $26.95. ISBN 0-8038-2007-0.

This reference work is based on the author's extensive research since 1969. It is a comprehensive chronology by year that includes both the statistical and narrative history of the Negro Leagues. The years 1862 to 1948 are detailed one-by-one through careful research, bringing this period of baseball history to the forefront. Illustrated with many photographs. Contains a bibliography of books, articles, newspapers, and reference books. Indexed.

496. James, Bill. **Stats All-Time Major League Handbook.** 2nd ed. Morton Grove, Ill.: STATS Publishing, 2000. 2696 pp. $24.95. ISBN 1-884064-81-7.

Updated through the 1999 season, this massive statistical compilation contains complete year-by-year statistics for every player in major league history. Contains a career register for every player since 1876.

497. James, Bill, and Jim Henzler. **Win Shares.** Morton Grove, Ill.: STATS Publishing, 2002. 728 pp. $29.95. ISBN 1-931584-03-6.

The authors introduce an innovative approach for calculating a player's performance and value each season, measuring the player's total contributions across positions, teams, and eras. In addition to a very detailed explanation of this statistical method of determining a player's status, the book includes a ranking of over 60,000 players through the 2001 season.

498. Johnson, Lloyd, Miles Wolff, and Steve McDonald, eds. **The Encyclo pedia of Minor League Baseball: The Official Record of Minor League Baseball.** Durham, N.C.: Baseball America, 1997. 666 pp. $48.95. ISBN 0-9637189-8-3.

In this comprehensive and enjoyable volume, the period of 1883 to 1996 is presented. Minor league baseball is analyzed in a year-by-year review of the leagues, teams, managers, and players, with statistics and standings. Detailed information is included on the cities and their leagues, as are records of individual players.

499. Koppett, Leonard. **The Man in the Dugout: Baseball's Top Managers and How They Got That Way.** Expanded ed. Philadelphia, Pa.: Temple University Press, 2000. 352 pp. $29.50. ISBN 1-56636-745-6.

Includes managers up to the year 2000 and back as far as 1950. Interviews with the managers themselves guide the author's analysis of why and how they have lived their careers.

500. Lee, Bill. **The Baseball Necrology: The Post-Baseball Lives and Deaths of Over 7,600 Major League Players and Others.** Jefferson, N.C.: McFarland, 2003. 517 pp. $55.00. ISBN 0-7864-1539-8.

This reference work of 7600 entries looks at the lives of baseball players, as well as other persons involved with baseball (writers, umpires, administrators) after their careers in baseball ended. Players in the Negro Leagues are included. Each entry provides the number of years involved in the major leagues, primary position played, hall of fame indication, date and place of birth and death, military service, obituary information about life after baseball, cause of death if known, and burial place. A unique feature is an appendix that presents burial locations, arranged by state, then city, then cemetery. A brief bibliography is also included.

501. Light, Jonathan Fraser. **The Cultural Encyclopedia of Baseball.** Jefferson, N.C.: McFarland, 1997. 888 pp. $75.00. ISBN 0-7864-0311-X.

In this nonstatistical account of the rich world of baseball, the author provides alphabetically arranged narrative entries that cover the players, managers, promoters, media figures, umpires, stadiums, salaries, trades, and many more baseball topics. Quotations, anecdotes, and photographs add to the interesting text to make this an enjoyable way to examine baseball history and culture.

502. Loverro, Thom. **The Encyclopedia of Negro League Baseball.** Facts On File Sports Library. New York: Facts On File, 2003. 368 pp. $75.00. ISBN 0-8160-4430-9.

This notable encyclopedia begins with a forward by Wilmer Fields, president of the Negro League Baseball Players Association and pitcher for the Homestead Grays from 1939 to 1950. This record of Negro League baseball contains more than 3000 entries of varying lengths, some several pages long, but many of them only one sentence that concisely identifies a player's unique role in the history of baseball. Illustrated with over sixty black-and-white photographs. Contains a bibliography of books, Web sites and other sources. Indexed by individual's names, team's names, and subjects.

503. Lowry, Philip J. **Green Cathedrals: The Ultimate Celebration of All 271 Major League and Negro League Ballparks Past and Present.** Reading, Mass: Addison-Wesley, 1992. 275 pp. $24.90. ISBN 0-201-56777-6.

This beautifully illustrated presentation of major league and Negro League ballparks allows a nostalgic look at the history, architecture and detail of many early ballparks and also many newer ones. The carefully researched entries include anecdotes, statistics, historic photographs, and baseball trivia.

504. Madden, W. C. **The All-American Girls Professional Baseball League Record Book: Comprehensive Hitting, Fielding, and Pitching Statistics.** Jefferson, N.C.: McFarland, 2000. 294 pp. $39.95. ISBN 0-7864-0597-X.

This reference work contains the hitting, fielding, and pitching records of women who played in the AAGPBL. A brief history of the league, team rosters, and playoff records are also included.

505. Madden, W. C. **The Women of the All-American Girls Professional Baseball League: A Biographical Dictionary.** Jefferson, N.C.: McFarland, 1997. 288 pp. $48.60. ISBN 0-7864-0304-7.

This source profiles over 600 women who were involved in the league. Entries contain basic data, career statistics, and information on the individual's life before and after participating in the league. Includes a brief history of the league and an index of players by family and married names. Illustrated with black-and-white photographs and drawings.

506. Nathan, David H., ed. **The McFarland Baseball Quotations Dictionary.** Jefferson, N.C.: McFarland, 2000. 294 pp. $45.00. ISBN 0-7864-0888-X.

This collection of over 4000 baseball quotations will amuse and entertain readers who aren't even baseball fans. Arranged within a diverse group of subject categories, the entries also provide a context for the quotations and occasionally the year it took place. Includes a subject index and a name index. This is a revised edition of *Baseball Quotations* (1991) by the same author.

507. **NCAA Baseball Rules.** 2004 ed. Indianapolis, Ind.: National Collegiate Athletic Association, 2003. 119 pp. $7.50. ISBN 0736-5209.

This official NCAA rule book is published annually and contains both administrative and conduct rules. Includes a code of ethics for players and coaches, a summary of major rule changes for the year, a list of differences between NCAA rules and those of professional baseball, and contact information for help with rule interpretation. Illustrated with diagrams and drawings. Indexed.

508. Neft, David, Richard M. Cohen, and Michael L. Neft. **The Sports Encyclopedia: Baseball.** 23rd ed. New York: St. Martin's Griffin, 2003. 801 pp. $22.95. ISBN 0-312-30478-1.

This comprehensive baseball source provides the history of every player, team, and season from 1902 through the current year. It includes detailed statistics as well as brief essays to enliven the work. Arranged chronologically by year, each season's coverage begins with an overview of the season and major highlights. Includes alphabetical registers of batters and pitchers, hall of fame members, yearly pennant winners, yearly batting and pitching leaders, and other leaders.

509. Nemec, David. **The Great Encyclopedia of 19th-Century Major League Baseball.** New York: Donald I. Fine Books, 1997. 852 pp. $49.95. ISBN 1-55611-500-8.

This reference work covers baseball's early years, from 1871 to 1900, giving each season's annual report in chronological order. Each year's report begins with an essay that highlights major events of leagues, teams, and individuals and includes the season's statistical record and sidebars containing additional detailed information. A player register is included, as is a pitcher register, manager roster, and umpire roster. Nineteenth-century single-season and career leaders are listed. Illustrated with black-and-white photographs and drawings. Contains a bibliography and an index.

510. Nemec, David. **The Rules of Baseball: An Anecdotal Look at the Rules of Baseball and How They Came to Be.** New York: Lyons & Burford, 1994. 270 pp. $24.95. ISBN 1-55821-279-5.

This book explores the history of the rules and provides the details that illustrate why and how they have changed and developed over the years. Filled with anecdotal accounts of events that have been critical in the history of baseball. Includes in-depth definitions of many terms. Illustrated with over fifty historic black-and-white photographs. Indexed.

511. Nistler, Tony, and David Walton. **Baseball Register.** 2003 ed. St. Louis, Mo.: Sporting News Publishing, 2002. 653 pp. $15.95. ISBN 0-89204-699-6.

Produced annually since 1940, the *Baseball Register* is a standard reference work with essential information on every active major and minor league player and major league manager. It gives career statistics, basic biographical information, and other significant facts. Alphabetical in arrangement, this source is appropriate for any audience. The cover indicates that it "includes information from the former STATS, Inc. *Major League Handbook.*"

512. **Official Baseball Rules.** 2004 ed. St. Louis, Mo.: Sporting News Publishing, 2004. 104 pp. $7.95. ISBN 0-89204-733-X.

This pocket-sized volume contains the official major league baseball rules, the ones used by managers, coaches, players, and umpires in the major leagues and elsewhere to settle disputes. It includes rule changes in effect for the current season. In addition to rules, the volume contains the objectives of the game, diagrams of the official playing field with dimensions, description of approved equipment, and a glossary of terms. Indexed.

513. **Official Major League Baseball Fact Book.** 2003 ed. St. Louis, Mo.: Sporting News Publishing, 2003. 421 pp. $19.95. ISBN 0-89204-701-1.

Usually published in February to introduce the new season, this annual source includes a season preview with each team's schedule, the spring roster, stadium information (including a diagram of the stadium), ticket and broadcast information, and a front-office directory. The past season is also covered in depth with final standings, leaders and award winners, and the team and individual statistics for the season and championship play. There is a chronological list of hall of famers, as well as a season-by-season historical review from 1876 to the present. A final section of this book contains records for major leaders in various categories and data from baseball's most memorable games. Illustrated with many black-and-white photographs.

514. Okrent, Daniel, and Harris Lewine, eds. **The Ultimate Baseball Book: The Classic Illustrated History of the World's Greatest Game.** Boston: Houghton Mifflin, 2000. 448 pp. $29.95. ISBN 0-618-05668-8.

This well-illustrated encyclopedia of baseball history is arranged chronologically, with each chapter covering a decade from 1876 to 1999. Essays provide lively profiles as well as reviews of baseball highlights during the decade, presented in a nostalgic style. The volume contains historical text by David Nemec. Illustrated with historical black-and-white photographs and drawings. Indexed.

515. Pietrusza, David, Matthew Silverman, and Michael Gershman, eds. **Baseball: The Biographical Encyclopedia.** Kingston: Total Sports Publishing, 2000. 1298 pp. $29.95. ISBN 1-894963-09-1.

This impressive biographical source contains brief profiles of 2000 of the most important persons involved with baseball. Each entry contains personal data, career statistics, and a small photograph of the individual. Considered a companion volume to *Total Baseball.*

516. Porter, David L., ed. **Baseball.** Vol. 1 of **Biographical Dictionary of American Sports.** Rev. and expanded ed. 3 vols. Westport, Conn.: Greenwood Press, 2000. $340.95. ISBN 0-313-29884-X (set).

Arranged alphabetically, this incredible three-volume work contains 1450 signed baseball entries, including the 973 entries that appeared in the author's three earlier volumes on baseball, which have been revised and updated. Profiles are given for athletes, coaches, promoters, and administrators who were influential in baseball. Most entries are one page in length and cover the person's career highlights as well as other interesting details; for each, a bibliography of sources is provided. Appendices contain a great deal of additional information, such as a list of entries by main position played and by place of birth; major league managers, executives, and umpires; National Baseball Hall of Fame members; and lists of entries from the Negro League and All-American Girls Professional Baseball League. Indexed.

517. Rielly, Edward J. **Baseball: An Encyclopedia of Popular Culture.** Santa Barbara, Calif.: ABC-CLIO, 2000. 371 pp. $75.00. ISBN 1-57607-103-0.

Covering the social and cultural aspects of baseball, this encyclopedia is a unique and interesting source. It begins with a list of the topics covered: people, teams, places, and things as diverse as artificial turf, baseball cards, Cuban baseball, railroads, women in baseball, and the World Series. Each entry includes a brief essay, cross-references, and a list of sources for additional reading. Illustrated with black-and-white photographs. Includes a full bibliography and an index.

518. Riley, James A. **The Biographical Encyclopedia of the Negro Baseball Leagues.** New York: Carroll & Graf, 2002. 952 pp. $25.00. ISBN 0-7867-0959-6.

This outstanding reference source contains detailed information on over 4000 African-American athletes who were involved in the Negro Baseball Leagues during the period of 1872 to 1950. Included are individuals who played with a major league–quality team or who made a historical impact during their career. Entries vary in length from one paragraph to one to two pages and include the person's name, nicknames, career dates, teams, position, vital statistics, biographical sketch, and performance data. Illustrated with historical black-and-white photographs and contains an addendum with information about newly identified persons and new information about those in the earlier edition (1994). Includes a bibliography of sources consulted, an index.

519. Sickels, John. **Stats Minor League Scouting Notebook.** 2002 ed. Morton Grove, Ill.: STATS Publishing, 2002. 298 pp. $19.95. ISBN 1-931584-00-1.

In this annual publication, the author uses his own "Seven Skills" evaluation criteria to identify and grade those baseball players likely to play in the major leagues. The entries for prospects are arranged alphabetically and provide the players' height, weight, age, date of birth, a statistical analysis of performance, and a summary statement of strengths and weaknesses. Also includes the author's top-fifty prospects. Contains a glossary of terms, an appendix that lists minor league teams, and an index by team.

520. Skipper, John C. **A Biographical Dictionary of the Baseball Hall of Fame.** Jefferson, N.C.: McFarland, 2000. 346 pp. $45.00. ISBN 0-7864-0603-8.

This source examines the lives and statistical career accomplishments of members of the National Baseball Hall of Fame. Includes those inducted through the year 1999. Arranged alphabetically by name, the entries are one to two pages long and include an essay that describes the major facts and feats that distinguish the person's career, followed by the statistics. Includes a bibliography and an index.

521. Skipper, John C. **A Biographical Dictionary of Major League Baseball Managers.** Jefferson, N.C.: McFarland, 2003. 380 pp. $45.00. ISBN 0-7864-1021-3.

The more than 600 entries in this reference work provide great coverage of major league managers. The entries include dates of birth and death, the teams and dates they managed, win-loss records, winning percentages, and standings. Appendices provide additional information, such as most and fewest games managed, wins and winning percentage, and a chronological list of the managers. Illustrated with photographs. Includes a bibliography and an index.

522. Smith, Myron J. **Baseball: A Comprehensive Bibliography, Supplement 1, 1985–May 1992.** Jefferson, N.C.: McFarland, 1993. 422 pp. $68.50. ISBN 0-89950-799-9.

This supplement to the author's original bibliography contains over 8000 new entries. The volume provides an impressive list of journals consulted. The topical arrangement and thorough indexing make it easy to find sources quickly. Each section is introduced with a paragraph of explanation. Indexed by author and subject.

523. Smith, Myron J. **Baseball: A Comprehensive Bibliography, Supplement 2, 1992 through 1997.** Jefferson, N.C.: McFarland, 1998. 310 pp. $25.00. ISBN 0-7864-0531-7.

In the second supplement to the author's original comprehensive bibliography, he updates his work with over 5000 new entries. Covers all aspects of baseball and a wide variety of types of sources. Includes Web sites, with the caveat that they change frequently.

524. Smith, Ron. **The Ballpark Book: A Journey through the Fields of Baseball Magic.** Rev. ed. St. Louis, Mo.: Sporting News Publishing, 2003. 336 pp. $39.95. ISBN 0-89204-703-8.

This popular reference pays tribute to fifty-two ballparks, describing the history and details of each in colorful essays filled with facts and trivia. They are arranged by eras: the classics (Fenway and Wrigley), the middle ages (Dodger and Shea), the turf era (Riverfront and Three Rivers), the dome era (Metrodome and SkyDome), the new wave era (Coors and Camden Yards), and those ballparks that are gone but not forgotten (Comiskey and Candlestick). Well illustrated with hundreds of color photographs and drawings.

525. Solomon, Burt. **The Baseball Timeline: In Association with Major League Baseball.** 1st American ed. New York: Dorling Kindersley, 2001. 1216 pp. $50.00. ISBN 0-7894-7132-9.

This fascinating history of baseball is a worthy addition to the baseball reference shelf, though in its introduction the author suggests that it is "a book to have on hand while you watch, talk, or think about baseball, not a work to store on a shelf." Very accessible to the casual browser, it can be approached from any point from the very early years to the year 2000 because it is arranged by year and then day. Each year's coverage begins with major world news headlines and concludes with "best of year" statistics. Throughout the volume, extra information is provided outside the main text in boxes marked with symbols for subjects such as equipment, culture, trivia, rules changes, and league changes. Well illustrated with many black-and-white and color photographs. Includes a bibliography and a detailed index with entries by season under the team names and topics.

526. **Stats Player Profiles.** 2002 ed. Morton Grove, Ill.: STATS Publishing, 2001. 532 pp. $19.95. ISBN 1-884064-94-9.

This notable source provides detailed statistical analysis of the performance of current individual baseball players and teams in a variety of situations and environments throughout the season. These statistics are reported to be the ones the managers use during professional play.

527. Thorn, John, Phil Birnbaum, and Bill Deane, eds. **Total Baseball: The Ultimate Baseball Encyclopedia.** 8th ed. Toronto, ON: Sport Classic Books / Total Sport Publishing, 2004. 2688 pp. $59.95. ISBN 1-894963-27-X.

Considered by many to be the official encyclopedia of the game, this extensive reference work is complete in thirteen sections. The first twelve sections contain narrative essays covering aspects of history, the players, highlights, and the leagues. Also included is a complete analysis, with statistics, of postseason play from 1884 through 2003. The last section contains the registers, leaders, and rosters, as well as appendixes that cover attendance, 39 years of the Amateur Draft, the evolution of baseball records, all-time leaders, the annual record, the manager roster, and umpire roster. Includes a glossary of statistical terms and abbreviations for teams and leagues. The new "completely revised and updated" edition includes many unique feature articles and color photographs.

528. Tomlinson, Gerald, ed. **How to Do Baseball Research.** Cleveland, Ohio: The Society of American Baseball Research (SABR), 2000. 163 pp. $16.00. ISBN 0-910137-83-8.

In ten well-written chapters the authors provide a sound research strategy that will guide researchers of all ages. Chapters in the guide provide keys to good research; an introduction to libraries and archives; information on using print sources, the computer, and statistics; methods of checking facts; finding and using pictures and photographs; writing for SABR; and preparing a manuscript.

529. Walter, Bernie. **The Baseball Handbook: Winning Fundamentals for Players and Coaches.** Champaign, Ill.: Human Kinetics, 2002. 241 pp. $19.95. ISBN 0-7360-3985-6.

Intended for coaches and players, this comprehensive instruction guide covers offense, defense, pitching, base running, and special situations. Written by an experienced, award-winning coach, the method is proven on the field. Illustrated with photographs, diagrams, and charts.

530. Wirkmaa, Andres. **Baseball Scorekeeping: A Practical Guide to the Rules.** Jefferson, N.C.: McFarland, 2003. 270 pp. $29.95. ISBN 0-7864-1448-0.

In this unique guide to the serious work of scorekeeping, chapters clearly explain the duties, responsibilities, and authority of the official scorer; the official scorer's reports; and details such as player listings, substitute batters and runners, out-of-turn batters, called and forfeited games, runs batted in, base hits, stolen bases, sacrifices, putouts, assists, double and triple plays, errors, wild pitches and passed balls, bases on balls, strikeouts, earned runs, winning and losing pitchers, saves, statistics, percentage records, minimum standards for individual championships, and consecutive performance streaks. Indexed.

Web Sites

531. **International Baseball Federation (IBAF).** http://www.baseball.ch (accessed December 3, 2004).

As the international governing body for baseball, the IBAF site provides information about international competition, including official Olympic competition in baseball. The site contains the official rules, news, schedules, results of international competition, rankings, a directory of member countries with links, photographs, publications, and much more.

532. **National Baseball Hall of Fame and Museum, Inc.** http://www.base ballhalloffame.org/ (accessed December 3, 2004).

The site contains information to help plan a visit to the hall of fame in Cooperstown, New York, but also offers a great deal of information for the virtual visitor. Provides history, an events calendar, details of exhibits, profiles of the hall of famers, and much more.

533. **Negro League Baseball.** http://www.NegroLeagueBaseball.com (accessed December 3, 2004).

A great site for Negro League history, offers detailed information on the teams and players, a time line, an FAQ, a trivia quiz, and much more.

534. **Society for American Baseball Research.** http://www.sabr.org/ (accessed December 3, 2004).

Established in 1971 in Cooperstown, New York, the mission of SABR is to promote the study of baseball. Their Web site offers a world of information, including links to the group's twenty-four research committees, each with its own focus.

535. **USA Baseball.** http://www.usabaseball.com (accessed December 3, 2004).

The national governing body for baseball maintains a comprehensive Web site with player information, schedules, rules, results, statistics, and records.

Cricket

Reference Sources

536. Arnold, Peter, and Peter Wynne-Thomas. **The Ultimate Encyclopedia of Cricket: The Definitive Illustrated Guide to World Cricket.** Rev. and updated ed. London: Carlton, 2003. 208 pp. $29.95. ISBN 1-84442-929-6.

Profiles the top cricketers and major competitions internationally, including the World Cup. Also describes famous cricket grounds and details the greatest matches. Provides details of equipment that has been used over time, the culture of the game, and many stories that have shaped the direction of cricket over the years. Contains a section of records for such feats as most runs in a season, highest and lowest team totals, best bowling in a match, and all-around records. Also includes a chronology of important events in the development of the game from 1598 to 2002. Well illustrated with many black-and-white and color photographs. Indexed.

537. Browning, Mark. **A Complete History of World Cup Cricket, 1975–1999.** New York: Kangaroo Press / Simon & Schuster, 1999. 352 pp. $22.00. ISBN 0-7318-0833-9.

Tracing the history and development of cricket's World Cup, each game in the tournament is described with colorful profiles of the personalities, teams, controversies, triumphs, and complete statistics. Illustrated with high-quality color photographs of action during the matches. Contains a bibliography and an index.

538. Cashman, Richard I., Warwick Franks, Jim Maxwell, Brian Stoddart, Amanda Weaver, and Ray Webster, eds. **The Oxford Companion to Australian**

Cricket. With the Australian Society of Sports History. Melbourne: Oxford University Press Australia, 1996. 640 pp. ISBN 0-19-553575-8.

This comprehensive encyclopedia of Australian cricket provides both biographical information and statistics for women and men who played at the state or national level. Reflects all aspects of the sport and includes feature articles by prominent authors on such topics as captaincy and the first women's tour. Includes a select bibliography that updates the 1991 work of E. W. Padwick. Directories list the thematic articles and feature articles and their authors, names and locations of Australian grounds, and names of other countries that are important in cricket. Illustrated with black-and-white photographs and drawings.

539. Eastaway, Robert. **What Is a Googly? The Mysteries of Cricket Explained.** London: Robson Books, 2003. 152 pp. $11.00. ISBN 1-86105-629-X.

In this beginner's guide to cricket, the author explains terminology and the fundamentals of play. Covers basic rules, equipment, strategy, scoring and statistics, individual playing styles, and cricket lore. Also contains a history of the game, a glossary of terms, and a list of readings for further study.

540. Foley, Keith. **A Dictionary of Cricketing Terminology.** Lewiston, N.Y.: Edwin Mellen Press, 1998. 441 pp. $109.95. ISBN 0-7734-8266-0.

This alphabetically arranged dictionary of cricket terminology provides definitions for over 3500 terms. Quotations from cricketing literature and journalism are used to illustrate the definitions. A bibliography of sources consulted is given at the end of the work.

541. Padwick, E. W., et al. **A Bibliography of Cricket.** 2nd ed. 2 vols. London: Library Association Publishing for the Cricket Society, 1991. ISBN 0-85365-902-8 (v. 1); 0-85365-528-6 (v. 2).

The classic source on cricket, and a model for other comprehensive sport bibliographies, Padwick's work reveals the rich history of the sport of cricket. Volume 1 of this edition is actually the second edition of Padwick's original work, published in 1984, which covers to the end of 1979. Volume 2 of this edition covers publications from 1980 to 1989 and also 816 items published before 1980 that were not included in the earlier work. Volume 2 was complied by Stephen Eley and Peter Griffiths, with considerable guidance from Padwick. Covers international cricket fully.

542. Rundell, Michael. **The Dictionary of Cricket.** 2nd ed. New York: Oxford University Press, 1995. 218 pp. $25.00. ISBN 0-19-866198-3.

This A to Z dictionary of cricket terminology is a fascinating look into a fascinating sport. Terms are defined fully, and entries give additional information on the technical, legal, historical, or etymological implications of the vocabulary. Examples of the terms' use in the cricket literature are also given to illustrate the entries. The sources of these quotations are listed at the end of the volume.

543. Smith, T.E. **Tom Smith's New Cricket Umpiring and Scoring.** Jubilee ed. London: Weidenfeld & Nicolson, 2004. 256 pp. $15.95. ISBN 0-297-84724-4.

With coverage of everything from test matches to club cricket, this is the reference book that umpires and scorers consult during play. It contains the complete 2000 Code of the Laws of Cricket, with interpretation and 2003 amendments, and is authorized by the Association of Cricket Umpires and Scorers as a textbook.

Instructional Sources

544. Australian Cricket Board. **Coaching Youth Cricket.** Champaign, Ill.: Human Kinetics, 2000. 185 pp. $15.95. ISBN 0-7360-3330-0.

This coaching manual is intended for new or inexperienced coaches who are teaching cricket to athletes aged six to fourteen. It provides the coach with tools for effective communication and team building, a practice plan, and complete information about the game of cricket. Covers the basic skills of throwing, bowling, catching, wicket keeping, batting, and running between wickets. Includes over fifty drills to reinforce the skills being introduced. Illustrated with over 150 drawings and charts.

545. Bull, Stephen J., Scott Fleming, and Jo Doust. **Play Better Cricket.** Eastbourne, U.K.: Sports Dynamics, 1992. 98 pp. ISBN 0-951-9543-0-X.

The front cover indicates that this book has been "approved by the National Cricket Association." This training manual for cricket players covers both the mental and physical aspects of the game. Chapters provide information on goal setting, mental preparation for match play, team building, fitness and training methods, warm-up, nutrition, biomechanics of fast bowling, and principles of training. Illustrated with drawings and charts. Includes a list of references for further reading. Indexed.

546. Melville, Tom. **Cricket for Americans: Playing and Understanding the Game.** Sports and Culture. Bowling Green, Ohio: Bowling Green State University Popular Press, 1993. 214 pp. $25.95. ISBN 0-87972-606-7.

This guide is intended to help Americans understand and play the game of cricket for the first time. Contains chapters on techniques of play, the rules of cricket, the role of the umpires, the rich language of the game, and how to read and understand the scorecard and statistics. Also describes how to teach the game to others, the history of cricket in America, and how the game is organized around the world. Illustrated with a collection of black-and-white photographs that features some of the world's most famous cricket grounds. Includes a glossary of terms, a bibliography, and the laws of cricket.

Web Sites

547. **International Cricket Council (ICC).** http://www.cricket.org (accessed March 31, 2004).

The ICC is the governing body for international Test Match and One Day International (ODI) cricket. Their Web site provides comprehensive information on the international game, its players, and a directory of member nations. Also contains history, rules and regulations, and much more.

548. United States of America Cricket Association. http://www.usaca.org (accessed January 2, 2004).

The United States of America Cricket Association (USACA) is the governing body for cricket in the United States. Their Web site offers information on tournaments, educational programs, leagues and clubs, equipment, and players. It provides a history of cricket and the official laws of cricket.

Croquet

Reference Sources

549. Drazin, David H., comp. **Croquet: A Bibliography; Specialist Books and Pamphlets Complete to 1997.** New Castle, Del.: Oak Knoll Press / St. Paul's Bibliographies, 2000. 508 pp. $99.95. ISBN 1-58456-008-8.

This is the first volume of at least two planned by the author to comprehensively describe the complete literature of croquet. The content of this scholarly volume is specialist books and pamphlets on croquet and patents on inventions related to the game of croquet. Each of the more than 1000 entries contains a complete bibliographic description plus notes. The work is indexed in three ways: by title, by authors and other contributors, and by publishers and printers.

550. Mabee, Carlton H. **A Guide to Croquet Court Planning, Building, and Maintenance.** Kennebunkport, Maine: Bass Cove Books, 1991. 119 pp. $45.00. ISBN 0-9630074-0-8.

Written by a former national champion and chair of the Courts and Greens Committee of the USCA, the author is well qualified to write about all aspects of croquet greens from court construction to long-term maintenance. This is the definitive manual and reference book on croquet courts. Illustrated.

551. Rhoades, Nancy L. **Croquet: An Annotated Bibliography from the Rendell Rhoades Croquet Collection.** Metuchen, N.J.: Scarecrow Press, 1992. 244 pp. $50.00. ISBN 0-8108-2571-6.

This amazing source contains over 650 entries that describe a wide variety of croquet material from the extensive collection of the late Dr. Rendell Rhoades. It includes books, pamphlets, periodicals, catalogs, trading cards, newspapers, photographs, postcards, scrapbooks, art prints, and advertisements. It also offers a chronological list of books on croquet.

Instructional Sources

552. Boga, Steven. **Croquet.** Mechanicsburg, Pa.: Stackpole Books, 1995. 90 pp. $10.00. ISBN 0-8117-2489-1.
The front cover of the book indicates that it is "a handbook of all the rules, strategies, techniques, and tips you need to be a better player."

553. Lamb, W. E. **Croquet.** 3rd ed. With the Croquet Association. Know the Game. London: A & C Black, 2002. 48 pp. $10.00. ISBN 0-7136-6006-6.
A basic, illustrated guide to playing croquet. Indexed.

554. Osborn, Jack, and Herbert Bayard Swope. **Croquet: The Sport.** Palm Beach Gardens, Fla.: Farsight Communications, 1989. 271 pp. $24.95; $15.95 (pbk.). ISBN 0-9624568-0-2; 0-9624568-1-0 (pbk.).
Written by the founder of the U.S. Croquet Association, this extensive guide presents the sport of croquet as played at USCA clubs and covers everything the beginning player needs to know, including the sport's history, customs, and etiquette. Includes information on tactics, strategy and shot making. The work is clearly written and well illustrated.

Web Site

555. **United States Croquet Association.** http://www.croquetamerica.com (accessed April 1, 2004).
This is the official Web site of the U.S. Croquet Association, a primary organizing force in U.S. croquet. It offers excellent information on the history of the game, equipment, leagues, clubs, schools, major events, how to play, official international and U.S. rules, and more.

Field Hockey

Instructional Sources

556. Adelson, Bruce. **The Composite Guide to Field Hockey.** Philadelphia, Pa.: Chelsea House, 2000. 64 pp. $25.00. ISBN 0-7910-5872-7.
Intended for a young adult audience, this brief guide to the sport will be most appropriate in public and school libraries. Includes the history and development of the game and provides the fundamentals of play and the rules. Illustrated with black-and-white photographs.

557. Anders, Elizabeth. **Field Hockey: Steps to Success.** With Sue Myers. Champaign, Ill.: Human Kinetics, 1999. 193 pp. $17.95. ISBN 0-88011-673-0.
In a step-by-step approach, this guide helps beginners and intermediate players develop their skills and tactics in field hockey. Chapters cover moving with the stick, passing and receiving, ball control, tackling, attack and defense,

shooting, goalkeeping, and team strategies. Contains a method for rating progress. Illustrated with over 110 detailed drawings and diagrams. Contains a glossary of terms and contact information for field hockey organizations.

558. Swissler, Becky. **Winning Field Hockey for Girls.** Winning Sports for Girls. New York: Facts On File, 2003. 201 pp. $35.00; $18.95 (pbk.). ISBN 0-8160-4724-3; 0-8160-4725-1 (pbk.).

This comprehensive guide to field hockey begins with a history of the sport and of women's participation in the United States. Detailed coverage follows on the rules, equipment, basic skills and drills for dribbling, passing, receiving, shooting, tackling, and goalkeeping, offensive and defensive strategy, and conditioning. Illustrated with black-and-white photographs and diagrams of the field. Includes a list of resources and sources for further reading. Indexed.

Web Sites

559. **International Hockey Federation / Federation Internationale de Hockey (FIH).** http://www.fihockey.org (accessed March 4, 2004).

As the international governing body for field hockey, the FIH supports and promotes field hockey for men and women and also regulates international competition. Their Web site contains the history of field hockey and of the organization, official rules and regulations, statutes and bylaws, news, events, results, rankings, a photo gallery, information on coaching, tournament management, approved equipment, medical aspects, names of publications, and a directory of affiliated national associations. Also includes women's field hockey and links to Olympic qualifying tournaments.

560. **United States Field Hockey Association (USFHA).** http://www.usfieldhockey.com (accessed March 4, 2004).

U.S. Field Hockey is the national governing body for field hockey in the United States and is a member of the USOC and the FIH. Its mission is to support and develop the sport and its players, prepare teams for international competition, and represent the nation to the rest of the world. The organization's Web site offers a hall of fame, databases of events and results, rules, links to camps and clubs, and much more.

Handball

Instructional Source

561. Clanton, Reita E., and Mary Phyl Dwight. **Team Handball: Steps to Success.** Steps to Success Activity Series. Champaign, Ill.: Human Kinetics, 1997. 168 pp. $17.95. ISBN 0-87322-411-6.

This instructional source teaches the essential skills of team handball in twelve clearly described, sequential steps. Also offers sixty-two drills that reinforce the skills, illustrated with step-by-step drawings. Includes a bibliography.

Web Sites

562. International Handball Federation (IHF). http://www.ihf.info/ (accessed March 4, 2004).

The international governing body for handball competition, the IHF maintains a comprehensive Web site containing news, a calendar of events, and schedules and results of competition at a variety of levels for both men and women and juniors. There is information on training, marketing, and the history of handball, as well as a directory of national member federations.

563. United States Team Handball Federation. http://www.usateamhandball. org (accessed March 23, 2004).

As the national governing body for team handball in the United States, this organization maintains a Web site with such information as news, a calendar of events, general information about the sport, including history and simplified rules, links to the men's and women's Olympic teams, coach/referee programs, resource kits for starting a club or learning about the game, a directory of clubs, and much more great information.

Lacrosse

Reference Sources

564. National Collegiate Athletic Association. **NCAA Men's Lacrosse Rules.** 2004 ed. Indianapolis, Ind.: National Collegiate Athletic Association, 2003. 96 pp. $7.25. ISSN 0742-4361.

In this annually issued official rule book, the major rule changes for the year are noted. Covers the field and equipment specifications, time, scoring, fouls, and penalties. Illustrated with drawings of officials' signals and equipment and with diagrams of the playing field. Indexed.

565. US Lacrosse. **Women's Rules: Official Rules for Girls' and Women's Lacrosse.** 2004 ed. Baltimore, Md.: US Lacrosse, 2004. 92 pp. $6.00.

The official rules of women's lacrosse for 2004. The book includes official girl's youth rules. To purchase, see http://www.lacrosse.org (accessed December 3, 2004).

Instructional Sources

566. American Sport Education Program. **Coaching Youth Lacrosse.** 2nd ed. Champaign, Ill.: Human Kinetics, 2003. 288 pp. $16.95. ISBN 0-7360-3794-2.

Intended for coaches of athletes who are six to fourteen years old, both boys and girls, this informative guide to coaching lacrosse utilizes the games approach to make practice more enjoyable. It includes many practical suggestions to assist the volunteer coach in fulfilling her role. It contains chapters on communication, safety, the games approach for teaching skills and tactics, game-day, equipment variations, rules, and sample plans for practices. Illustrated with black-and-white photographs and diagrams.

567. Hinkson, Jim. **Lacrosse Fundamentals.** Rev. and updated ed. Chicago, Ill.: Warwick Publishing, 2000. 176 pp. $16.95. ISBN 1-894020-77-4.

Intended for players, fans, coaches, and teachers, this guide to lacrosse presents the basic skills in a step-by-step approach. The author describes and demonstrates the fundamental skills of the game and provides illustrations along the way for increased comprehension. Equipment is identified, and techniques and strategies are reinforced with practice drills.

568. Hinkson, Jim, John Jiloty, and Robert Carpenter. **Lacrosse for Dummies.** For Dummies. Etobicoke, ON: John Wiley Canada, 2003. 374 pp. $21.99. ISBN 1-894413-49-0.

This comprehensive book includes the fundamentals of playing and coaching lacrosse, rules of the game, and a chapter on following the sport as a fan. Detailed chapters provide in-depth information on the techniques and strategies of playing lacrosse and on developing coaching skills. Provides brief profiles of the ten greatest National Lacrosse League players. Illustrated with drawings and diagrams, as well as several humorous cartoons. Appendices contain a substantial glossary of terms and a set of sample contracts for coaches, parents, and players. Indexed.

569. Tucker, Janine. **The Baffled Parents Guide to Coaching Girls' Lacrosse.** The baffled parents' guides. With Maryalice Yakutchik. Camden, Maine: Ragged Mountain Press / McGraw Hill, 2003. 186 pp. $14.95. ISBN 0-07-141225-5.

In this guide for youth coaches at every level, the authors present all the fundamental skills, drills, equipment choices, rules, and strategies that every player needs to learn. What is more impressive is that they discuss how to teach effectively and motivate girls so that they can learn the game, gain confidence, and have fun. Well illustrated with black-and-white photographs and diagrams. Also contains illustrated coach's signals, a glossary of terms, and a list of resources for further information. Indexed.

Web Sites

570. **International Lacrosse Federation (ILF).** http://www.intlaxfed.org/ (accessed April 4, 2004).

As the international governing body for lacrosse competition, the ILF offers a well-organized and informative Web site with history, rules, bylaws, number of active players in the world, an international events calendar, news, and reports of tournaments and championships. Also includes links to member nations' Web sites.

571. **National Lacrosse League.** http://www.nll.com (accessed March 28, 2004).

The national league for professional lacrosse players maintains an informative Web site that includes a schedule, news, results, standings, statistics, team rosters, career stats, playoff information, franchise history, an all-time player register, and much more.

572. **US Lacrosse.** http://www.lacrosse.org/ (accessed January 2, 2004).

The national governing body for men's and women's lacrosse competition in the United States, the organization maintains a comprehensive Web site. It provides a history of the sport, an events calendar, news, rules, and programs of the organization. Includes information about the Lacrosse Museum and National Hall of Fame. National Lacrosse Hall of Fame members' profiles are included. Users can order instructional guides, rule books, and other books on lacrosse at the site.

Softball

Reference Sources

573. Amateur Softball Association/USA Softball. **The Official Rules of Softball.** 2004 Team ed. Oklahoma City, Okla.: Amateur Softball Association of America, 2004. 348 pp. $9.95.

The ASA's official rules book contains the full rules, softball diamond dimensions, any changes in the playing rules, points of emphasis, and an index to the rules, as well as also the ASA Code, the umpire manual, and a list of National Softball Hall of Fame members and other champions. Provides much administrative information on the organization and on procedures for holding tournaments.

574. **NCAA Softball Rules.** 2004 ed. Indianapolis, Ind.: National Collegiate Athletic Association, 2003. 228 pp. $7.50. ISSN 1089-0106.

In this annually issued official rule book, the major rule changes for the year are noted. Covers the field of play and equipment specifications, time, scoring, and definitions of terms. Umpire's signals are illustrated with drawings. Also illustrated with several diagrams of the playing field, feet and lines chart, and guidelines on lightning. Indexed.

575. **NCAA Softball Umpire Manual.** With Jeff Hansen. Indianapolis, Ind.: National Collegiate Athletic Association, 2003. 152 pp. $12.50.

This is the first edition of the NCAA's softball umpire's manual and is another practical addition to the NCAA's offering of official rules manuals that govern play at member institutions. Illustrated.

Instructional Sources

576. Garman, Judi. **Softball Skills and Drills.** Champaign, Ill.: Human Kinetics, 2001. 217 pp. $18.95. ISBN 0-7360-3364-5.

Intended for coaches and players, this guide to skills and drills has improvement in performance as its goal. Beginning with the fundamentals, the clear instructions assist in mastering the skills of hitting, bunting, slap hitting, base running, fielding, throwing, pitching, and catching. Includes over 170 detailed drills that reinforce the skills and techniques being taught. Illustrated with many black-and-white photographs and drawings. Includes offensive and defensive skills checklists and a master drill index.

577. Kneer, Marian E., and Charles L. McCord. **Softball: Slow and Fast Pitch.** 6th ed. Sports and Fitness series. Boston: McGraw-Hill, 1995. 147 pp. $9.60. ISBN 0-697-15255-3.

The game of softball is treated comprehensively in this detailed guide to both the slow- and fast-pitch versions. A general overview of the game, playing field, equipment, and differences between slow and fast pitch are first discussed. The history of the game is presented and common terms are defined, followed by detailed coverage of offensive skills, defensive skills, defensive position of play, patterns of play, the rules, umpiring and scorekeeping, coaching, and managing. Illustrated with black-and-white photographs and diagrams. Includes a list of references, questions and answers that test the reader on the content of the text, and an index.

578. Monteleone, John, and Deborah Crisfield. **The Louisville Slugger Complete Book of Women's Fast-Pitch Softball.** New York: Owl Books / Henry Holt, 1999. 219 pp. $19.95. ISBN 0-8050-5809-5.

This book is an instruction source that provides more than an introduction. Covers the full offensive game, the defensive game, game-time tactical and strategic decision making pitching, and physical fitness, including conditioning and strength training. Illustrated with black-and-white photographs of women in action.

579. Potter, Diane L., and Gretchen A. Brockmeyer. **Softball: Steps to Success.** 2nd ed. Steps to Success Activity Series. Champaign, Ill.: Human Kinetics, 1999. 175 pp. $17.95. ISBN 0-87322-794-8.

This basic guide to softball provides sequential instruction of softball skills in the optimal order for greatest learning. Offers an introduction to catching and throwing, fielding, pitching, hitting, base running, position play, and offensive and defensive tactics. Provides information on modified games and on coed slow-pitch softball. Illustrated with drawings. Includes a self-assessment tool and a glossary of terms.

580. United States Olympic Committee. **A Basic Guide to Softball.** An Official U.S. Olympic Committee Sports Series. Torrance, Calif.; Milwaukee, Wisc.: Griffin Publishing Group; distributed by Gareth Stevens Publishing, 2001. 150 pp. $22.60; $9.95. ISBN 0-8368-2798-8; 1-58000-074-6.

This guide provides basic information intended to help the novice user get started with the sport. Covers history, fundamentals of the sport, information on the Olympics and other competitions, equipment, safety, and nutrition and training. Includes rules for fast pitch, modified pitch, slow pitch, and 16-inch slow pitch. Contains a team roster and member biographies for the U.S. softball team from the 2000 Summer Olympics, as well as results for these games. Illustrated with drawings and black-and-white photographs. Includes a glossary and contact information for important softball organizations.

Web Sites

581. **Amateur Softball Association.** http://www.asasoftball.org (accessed March 19, 2004).

The ASA is the national governing body for softball competition in the United States. Their Web site provides a tournament calendar, news, press releases, the 2004 ASA Code available to download, information for umpires and about certified equipment, and a link to the National Softball Hall of Fame, along with a member directory.

582. **International Softball Federation (ISF).** http://www.international softball.com/ (accessed March 4, 2004).

The ISF, the international governing body for softball competition, maintains a comprehensive Web site. It includes educational information on coaching, umpiring, equipment, and skill analysis, as well as the official rules, news, results from championships, press releases, and an events calendar. There is also a hall of fame on the site and information on the upcoming Olympic Games. It includes a directory of member organizations worldwide, and contact information for donating used equipment to those in need.

Chapter 9

Large-Ball Sports

Played on a field or court, the sports covered in this chapter all involve the use of a large ball. This chapter lists information sources on basketball, football, rugby, soccer, and volleyball. Football's popularity in the United States and soccer's popularity in the rest of the world make for a large body of literature that provides information on all aspects of these games, from the rules and regulations to the statistics, players, and history of sporting competition.

Basketball

Reference Sources

583. Bjarkman, Peter C. **The Biographical History of Basketball.** Lincolnwood, Ill.: Masters Press, 2000. 590 pp. $24.95. ISBN 1-57028-134-3.
This biographical reference provides brief profiles that summarize the careers of 500 of the most important persons in basketball, including coaches and administrators, as well as players. The author also includes his list of the most significant players and other major personalities in basketball. Also offers historical information on the development of the game over the years. Includes a bibliography of sources. Illustrated with black-and-white photographs and tables.

584. Brenner, Morgan G. **College Basketball's National Championships: The Complete Record of Every Tournament Ever Played.** American Sports History, no. 13. Lanham, Md.: The Scarecrow Press, 1999. 1037 pp. $98.50. ISBN 0-8108-3474-X.
A favorite for "March Madness," this reference source details men's and women's national basketball tournaments from 1937 to 1998. It includes major association tournaments like the NCAA Division I tournament but also many lesser-known association and nonassociation national championship tournaments such as the National Catholic College Tournament. Contains a trivia section with rankings such as the teams with the most final-four appearances,

fewest known wins in a season, most number-one seeds, and so forth. Also lists national champions by association, by year, and by school. In all, the author has compiled the standings of 493 association and 105 nonassociation tournaments.

585. Carter, Craig, and Rob Reheuser, eds. **The *Sporting News* Official NBA Guide.** 2002–2003 ed. St. Louis, Mo.: Sporting News Publishing, 2003. 748 pp. $16.95. ISBN 0-89204-680-5.

This classic basketball reference presents a team-by-team roster of players for the current season, all the other essential team information, including photos of the team administrators; the current schedule; a review of the previous season's results; and other highlights. Also includes the official rules of the NBA and its history and records in a year-by-year overview. Illustrated with black-and-white team photographs, some action shots, and a diagram of the court with dimensions.

586. Dortch, Chris. **Blue Ribbon College Basketball Yearbook.** 2002–2003 ed. Herndon, Va.: Brassey's, 2002. 384 pp. $21.95. ISBN 1-57488-431-X.

This valuable reference covers all the NCAA Division I college teams, providing a detailed review of each college or university basketball program. The top forty teams are given closer attention and more detailed coverage. Teams and players are analyzed on a variety of points and given a grade. Each conference is also reviewed. Indexed by team and conference.

587. Douchant, Mike. **Encyclopedia of College Basketball.** New York: Gale Research, 1995. 615 pp. $85.00. ISBN 0-8103-9640-8.

This reference encyclopedia contains several chapters on the historical development of college basketball. It includes coverage of women's basketball, small colleges, the Olympics, player and team profiles, statistics, and trivia. It contains decade-by-decade and year-by-year highlights and statistics of each season and a review of the NCAA tournament since 1938. Illustrated with many black-and-white photographs, diagrams, charts, and brackets. Indexed.

588. Johnson, Gary K. **NCAA Men's Basketball Finest.** 2nd ed. Indianapolis, Ind.: National Collegiate Athletic Association, 1998. 223 pp. $12.00. ISSN 1521-2955.

This history-oriented reference contains year-by-year and career statistics of more than 390 Division I basketball players and more than 100 coaches. The criteria for inclusion is detailed in the book's foreword but includes those players who have won national honors, made national statistical achievements, or shared or held a national career or season record. Criteria for coaches are also clearly defined. Entries for players and coaches are listed alphabetically in separate sections. Illustrated with a set of color photographs and a black-and-white photograph with each entry.

589. Kalb, Elliott. **Who's Better, Who's Best in Basketball? Mr. Stats Sets the Record Straight on the Top 50 NBA Players of All Time.** New York: Contemporary Books / McGraw-Hill, 2004. 410 pp. $14.95. ISBN 0-07-141788-5.

Written by a noted sports statistics authority, this lively guide is a treasure trove for fans of professional basketball. It profiles the author's ranked list of the top fifty NBA players of all time, detailing each player's history, comparing the player's rating with others' ratings, and including the records along the way that are the proof. An appendix contains lists by position, best players by era, and best single seasons. Illustrated with a representative set of color and black-and-white photographs of players.

590. Marcus, Jeff. **Biographical Directory of Professional Basketball Coaches.** American Sports History, no. 23. Lanham, Md.: Scarecrow Press, 2003. 443 pp. $79.95. ISBN 0-8108-4007-3.

This directory of professional coaches gives the year-by-year coaching records for every pro, major league coach in basketball since 1927. Arranged in alphabetical order by coach's name, the entries provide biographical profiles of each coach's career, regular season records, and playoff records. Includes the ABL, NBL, BAA, and ABA, as well as the NBA. Contains a selected bibliography.

591. Maxwell, John, Jeanne Tang, Rita Sullivan, and Peter Steber, eds. **Official WNBA Guide and Register.** 2003 ed. St. Louis, Mo.: Sporting News Books, 2003. 550 pp. $17.95. ISBN 0-89204-709-7.

Included in this annual statistical reference are complete rosters for every WNBA team; a complete statistical history of each player; complete schedules; league and team records; and team directories and ticket information. Includes the official WNBA rules and an index for the rules. Contains complete information for the current season and more brief reviews of earlier seasons. Includes an alphabetical listing of profiles of veteran players, rookies, and newcomers, as well as head coaches. Illustrated with black-and-white photographs of the teams and individual players and coaches.

592. McKeag, Douglas B., ed. **Basketball.** Handbook of Sports Medicine and Science. Malden, Mass.: Blackwell Science, 2003. 225 pp. $34.95. ISBN 0-632-05912-5.

This series is published under the auspices of the International Olympic Committee and covers the epidemiology of injury in basketball; physiological and nutritional aspects; preventive medicine; and information for special groups of players such as diabetics and asthmatics. The articles in the handbook are intended for use by physicians, trainers, and coaches but would also be useful for athletes or for parents of children who are participating in athletics. Illustrated with diagrams, tables, and black-and-white photographs. Each chapter contains a list of references for further reading. Indexed. This series is most appropriate for college and university collections in sports medicine.

593. **NCAA Men's and Women's Basketball Rules and Interpretations.** 2004 ed. Indianapolis, Ind.: National Collegiate Athletic Association, 2003. 174 pp. $7.50.

The full official rules are presented, along with court and equipment specifications, a court diagram, and appendices that detail the policy on fight reporting, tobacco use, officiating guidelines, and the official basketball signals. Illustrated with photographs of the NCAA rules committees and diagrams. Indexed.

594. **Official NCAA Men's Basketball Records.** 2003 ed. Indianapolis, Ind.: National Collegiate Athletic Association, 2002. 362 pp. $12.00. ISBN 1089-5280.

This annual publication contains individual and team records for all NCAA Divisions, including single-game, season, and career statistics. Also includes coaching records, championship results, attendance records, award winners, the 2002 Conference standings, and a history of playing rules from 1891 to the present. Illustrated with black-and-white photographs.

595. **Official NCAA Men's Final Four Tournament Records.** 2002 ed. Indianapolis, Ind.: National Collegiate Athletic Association, 2001. 225 pp. $12.00.

This annual publication contains individual and team records; records for all rounds of the NCAA tournament; coaching records, including the records of every head coach in the tournament; complete tournament brackets through the previous season; and sites, dates, seeds, and scores since 1939. Also includes attendance history and records; all-time site and arena history; tournament game arenas by state; and future dates and sites.

596. **Official NCAA Women's Basketball Records.** 2004 ed. Indianapolis, Ind.: National Collegiate Athletic Association, 2003. 346 pp. $12.00. ISBN 1089-5299.

This annual publication contains individual and team records for all NCAA divisions, including single-game, season, and career statistics. Also includes coaching records, championship results, attendance records, award winners, the 2003 Conference standings, and a history of playing rules from 1891 to the present. Illustrated with black-and-white photographs.

597. **Official NCAA Women's Final Four Tournament Records.** 2002 ed. Indianapolis, Ind.: National Collegiate Athletic Association, 2002. 139 pp. $12.00. ISBN 0267-1017.

This annual publication contains individual and team records; records for all rounds of the NCAA tournament; coaching records, including the records of every head coach in the tournament; complete tournament brackets through the previous season; and sites, dates, seeds, and scores since 1982. Also includes attendance history and records; all-time site and arena history; tournament game arenas by state; and future dates and sites.

598. Oliver, Dean. **Basketball On Paper: Rules and Tools for Performance Analysis.** Washington, D.C.: Brassey's Inc., 2004. 360 pp. $27.95. ISBN 1-57488-687-8.

This statistical guide examines how to analyze a player's performance and value in the team setting. Significant teams and players are evaluated and analyzed as examples.

599. Shouler, Ken, Bob Ryan, Sam Smith, Leonard Koppett, and Bob Belotti. **Total Basketball: The Ultimate Basketball Encyclopedia.** Toronto, ON: Sport Classic Books / Sport Media Publishing, 2004. 1488 pp. $49.95. ISBN 1-894963-01-6.

This comprehensive reference source on basketball provides a thorough history of the game from its invention to the present. It contains NBA team histories, league histories, and coverage of the ABA, women's basketball, and Olympic competition. It contains narrative essays on aspects of the game, biographies of top players, complete results and records, and a statistical register for every NBA player. Illustrated with 175 color and black-and-white photographs.

600. Skaine, Rosemarie. **Women College Basketball Coaches.** Jefferson, N.C.: McFarland, 2001. 197 pp. $28.50. ISBN 0-7864-0920-7.

Much more than a source for biographies, this title analyzes the role of women coaches in the history and development of college sports. Provides a history of Title IX legislation. Includes profiles of some twenty-eight selected coaches and other major contributors to college basketball for women. Illustrated with tables of data and black-and-white photographs of some of the most important figures. Indexed.

601. Smith, Ron, Ira Winderman, and Mary Schmitt Boyer. **The Complete Encyclopedia of Basketball.** London: Carlton Books, 2001. 576 pp. $45.00. ISBN 1-84222-114-0.

With colorful historical profiles of the teams, the players, the coaches, and the arenas, this valuable reference source focuses on the NBA but also provides coverage of college basketball, women's basketball, international basketball, and the Olympic Games. Contains chapters on the rules of the game and the business side of the sport. Provides brief biographies of members of the basketball hall of fame, as well as NBA records, and a chronology of professional basketball. Well illustrated with many color photographs. Includes a glossary of terms and an index.

602. Walton, David, and John Gardella, eds. **The** *Sporting News* **Official NBA Register.** 2002–2003 ed. St. Louis, Mo.: Sporting News Publishing, 2002. 471 pp. $16.95. ISBN 0-89204-682-1.

This classic basketball source lists the career statistics of every player in the NBA. Veteran players and newcomers are treated separately. The entries also include a small photograph of the person's face, basic personal data, collegiate record, and a brief statement of career highlights. Includes special coverage of the greatest players and head coaches and a list of NBA statistical leaders.

Instructional Sources

603. Krause, Jerry. **Basketball.** Winning Edge. Boston: WCB / McGraw-Hill, 1999. 178 pp. ISBN 0-8151-5184-5.

Intended for anyone who plays or watches basketball and for physical activity courses in high school or college, this is a basic guide to the game and how to play it. Includes a history of the game, information on facilities and equipment, and the rules of the game. Basic movements and skills are detailed, and the concepts of teamwork and team strategy are explored. Contains assessment tools throughout the text to help readers improve their skills. Contains a glossary of terms, a bibliography of sources for further reading, and an index. Illustrated with photographs and diagrams.

604. Krause, Jerry V., Don Meyer, and Jerry Meyer. **Basketball Skills and Drills.** 2nd ed. Champaign, Ill.: Human Kinetics, 1999. 206 pp. $34.95. ISBN 0-7360-3357-2.

Intended for coaches, players, or players' parents, the fundamental skills described in this work will be most applicable to players at elementary, middle, and secondary school level. Includes both basic and advanced sections of skills and drills, and those required by the team as well as the individual player. Provides information on body control, ball handling, shooting, moving the ball, defense, rebounding, and team offense and defense. Includes a list of drills by type of skill. Illustrated with court diagrams, drawings, and photographs.

605. Summitt, Pat Head, and Debby Jennings. **Basketball: Fundamentals and Team Play.** 2nd ed. Sports and Fitness. Madison, Wisc.: Brown and Benchmark, 1996. 101 pp. $9.60. ISBN 0-697-15247-2.

This basic guide to basketball play begins with a brief history of the sport, then covers a complete conditioning program, the fundamental skills, team strategies, and the rules of the game. Illustrated with black-and-white photographs and court diagrams. Includes a glossary of terms, a question-and-answer section, and an index.

Web Sites

606. **Federation Internationale de Basketball (FIBA).** http://www.fiba.com (accessed March 19, 2004).

The International Basketball Federation (FIBA) is the international governing body for basketball competition. Its Web site provides a directory of member organizations, news, press releases, an events calendar, results of competition, world rankings, information on training, equipment, and sports medicine, publications that include official rules and statutes, and much more.

607. **Naismith Memorial Basketball Hall of Fame.** http://www.hoophall.com (accessed March 19, 2004).

This informative Web site contains history, news, events, exhibits, education, trivia, and everything you need to plan a visit. The site also provides detailed profiles of over 250 basketball hall of famers.

608. **National Basketball Association.** http://www.nba.com (accessed March 20, 2004).

This official NBA Web site has all the news, statistics, standings, transactions, schedules, player profiles, coach profiles, links to the NBA teams' Web sites, and just about anything else a fan wants to know.

609. **National Wheelchair Basketball Association.** http://www.nwba.org (accessed March 20, 2004).

The NWBA is the national governing body for wheelchair basketball, and their comprehensive site contains results and records, news, a hall of fame, and much more.

610. **USA Basketball.** http://www.usabasketball.com (accessed March 26, 2004).

As the national governing body for men's and women's basketball, this organization is responsible for selecting and training teams to represent the United States in international competition. The site contains information on history, rules, and both men's and women's programs.

611. **Women's Basketball Hall of Fame.** http://www.wbhof.com (accessed March 27, 2004).

The Women's Basketball Hall of Fame's Web site contains news, information on events, and directions for visitors to the Hall. It also contains a historical time line of women's participation in basketball, photos and profiles of the hall of fame inductees, and much more.

612. **Women's National Basketball Association (WNBA).** http://www.wnba.com (accessed March 27, 2004).

The WNBA's Web site contains history, news, statistics, standings, schedules, playoff information, team information, and player and coach profiles, all in an easy-to-navigate format that fans will appreciate.

Football

Reference Sources

613. Adler, Larry, comp. **Football Coach Quotes: The Wit, Wisdom, and Winning Words of Leaders on the Gridiron.** Jefferson, N.C.: McFarland, 1992. 212 pp. $37.50. ISBN 0-89950-542-2.

Arranged alphabetically by coach, the quotations are numbered and touch on a variety of interesting topics, sometimes related to football, and sometimes stretching away from it. Each coach is identified by the teams he was associated with, dates, and record, when available. Includes a useful bibliography of sources and an index.

614. Carroll, Bob, Michael Gershman, David Neft, and John Thorn, eds. **Total Football II: The Official Encyclopedia of the National Football League.** Rev. and updated ed. New York: HarperCollins, 1999. 1812 pp. $59.95. ISBN 0-06-270174-6.

This truly comprehensive guide to the National Football League contains a complete player register with statistics for over 17,000 football players since its beginning in 1924. It also provides over 500 pages of history on the teams and leagues, most memorable games, greatest coaches and players, awards, game strategy, media coverage, and other notable factors in football. A number of appendices provide even more information on football firsts, game scores, famous quotations, and the list goes on.

615. Carter, Craig, and Tony Nistler, eds. **The *Sporting News* Pro Football Guide.** 2003 ed. With Sporting News/STATS. St. Louis, Mo.: Sporting News Books, 2003. 456 pp. $17.95. ISBN 0-89204-707-0.

A standard source of information on the National Football League, the *Guide* offers a league directory and complete team information for all NFL teams. It provides the current season's schedule, college-draft selections, and procedures for playoffs. It gives a week-by-week review of the previous season, with information on standings, championships, player participation and attendance at games. It features the previous year's statistics, as well as a section on historical statistics, records, and awards. Includes information from the former *Stats Pro Football Handbook.*

616. **Denver Broncos Media Guide.** Denver, Colo.: Denver Broncos Football Club, 2004. 600 pp. $15.00.

College and professional sports media guides are a great source of information about the team and the current season. Each team produces its own guide, and it is the same reference that members of the press use to get their facts. As an example, this guide for the Broncos contains nearly 600 pages of scores, statistics, team records, and game summaries all the way back to the team's inaugural 1960 season. Consult the team's Web site for information about purchasing a copy.

617. Dortch, Chris. **Blue Ribbon College Football Forecast.** 2002–2003 ed. Washington, D.C.: Brassey's, 2002. 384 pp. $21.95. ISBN 1-57488-432-8.

This annual guide to college football gives a complete breakdown of all 117 NCAA Division 1-A teams. It provides annual statistics from the previous season and other information such as changes in coaching staff and team schedules. It also offers a preseason top-twenty-five list and selections for offensive and defensive All-Americans.

618. **Football Rules Simplified and Illustrated.** Indianapolis, Ind.: National Federation of State High School Associations, 2001. $6.50. ISSN 0731-9533.

This simplified version of the official NFHS rules is intended for high school football officials, coaches, players, and spectators. It is illustrated with cartoon-like drawings on every page to clearly show the significance of each rule.

619. Fossey, Keith R. **The Football Scholarship Guide.** Kenosha, Wisc.: Pigskin Press, 1992. 308 pp. $24.95. ISBN 0-9633495-0-3.

Intended for student-athletes and their parents, this source is part directory and part self-promotion plan. The self-promotion plan introduces the reader to the world of college football and the process by which scholarships are awarded. It offers a detailed action plan for aggressively moving through the stages of the recruiting season, defining the roles of everyone involved. The directory part presents college football by region, identifying colleges by conference, division, and national association. Entries provide contact and demographic information and note whether or not the college traditionally offers football scholarships.

620. Harrington, Denis J. **The Pro Football Hall of Fame: Players, Coaches, Team Owners, and League Officials, 1963–1991.** Jefferson, N.C.: McFarland, 1991. 354 pp. $35.00. ISBN 0-89950-550-3.

This biographical reference profiles members of the Pro Football Hall of Fame through the 1991 class. It offers a brief history of pro football and of the hall of fame, then gives the entries in alphabetical order within position category. Entries contain basic data and an essay that highlights career accomplishments, plus additional interesting details. Black-and-white photographs are included for some of the enshrinees. Indexed.

621. National Football League. **Official Rules of the NFL.** 2005 ed. Chicago: Triumph Books, 2004. 216 pp. $9.95. ISBN 1-57243-684-0.

Contains the complete official playing rules for the season, with terms and concepts clearly defined, scoring explained, and duties of the officials outlined. Illustrated with drawings of the field, with dimensions and markings, and with official referee signals.

622. Neft, David S., Richard M. Cohen, and Rick Korch. **The Football Encyclopedia: The Complete History of Professional Football from 1892 to the Present.** New York: St. Martin's Press, 1994. 1080 pp. $49.95. ISBN 0-312-11435-4.

This source for historical statistics provides a yearly analysis of pro football from 1920 to 1993. It also offers an essay summarizing activity during the years prior to 1920 when the sport was in its beginnings. Each year is covered with an essay, the statistics, and a summary of Super Bowl highlights with statistics. A great source of data for the expanse of time covered. The work ends with a set of football caricatures by Bob Carroll.

623. Neft, David S., Richard M. Cohen, and Rick Korch. **The Sports Ency-clopedia: Pro Football, the Modern Era, 1974–1998.** 17th ed. New York: St. Martin's Griffin, 1999. 633 pp. $19.99. ISBN 0-312-20438-8.

This excellent statistical source provides scores from every game, team and individual players' statistics, and season summaries during the specified range of years. It also provides yearly highlights for each team and coverage of awards, leaders, and championships.

624. Nistler, Tony, David Walton, and Steve Meyerhoff. **The *Sporting News* Pro Football Register.** 2003 ed. With Sporting News / STATS. St. Louis, Mo.: Sporting News Books, 2003. 520 pp. $17.95. ISBN 0-89204-708-9.

This book focuses on the players and coaches of the current season. Entries on the players are arranged alphabetically and include all the basic career information, with high school and college play, statistics and transactions. An important source for those involved with choosing fantasy teams.

625. Porter, David L., ed. **Football.** Vol. 2 of **Biographical Dictionary of American Sports.** Westport, Conn.: Greenwood Press, 1987. 763 pp. $102.95. ISBN 0-313-25771-X.

This carefully researched reference includes over 500 signed entries, which are listed alphabetically. Profiles are given for athletes, coaches, promoters, and administrators who were influential in college and professional football. Most entries are one page in length and cover the person's career highlights as well as other interesting details; for each, a bibliography of sources is provided. Appendices contain a great deal of additional information, such as a list of football entries by position played and by place of birth; college and pro football hall of fame members; and college and pro football conferences, leagues, and associations. Indexed.

626. Smith, Myron J., comp. **The College Football Bibliography.** Bibliographies and Indexes on Sports History, no. 2. Westport, Conn.: Greenwood Press, 1994. 951 pp. $165.95. ISBN 0-313-29026-1.

In this expansive bibliographic reference, the author organizes the literature of college football from the 1880s to 1993. The work contains over 12,000 entries on all aspects of college football. Included are nearly all types of print sources, except newspapers; a list of the journals consulted is provided as an appendix. Some of the entries are annotated, and they are arranged in the work primarily by topic. This is a comprehensive yet accessible tool, and it is appropriate for public and academic libraries that serve college football fans. Indexed by author and subject.

627. Smith, Myron J. **Professional Football: The Official Pro Football Hall of Fame Bibliography.** Westport, Conn.: Greenwood Press, 1993. 414 pp. $103.95. ISBN 0-313-28929-X.

This extensive bibliography of nearly 15,000 entries covers the literature of pro football in the United States primarily, with lesser coverage of Canada and Australia. The intended audience is not the specialist but rather the average person with an interest in football, from middle school through adulthood. Some but not all, of the entries are annotated. The coverage is comprehensive, with no aspect left untouched from the turn of the century to mid-1991. The arrangement of entries is by source type and topic, so the table of contents is an important tool for access, as is the author/subject index.

628. Smith, Ron. **The *Sporting News* Selects Football's 100 Greatest Players.** St. Louis, Mo.: Sporting News Publishing, 1999. 224 pp. $29.95. ISBN 0-89204-624-4.

Profiles 100 of the best pro-football players of the century, chosen by twelve editors of the *Sporting News.* Each brief profile contains performance statistics and large, historical photographs, many of which are in color. Contains a chronological breakdown of the top 100, as well as an alphabetical listing of the players. Also contains breakdowns of the top 100 by position, college, primary teams, birthdates, birthplaces, and seasons/games played. Provides a top-100 roll call, or page index, by position and then alphabetically by last name.

629. Stewart, Alva W. **College Football Stadiums: An Illustrated Guide to NCAA Division I-A.** Jefferson, N.C.: McFarland, 2000. 246 pp. $35.00. ISBN 0-7864-0902-9.

This directory of college football stadiums covers 114 schools in the NCAA Division I-A. Included for each stadium is information on the stadium itself, such as history, date and sometimes cost of original construction, special features, seating capacity, and type of playing surface. Also included for each school is team name, mascot, colors, song; date of the first intercollegiate football game; and a list of football coaches and athletic directors. A black-and-white photo of each stadium, plus a photo of the mascot or image of the team logo, is included for nearly every team.

Web Sites

630. **College Football Hall of Fame.** http://www.collegefootball.org/ (accessed April 2, 2004).

Located in South Bend, Indiana, this hall of fame has developed an informative Web site, with a schedule of events, an online tour of the hall, an online directory, and profiles of all the hall of famers, and an education program.

631. **National Football League.** http://www.nfl.com (accessed December 3, 2004).

The official site of the NFL provides all the information a fan needs: news, scores, statistics, schedules, standings, and links to further information on all the teams and players.

632. **Professional Football Hall of Fame.** http://www.profootballhof.com/ (accessed March 3, 2004).

The Pro Football Hall of Fame in Canton, Ohio, maintains a great Web site, with biographical information on all of the hall of famers and enshrinement, a virtual tour, history, and information on planning a visit. Also offers links to many other NFL sites.

Rugby

Reference Sources

633. Andrews, Malcom. **The ABC of Rugby League: The Code's First Real Encyclopaedia.** Sydney, Australia: ABC Enterprises/Australian Broadcasting Corporation, 1992. 602 pp. ISBN 0-7333-0176-2.

This encyclopedia provides comprehensive coverage of rugby league and its history in Australia. Alphabetical in arrangement, entries describe all aspects of the sport, from Aboriginal footballers to Kangaroos statistics for 1908 through 1991 to Yugoslavia's brief run with the rugby league. Covers Australian clubs, with profiles of great players, coaches, and administrators. Illustrated with statistical tables and black-and-white photographs.

634. Bath, Richard, ed. **The Ultimate Encyclopedia of Rugby: The Definitive Illustrated Guide to World Rugby Union.** London: Carlton / Hodder & Stoughton, 1997. 224 pp. ISBN 0-340-69528-5.

Facts are easy to find in this well-organized encyclopedia of rugby. The content is arranged in chapters that cover origins of the game; the main competitions around the world; the FIRA-affiliated countries, with number of clubs and players for each; and profiles of thirty of the greatest clubs and teams. Includes a chronology of rugby, from the first record of its being played in London in 1175 up to important events in 1997. Indexed and illustrated with mostly color photographs, all clearly captioned.

635. Cleary, Mick, and John Griffiths. **International Rugby Yearbook, 2003–2004.** London: CollinsWillow / HarperCollins, 2003. 512 pp. $29.95. ISBN 0-00-714047-9.

The front cover of the book indicates that it is "the definitive World Rugby Union sourcebook." This fact-filled publication contains the International Rugby Board (IRB) directory of world unions, feature articles by leading rugby writers, results from the season for premier test-playing nations (both domestic and international levels), and detailed coverage of the major international competitions, including the Women's World Cup. Contains a review of the previous season and fixture list, and profiles of the IRB top five players of the year. Illustrated with black-and-white photographs.

636. Davies, Gerald. **The History of the Rugby World Cup.** London: Sanctuary Publishing, 2003. 379 pp. $18.95. ISBN 1-86074-445-1.

This detailed analysis of the Rugby World Cup covers every tournament since its inception in 1987 up to the 2003 tournament in Australia. It provides commentary, match statistics, and interviews with the players and coaches who have been instrumental in the tournament's development. Provides in-depth coverage of the final stages of the tournaments. Illustrated with a 16-page insert of color action photographs with captions. A treat for rugby fans!

637. Gate, Robert. **Rugby League Hall of Fame.** Stroud, U.K.: Tempus Publishing, 2003. 224 pp. $35.00. ISBN 0-7524-2693-1.

The author of this source was instrumental in founding the original Rugby League Hall of Fame. This source celebrates the legendary players who have achieved star status in the sport over several decades. Biographies include personal information as well as the players' detailed career accomplishments and statistics. Well illustrated with color photographs.

638. Hourcade, Bertrand. **Dictionary of Rugby: French-English, English-French.** Paris: La Maison du Dictionnaire Paris, 1998. 203 pp. ISBN 2-85608-126-6.

This bilingual dictionary of rugby terms is intended to improve communication between the French-speaking and English-speaking worlds of rugby. More than 6000 English and French words are listed. The first half of the volume is French to English, and the second half is English to French. This is a very useful reference for those involved in or spectators for the increasingly popular international sport of rugby.

639. Jansen, Zandberg, and Gideon Nieman. **Rugby World Cup Greats.** Cape Town, South Africa: Tafelberg, 1999. 156 pp. $129.95. ISBN 0-624-03819-X.

Beautifully illustrated with color photographs, this biographical source profiles a selection of fifty-eight of the world's greatest rugby players from the World Cup in 1987, 1991, 1995, and 1999. For each player, basic information is displayed in a box: full name, position, country, club and province, date of birth, height, weight, and number of test matches, points in test matches, World Cup tournaments, and points in World Cup tournaments. An essay is also included for each player, vividly describing the plays, events, and matches that led to his selection. Includes a bibliography of sources.

640. Jenkins, John M. **A Rugby Compendium: An Authoritative Guide to the Literature of Rugby Union.** Boston Spa, West Yorkshire, U.K.: British Library, 1998. 322 pp. $55.00. ISBN 0-7123-1096-7.

Using the collections of the British Library and the National Library of Wales, the author has compiled a fascinating bibliography of the literature of rugby union from throughout the English-speaking world, through 1997. Many of the entries are annotated, but not all. Covers standard rugby reference sources, as well as a huge body of specialist literature. Illustrated with a selection of the covers of source in miniature. Indexed by name, club, title, and subject.

641. Quinn, Keith. **The Encyclopedia of World Rugby.** Moffat, Scotland: Lochar Publishing, 1991. 328 pp. ISBN 0-948403-61-6.

Arranged alphabetically, in true encyclopedia style, this reference work strives to be comprehensive in its coverage of the world of rugby. Important persons, teams, and clubs are given attention, as are the countries from which they hail. This book is very dense with content, and it is an excellent source of historical information on rugby. The entries for nations are given especially detailed attention, with essays sometimes several pages long. Illustrated with color and black-and-white photographs. Contains an extensive bibliography and an index of names.

642. Robertson, Ian. **The Complete Book of the Rugby World Cup 1995.** London: Hodder & Stoughton, in association with Scottish Life, 1995. 192 pp. ISBN 0-340-64953-4.

This beautiful volume chronicles the month-long tournament that was held in South Africa in 1995. It begins with an essay describing the opening ceremony, including the text of Nelson Mandela's opening speech. Additional essays contain a great deal of history as well as interviews and describe the round of pools, quarterfinals, semifinals, playoffs, and the final game. An appendix contains the statistics for World Cup records (the final stages). Illustrated with color photographs.

643. Robinson, Derek. **Rugby: A Player's Guide to the Laws.** 4th ed. London: CollinsWillow, 2002. 192 pp. $13.95. ISBN 0-00-713614-5.

Revised and updated to include changes made in 2001, this guide to the rules of rugby is easy to read and contains over sixty illustrations, including dimensions of the playing field, to aid the reader. The book is arranged in sixteen short chapters, each explaining a specific aspect of the game or type of play. Appendices give variations for play with seven players on each team and for players under nineteen years of age. Indexed.

644. Sommerville, Donald. **The Encyclopedia of Rugby Union.** London: Arum Press, 1997. 192 pp. $24.95. ISBN 1-85410-481-0.

This encyclopedia provides an authoritative record of the great events, players, games, and achievements of rugby union and offers a glimpse of its future development. Includes chapters on the history of the game and the laws, teamwork, and tactics. Provides in-depth profiles of eight countries where rugby is prominent in the sporting scene and gives more brief profiles of other places in the world where competition is strong. Reviews the major world competitions and women's rugby, and profiles a number of great clubs and players. Statistics are provided through May 1997. Well illustrated with beautiful color and black-and-white photographs and drawings. Indexed.

Instructional Sources

645. Biscombe, Tony, and Peter Drewett. **Rugby: Steps to Success.** Steps to Success Activity Series. Champaign, Ill.: Human Kinetics, 1998. 159 pp. $17.95. ISBN 0-88011-509-2.

This guide to the fundamentals of rugby provides concise, sequential instruction on ball handling, passing and receiving, footwork, tackling, kicking, contact, the front five, the back five, the middle five, mini-units, and tactics and strategies. Includes seventy-four drills to reinforce the skills and a method for rating one's progress. Illustrated with over 170 diagrams and drawings. Contains a glossary of rugby terms.

646. Greenwood, James R. **Total Rugby: Fifteen-Man Rugby for Coach and Player.** 5th ed. London: A & C Black, 2003. 384 pp. $24.95. ISBN 0-7136-6672-2.

Written by one of the world's most highly regarded rugby coaches, this work puts forward a coaching philosophy that utilizes technical excellence to form detailed solutions to coaching problems. It discusses the development of total rugby, the game and its principles of attack and defense, and the technical skills that individuals, units, and teams must perfect to succeed. Provides information on team selection, coaching methods, and the psychological aspects of the sport. Also contains a chapter on fitness for rugby. Illustrated with black-and-white photographs and diagrams. Indexed.

647. Williams, Tony, and Gordon Hunter. **Rugby Skills, Tactics, and Rules.** Buffalo, N.Y.: Firefly Books, 2000. 167 pp. $19.95. ISBN 1-55209-546-0.

This informative and interesting guide to rugby describes the game, the positions of players, and the basic skills they require. Further detailed information is provided on the tactical and skill aspects of the game, as well as attack, defense, and coaching. Beautifully illustrated with over 150 captioned color action photographs of prominent players and teams. Includes the *Laws of the Game of Rugby Football*, as issued by the International Rugby Board, and a diagram of the playing field. Also includes a glossary and a list of useful addresses and Web sites. Indexed.

Web Sites

648. **International Rugby Board (IRB).** http://www.irb.com (accessed March 20, 2004).

The IRB, the international governing body for rugby competition and the world law-making body for the game of rugby union, maintains a well-organized and informative Web site. Included is information about the organization and its history, world news, rankings, events, laws and regulations, a section on training, refereeing, and coaching, and links to more information about all the world championships and other competitive events. Also includes a directory of national members throughout the world.

649. **USA Rugby.** www.usarugby.org (accessed December 3, 2004).

USA Rugby is the national governing body for rugby union in the United States, and the organization fields several men's and women's national teams. Their Web site is informative, with news, events, results, information on national teams and championships, coaches and referees, clinics and camps, and the rules of the game. Also provides links to regional unions and clubs.

Soccer

Reference Sources

650. Ager, David. **The Soccer Referee's Manual.** 4th ed. London: A & C Black, 2003. 150 pp. $17.95. ISBN 0-7136-6676-5.

Offering the latest instruction on soccer refereeing in clear, accessible language, this manual includes Federation Internationale de Football Association's (FIFA) most recent amendments to the official *Laws of the Game*. It also provides emphasis on how referees administer and apply the laws to control play. Offers expert advice and insights into the British Football Association's referee training, with over 100 questions and answers on the laws and their interpretation. Written by an acknowledged authority in refereeing, this is an invaluable reference for referees and for fans who want to improve their understanding of soccer. Illustrated with diagrams and charts. Includes an appendix on assessment and one on diet and fitness.

651. Allaway, Roger, Colin Jose, and David Litterer. **The Encyclopedia of American Soccer History.** American Sports History, no. 20. Lanham, Md.: Scarecrow Press, 2001. 454 pp. $65.00. ISBN 0-8108-3980-6.

This work looks at American soccer from the 1860s through the 1999 Women's World Cup and the 1999 Major League Soccer season. Arranged alphabetically, the entries cover the players, significant coaches, administrators, referees, teams, professional and semiprofessional leagues, games, championship events, and locations that have shaped soccer history in the United States. Appendices provide statistics and records, profiles of memorable games, and a bibliography. Appropriate for academic collections and also those that serve soccer fans.

652. Ballard, John, and Paul Suff. **The Dictionary of Football: The Complete A–Z of International Football, from Ajax to Zinedine Zidane.** London: Boxtree, 1999. 670 pp. $39.50. ISBN 0-7522-2434-4.

With over 6000 concise and informative entries, this is much more than a soccer dictionary. Covering not only the players, teams, clubs, and stadiums, it includes critical comment on the history, as well as the cultural, media, and legal aspects, of the world game. International terminology is clearly defined, and rules and regulations are treated concisely. Statistics, trophies, and records are included throughout the dense volume. Entries are listed alphabetically and cross-referenced. Illustrated with many historically significant black-and-white photographs. Produced in association with *World Soccer* magazine.

653. Cox, Richard William, Dave Russell, and Wray Vamplew, eds. **Encyclopedia of British Football.** Sports Reference Library. Portland, Ore.: Frank Cass, 2002. $64.50; $22.50 (pbk.). ISBN 0-7146-5249-0; 0-7146-8230-6 (pbk.).

Sponsored by England's National Football Museum, which opened in 2001, this overview of soccer in Britain presents the history of the sport from its beginnings through the present day. Includes over 250 entries, arranged alphabetically, on a variety of subjects such as organizations, clubs, events, major competitions, important individuals, and issues pertinent to soccer, such as social class, racism, drugs and alcohol, and commercialization. References are listed for each entry; many entries also list additional sources for further reading on the topic. A full list of the entries is presented at the beginning of the volume. It also provides a chronology of major events in British football, from 1508 to 2001, and a detailed index.

654. Crouch, Terry. **The World Cup: The Complete History.** London: Aurum Press, 2002. 504 pp. $16.95. ISBN 1-85410-843-3 (pbk.).

Covers the history of the World Cup, as well as the qualifying rounds that led up to each, from Uruguay in 1930 to France in 1998, plus the qualifying rounds for Japan and South Korea in 2002. A great statistical compendium, balanced with significant narrative for each World Cup. Not illustrated.

655. Duarte, Orlando. **The Encyclopedia of World Cup Soccer.** New York: McGraw-Hill, 1994. 435 pp. $24.95. ISBN 0-07-017944-1.

Beginning with a history of the start of FIFA and the World Cup, this work follows that history forward through the fifteenth World Cup in 1994, describing the major events, qualifying rounds, and triumphs of play. Includes statistics for each World Cup. Illustrated throughout the text with black-and-white photographs, plus a section of color photographs. Also includes listings of the top goal scorers in each World Cup, all World Cup scorers, goal scorers in every World Cup listed chronologically, number of goals by nation, and lists of referees and coaches from 1930 to 1990.

656. Ekblom, Bjorn, ed. **Football (Soccer).** Handbook of Sports Medicine and Science. Malden, Mass.: Blackwell Science, 1994. 240 pp. $44.95. ISBN 0-632-03328-2.

This series is published under the auspices of the International Olympic Committee Medical Commission. This volume covers the epidemiology of injury in the sport; physiological and nutritional aspects; preventive medicine; and information for special groups of players such as the female soccer player. The articles in the handbook are intended for use by physicians, trainers, and coaches but would also be useful for athletes themselves or parents of children who are participating in athletics. Illustrated with diagrams, tables, and black-and-white photographs. Each chapter contains a list of references for further reading. Indexed. This series is most appropriate for college and university collections in sports medicine.

657. Fortanasce, Vincent, Lawrence Robinson, and John Ouellette. **The Official American Youth Soccer Organization Handbook: Rules, Regulations, Skills and Everything Else Kids, Parents, and Coaches Need to Participate in Youth Soccer.** New York: Fireside / Simon & Schuster, 2001. 251 pp. $13.00. ISBN 0-7432-1384-X.

Endorsed by the American Youth Soccer Association, this handbook contains the complete rules of youth soccer, including offside, throw-ins, and

penalty kicks. Also provides information on prevention of injuries, the responsibilities of each position, and the AYSA's inclusive and positive philosophy, all
in an easy-to-understand format. Illustrated with diagrams of the playing field
and drawings of players and referees. Contains a glossary of youth soccer terms
and an index.

658. Goldblatt, David. **DK World Soccer Yearbook, 2002–3: The Complete
Guide to the Game.** New York: Dorling Kindersley, 2002. 496 pp. $30.00.
ISBN 0-7894-8943-0.

An amazing source, this annual soccer publication contains tremendous visual appeal with page after page of color photographs, maps, and tables that describe and illustrate the facts of soccer competition worldwide. Gives the results
from all the major divisions and the history and development of soccer generally speaking, as well as in the more than 200 FIFA-affiliated nations. Provides
more extensive coverage for nations like England, where soccer dominates the
national sporting scene. Briefly covers the World Cup, the Olympic Games and
women's soccer. Also contains further information on major cities, stadiums,
players, and managers. Arranged by geographic area and country. Contains a
bibliography and an index.

659. Hulmes, David. **The Best Book of Football Songs and Chants Ever!**
London: Carlton Books, 1998. 224 pp. $10.00. ISBN 1-85868-584-2.

This unique book provides a fascinating look into the culture of soccer, or
football, in the U.K.: their songs and chants. Contains over 300 memorable entries, arranged in the following chapters: English Football Club Songs, General
Songs, England Team Songs, Scottish Club Songs, and Scotland Team Songs.
Contains the classic as well as the contemporary. Illustrated with black-and-
white cartoons.

660. Jose, Colin. **The United States and World Cup Soccer Competition: An
Encyclopedic History of the United States in International Competition.**
American Sports History Series, no. 2. Metuchen, N.J.: Scarecrow Press, 1994.
332 pp. $45.00. ISBN 0-8108-2881-2.

A history of the World Cup from 1930 to 1990, this work includes the
record of the U.S. national soccer team in qualifying and final rounds of competition. Also includes a detailed record of every game played by U.S. men's
and women's national teams in international competition between 1885 and July
1993, at the senior level of play. Contains details of qualifying rounds of the
1994 competition and features an essay on the U.S. participation in the 1930
competition, written in 1931 by team manager Wilfred Cummings.

661. LaBlanc, Michael L., and Richard Henshaw. **The World Encyclopedia of
Soccer.** Detroit, Mich.: Gale Research, 1994. 430 pp. $42.00. ISBN 0-8103-
8995-9.

A substantial source, this encyclopedia begins with the history of soccer,
as well as the rules and tactics that are essential to an understanding of the game.
Entries profile the world's greatest players (many illustrated with photos) and

the nations and teams involved in world soccer. Coverage is also provided of FIFA, U.S. soccer organizations, and women's and Olympic soccer. Illustrated throughout with black-and-white photographs. Appendices include a soccer time line from 2500 B.C. to 1994, a glossary of terms, early rules, cup competition, and information on stadiums. Indexed.

662. Lover, Stanley F. **Official Soccer Rules Illustrated: A Quick Reference for All Coaches, Players, and Fans.** Chicago: Triumph Books, 2003. 134 pp. $12.95. ISBN 1-57243-554-2.

Intended for players, coaches, parents, and fans, this book of rules follows the worldwide FIFA pattern with the goal of providing a visual link between the official rules and actual play. It includes a brief glossary of terms and clearly explains all the basic components of play. Rules are explained in depth and illustrated; the roles of referees and match officials are discussed thoroughly. Illustrated with over 100 drawings of soccer play and diagrams of the playing field. Includes a soccer IQ test to gauge one's soccer knowledge.

663. MacDonald, Tom. **The World Encyclopedia of Soccer: A Complete Guide to the Beautiful Game.** Updated ed. London: Lorenz Books / Anness Publishing, 2003. 256 pp. $29.95. ISBN 0-7548-1124-7.

This substantial reference work begins with a history of international soccer, from its very early days to the present. Provides detailed biographies of the most prominent players and personalities in soccer and profiles thirty-six of the most important teams from FIFA member nations of the world. Also profiles forty of the major teams in club football. Includes World Cup results from 1930 through 2002, as well as international and national results. Beautifully illustrated with page after page of black-and-white and color photographs. Indexed.

664. **NCAA Men's and Women's Soccer Rules.** 2003 ed. Indianapolis, Ind.: National Collegiate Athletic Association, 2003. 97 pp. $7.50. ISSN 0735-0368.

In this annually issued official rule book, the major rule changes for the year are noted. Covers the field of play and equipment specifications, time, scoring, offside, and penalties. Officials' signals are illustrated with drawings. Also illustrated with several diagrams of the playing field. Indexed.

665. Oliver, Guy. **The Guinness Book of World Soccer: The History of the Game in Over 150 Countries.** 2nd ed. London: Guinness Publishing, 1995. 920 pp. ISBN 0-85112-654-5.

Arranged geographically, by governing body, this statistical compendium is divided into sections that cover the world governing body, the European governing body, the South American governing body, the African governing body, the CONCACAF, the Asian governing body, and Oceania. Provides the results of all major championships in each section, then goes on to provide detail on each country's activity. Includes an informative historical essay on the development of soccer in each country, a club directory for the country, and the records. Includes an appendix that matches European and South American club names with their country of origin, and a bibliography of sources.

666. Pickering, David. **The Cassell Soccer Companion: History, Facts, Anecdotes.** 1998 ed. London: Cassell, 1998. 342 pp. $14.95. ISBN 0-304-35097-4.

With the goal of providing a comprehensive guide to the colorful history of association football, the author covers the clubs and athletes, nicknames, technical terms, song lyrics, and many other topics that combine to form soccer culture. Arranged in alphabetical order, the concise entries in this collection vary in length from one sentence to one page. Full of facts, trivia, and anecdotes, this fascinating soccer guide will entertain fans and answer many unusual questions.

667. Radnedge, Keir. **The Complete Encyclopedia of Soccer: The Bible of World Soccer.** London: Carlton, 2000. 647 pp. $50.00. ISBN 1-84222-058-6.

In this comprehensive volume on soccer, the origins of the game are explored, and international tournaments and competitions are described and their results presented. International club competitions are also described and their results given, although special attention is shown to the great clubs in Europe, South America, and other parts of the world. Major FIFA soccer countries are also identified and described, as are the great players and great coaches. Chapters are devoted to international results and players' records in Great Britain and Ireland; German, French, Dutch, Spanish, Italian, Argentinean, and Brazilian international players' records are also listed. A final chapter is devoted to additional records and awards. Well illustrated with over 200 archival photographs in color and black-and-white. Includes a glossary of terms and an index.

668. Schwartz, Carl P. **Rules for Refs: Soccer '01–'02.** Racine, Wisc.: Referee Enterprises, 2001. 94 pp. $9.95. ISBN 1-58208-023-2.

The front cover of the book indicates that it gives "practical, authoritative information for the 2001–2002 soccer season." Provides complete coverage of FIFA, NCAA, and National Federation of State High School Associations (NFHS) rule changes and the key differences between these sets of rules. Offers case plays, rulings, interpretations, and explanations.

669. Seddon, Peter J., comp. **A Football Compendium: An Expert Guide to the Books, Films and Music of Association Football.** 2nd ed. With Cynthia McKinley, ed. Boston Spa, West Yorkshire, U.K.: The British Library, 1999. 815 pp. $60.00. ISBN 0-7123-1118-1.

In this massive bibliography of the literature of soccer, over 7000 sources are identified. Some entries are annotated, others are not, and many of the sources are quite unique. As such, this source will appeal to the specialist collector as much as to the academic doing specialized research on association football. And it will also appeal to the casual browser looking for something really fascinating. Illustrated with small reproductions of the covers of sources, as well as cartoons, sketches, and other illustrations depicting club logos or mascots. Indexed by name, club, title, and subject.

Instructional Sources

670. Buxton, Ted, Alex Leith, and Jim Drewitt. **Soccer Skills for Young Players.** Buffalo, N.Y.: Firefly Books, 2000. 128 pp. $14.95. ISBN 1-55209-329-8.

This training guide progresses through a series of seventy-one drills intended to teach the skills that are essential in soccer. The purpose of each drill is explained, and the required number of players, equipment needed, and skill level are indicated. Beautifully illustrated with color photographs and diagrams of the field of play. Includes a glossary of soccer terms and an annotated list of useful addresses of major associations and publications. Indexed.

671. Carr, David, and Michael Metzler. **Soccer: Mastering the Basics with the Personalized Sports Instruction System.** Personalized Sport Instruction. Boston: Allyn & Bacon, 2001. 129 pp. $17.00. ISBN 0-205-32371-5.

This workbook teaches the fundamentals of soccer and can be used in a formal course setting or by individuals who want to work at their own pace outside a course and chart their own progress. Each chapter presents a module of information about performance skills, shots, or the game itself and concludes with tasks that test what was learned. Includes the rules of soccer. Illustrated with photographs and diagrams.

672. Luongo, Albert M. **The Soccer Handbook for Players, Coaches and Parents.** Jefferson, N.C.: McFarland, 1996. 198 pp. $25.00. ISBN 0-7864-0159-1.

This handbook provides detailed coverage of the technical skills required for playing youth soccer. Includes lists of expected or average skill levels by age; a program of drills; and advanced techniques. Includes full description of the game itself and the role of different players. FIFA's 1995 *Laws of the Game* is reprinted in the appendix. Illustrated with black-and-white photographs and many drawings. Indexed.

673. Luxbacher, Joe. **Soccer: Steps to Success.** 2nd ed. Steps to Success Activity Series. Champaign, Ill.: Human Kinetics, 1996. 161 pp. $17.95. ISBN 0-87322-763-8.

An instructional source that teaches the game of soccer with ten sequential steps, each step is reinforced with drills to encourage quick improvement. Provides coverage of passing and receiving; dribbling, shielding, and tackling; individual attack and defense tactics; heading skills; shooting; goalkeeping; group attack; group defense; team tactics; and team organization. The steps are illustrated with 135 drawings, many of them showing the sequence of movement. Contains a glossary of terms.

674. National Soccer Coaches Association of America. **The Soccer Coaching Bible.** Champaign, Ill.: Human Kinetics, 2004. 316 pp. $21.95. ISBN 0-7360-4227-X.

This important coaching source contains contributions from thirty expert coaches and is intended for coaches at the club, high school, or college level.

Chapters detail the priorities and principles of coaching, program development, training, technique, player and team motivation, and growth opportunities for coaches. Illustrated with black-and-white line drawings and diagrams.

Web Sites

675. Federation Internationale de Football Association (FIFA). http://www .fifa.com/ (accessed March 4, 2004).

As the international governing body for soccer, FIFA's comprehensive Web site posts official rules and regulations of competition, substantial essays on the history of the game, its laws, and of the FIFA World Cup, information on a variety of other competitions, men's and women's world rankings, news, Olympic qualifiers, and much more. Also includes a directory of the more than 200 FIFA-affiliated organizations worldwide.

676. National Soccer Hall of Fame. http://www.soccerhall.org (accessed April 2, 2004).

This site offers visitor information, a virtual soccer museum, a library, news archive, tournament information, a history of U.S. soccer, and a player registry. Provides a database of hall of famers, accompanied by biographical information, statistics, and a photograph of each one.

677. Union of European Football Associations (UEFA). http://www.uefa.com (accessed December 3, 2004).

UEFA is the governing body of football (soccer) in Europe. This comprehensive site contains history, the organization's mission, administration, results of competitions, news on players and clubs, and much more—all available in eight languages. Provides links to national associations and clubs in the UEFA countries.

678. United States Soccer Federation. http://www.ussoccer.com (accessed March 21, 2004).

This is the national governing body for all forms of soccer in the United States, and the organization maintains a comprehensive Web site. Included on the site are news, schedules, rules, a referee administrative handbook, information on coaching clinics, a fan site, and much more.

Volleyball

Reference Sources

679. Annual Official USA Volleyball Reference Guide. United States Volleyball Association, no. 84, 2004 ed. Colorado Springs, Colo.: USA Volleyball, 2004. 218 pp.

This annually issued administrative guide provides information on the organization's corporate structure, a list of member organizations, and information on awards and recognitions, governance, administrative procedures, and past championship winners, archives, and a leadership directory. Referred to on the front cover of the book as the *2004 Official Guidebook.*

680. Fédération Internationale de Volley-ball. **100 Years of Global Link: Volleyball Centennial, 1895–1995.** Lausanne, Switzerland: Fédération Internationale de Volley-ball, 1996. 232 pp.

This beautifully illustrated volume begins with messages from many international volleyball dignitaries as they recognize the celebration of 100 years of volleyball. It presents the history of the game and the history of its governing body, the International Volleyball Federation (FIVB). Biographies are given for the thirty-six top international players of the century, and prominent coaches are mentioned briefly. Records and statistics are given for Olympic Games and other world championships, and beach volleyball is included. Contains a world map showing federations ranked by their competitive level, and the emblems of affiliated federations.

681. **Official United States Volleyball Rules.** 2003–2004 ed. United States Volleyball Association, Colorado Springs, Colo.: USA Volleyball, 2003. 242 pp. $6.95. ISBN 0-9704491-1-9.

This annual publication contains the full official rules and includes the *Official United States Beach Volleyball Rules* in the same volume, published on separately paged inverted pages. Official hand signals are illustrated with black-and-white photographs, and the court, playing area, typical playing positions and scoring methods are shown with diagrams. Also includes scorekeeping examples, abbreviations used, and metric conversions. Rules are indexed. Additional information is provided for players with disabilities, and contact information is given for assistance with rules interpretation.

682. **NCAA Women's Volleyball Rules and Interpretations.** Indianapolis, Ind.: National Collegiate Athletic Association, 2002. $7.50.

This annual rule book contains diagrams of playing areas, official signals, and official interpretations and rulings for women's volleyball at NCAA institutions.

683. **Official Women's NCAA Volleyball Records.** 2003 ed. Indianapolis, Ind.: National Collegiate Athletic Association, 2003. 140 pp. $12.00. ISSN 1089-0092.

This annual record book contains individual and team records for all NCAA divisions; All-Americans and other award winners; coaching records; the previous year's championship results, conference standings, and statistical leaders; and attendance leaders and records. Illustrated with black-and-white photographs from the season's play.

684. Reeser, Jonathan C., and Roald Bahr, eds. **Volleyball.** Handbook of Sports Medicine and Science. Malden, Mass.: Blackwell Science, 2003. 230 pp. $34.95. ISBN 0-632-05913-3.

Published under the auspices of the International Olympic Committee Medical Commission, this handbook covers the scientific and clinical aspects of volleyball. Includes information on biomechanics, the role of the medical professional, volleyball injuries, unique considerations for special groups of players (elite, female, disabled, etc.), and methods of performance enhancement. Illustrated with black-and-white photographs, line drawings, and tables. Chapters contain references and, occasionally, further sources of recommended reading. Indexed. Recommended primarily for academic collections.

685. Shewman, Byron. **Volleyball Centennial: The First 100 Years.** Spalding Sports Library. Indianapolis, Ind.: Masters Press, 1995. 325 pp. $19.95. ISBN 1-57028-009-6.

This volume covers the first 100 years of volleyball, so it is primarily a history of the game, both on the beach and indoors. Arranged chronologically, chapters provide volleyball highlights during a range of years and give details of significant events during each period. Good coverage of the Olympic Games between 1964 and 1992. Illustrated with many black-and-white photographs. An appendix provides U.S. national team finishes in major championships and NCAA champions for both men and women and lists of hall of fame inductees.

Instructional Sources

686. Dearing, Joel. **Volleyball Fundamentals: A Better Way to Learn the Basics.** Sports Fundamentals. Champaign, Ill.: Human Kinetics, 2003. 135 pp. $14.95. ISBN 0-7360-4508-2.

In this volleyball manual sequential instructions are given to teach essential skills and tactics of the game. Over fifty activities and drills reinforce the skills for better performance. Includes chapters on serving, receiving, setting, attacking, blocking, digging, team strategies, including the transition from defense to offense, and modified games. Provides information on scoring. Illustrated with black-and-white photographs, drawings, and diagrams.

687. Dunphy, Marv, and Rod Wilde. **Volleyball Today.** 2nd ed. Wadsworth's Physical Education Series. Belmont, Calif.: Wadsworth Publishing, 2000. 230 pp. . $24.95. ISBN 0-534-35836-5.

With comprehensive coverage of the fundamentals of volleyball, this text is appropriate for players at all levels. Includes discussion of the game, facilities, equipment, and safety; essential skills, including passing, bumping, setting, spiking, serving, blocking, transitions, and individual and team strategies; common injuries; and conditioning and nutrition. A chapter on beach and doubles volleyball is also included. An appendix contains the abridged international volleyball rules. Illustrated with color photographs and drawings. Contains a resource directory and an index.

688. Kiraly, Karch, and Byron Shewman. **Beach Volleyball.** Champaign, Ill.: Human Kinetics, 1999. 167 pp. $16.95. ISBN 0-88011-836-9.

This guide to the techniques, training, and tactics of volleyball provides a history of the game and its inclusion in the Olympics, followed by chapters devoted to the skills, training, and play. Covers the serve, pass, set, block, spike, and dig, as well as conditioning for flexibility, strength, plyometrics, speed, agility, and endurance. Includes twenty-three practice drills to reinforce the instruction. Also includes milestones of the noted author's volleyball career. Illustrated with black-and-white photographs. Indexed.

689. Kluka, Darlene A., and Peter J. Dunn. **Volleyball.** 4th ed. Winning Edge. Boston: McGraw-Hill, 2000. 232 pp. $10.30. ISBN 0-07-230030-2.

This instruction book begins with history and development of the game and its objectives. It provides information on facilities and equipment, rules and terminology, and the basic skills and more advanced strategies, including offensive and defensive tactics. Illustrated with black-and-white photographs, drawings, and diagrams. Appendices include a list of additional sources, and the original 1896 volleyball rules for comparison with today's game. Provides a glossary of terms and an index.

690. McGown, Carl, Hilda Ann Fronske, and Launa Moser. **Coaching Volleyball: Building a Winning Team.** Boston: Allyn & Bacon, 2001. 308 pp. $26.67. ISBN 0-205-30958-5.

This book on coaching volleyball will be useful for coaches of all playing levels, from beginning to advanced. After an introductory discussion of philosophy and team building, skills and drills are covered in detail, illustrated with diagrams and photographs. Contains chapters on the athlete's body and extensive information on strategy, competition, and dealing with typical problems. Includes sample charts and other documents that can be photocopied.

691. Poole, Jon, and Michael Metzler. **Volleyball: Mastering the Basics with the Personalized Sports Instruction System.** Personalized Sport Instruction. Boston: Allyn & Bacon, 2001. 129 pp. $17.00. ISBN 0-205-32370-7.

This guide to volleyball uses the PSIS to allow beginning students to progress through a sequence of skills and drills at their own individual pace. Can be used by students in a course or by self-learners as they work through the modules and master each skill. Provides clear instructions to make each skill understandable. Illustrated with black-and-white photographs and diagrams. Includes basic rules and terminology, as well as a progress chart.

692. Viera, Barbara, and Bonnie Jill Ferguson. **Volleyball: Steps to Success.** 2nd ed. Steps to Success Activity Series. Champaign, Ill.: Human Kinetics, 1996. 161 pp. $17.95. ISBN 0-87322-646-1.

This volleyball instruction source provides a step-by-step approach to help the reader learn fundamental skills and strategies required for the game. Includes ninety-nine drills to reinforce the instruction, along with performance goals, specific pointers, and a method of self-evaluation. Illustrated with over 190 drawings and diagrams.

Web Sites

693. Federation Internationale de Volleyball (FIVB). http://www.fivb.org (accessed January 2, 2004).

The International Volleyball Federation's official site contains information on the organization itself, its headquarters, corporate profile, and the FIVB World Congress, as well as extensive international volleyball news. Contains sections on the history and origin on the game, beach volleyball, basic play, rules, competitions, world rankings, a calendar of events, coverage of Olympic Games, and much more.

694. United States Volleyball Association. http://www.usavolleyball.org (accessed January 2, 2004).

This organization's official site contains volleyball news and results of competition, a comprehensive calendar of events, and an online gift shop. Provides the full text of several publications, such as athlete and coach competency handbooks; other publications can be ordered on the site. Includes a national directory of places to play volleyball, definitions of the regions, and a list of member organizations, extensive information on its disabled volleyball division, and information on camps, clinics, and championships, including Olympic competition. Contains both indoor and outdoor official rules and the association's administrative guidebook.

695. Volleyball Hall of Fame. http://www.volleyhall.org/ (accessed December 3, 2004).

The hall of fame Web site provides history of the game, a photo gallery, profiles of inductees and honorees, information on their archives, and many other links.

Combat Sports

Chapter 10

With roots in the ancient world, combat sports have always been popular as a method of settling disputes among competitors. They are now also seeing a great increase in popularity for their health benefits. Some of these activities are performed with a weapon and others use only bare hands and feet, but mastering these sports requires precise physical movement, great patience, and mental strategy. This chapter lists information sources on boxing, fencing, martial arts, and wrestling.

Boxing

Reference Sources

696. Benson, Douglas S. **Championship Boxing: A Statistical History of Modern Boxing's First Century, 1880–1980.** Chicago: D.S. Benson, 1995. 313 pp.

In this chronology of championship boxing, the author provides two modes of access: by weight class and then by year, and by year with all weight classes combined. The work also contains a graphic history of boxing, consisting of nearly a hundred pages of historic action photographs and drawings, arranged chronologically. Indexed by name of champion.

697. Blewett, Bert. **The A–Z of World Boxing: An Authoritative and Entertaining Compendium of the Fight Game from Its Origins to the Present Day.** London: Robson Books, 1996. 439 pp. $38.95. ISBN 1-86105-004-6.

This alphabetically arranged encyclopedia of boxing contains profiles of all the famous fighters in the ring and also includes entries on announcers and other important people in the sport. Topics as diverse as art, attire, deaths, fat fighters, firsts, posters, television, and unions are also included. Illustrated with many classic black-and-white photographs and drawings. Indexed.

698. **The Boxing Record Book.** Vol. 21. Sicklerville, N.J.: Fight Fax, 2004. $64.00.

This annual publication contains the complete records of all currently active boxers, including over 200 female fighters' records from all over the world. This extensive publication lists split and majority decisions, telephone numbers, and Boxing Writer's Association Award winners. The title-bout section provides a complete breakdown of round-by-round scoring of every International Boxing Federation, International Boxing Organization, World Boxing Association, World Boxing Council, and World Boxing Organization 2003 title bout, including referees, judges, promoters, and more.

699. Fleischer, Nat, and Sam Andre. **An Illustrated History of Boxing.** 6th revised and updated ed. New York: Citadel Press / Kensington Publishing, 2001. 641 pp. $24.95. ISBN 0-8065-2201-1.

First published as *A Pictorial History of Boxing* (London: Spring Books, 1959), this volume is primarily a rich collection of historic portraits and photographs from the world of boxing. Essays are included to explain the major events over time within each weight category, and illustrations are described in detail. The sixth edition was updated by Don Rafael. Indexed by boxer's name.

700. Mullan, Harry. **The Ultimate Encyclopedia of Boxing: The Definitive Illustrated Guide to World Boxing.** Edison, N.J.: Chartwell Books, 1996. 208 pp. ISBN 0-7858-0641-5.

This encyclopedia provides a brief essay on the origins of boxing and then profiles 200 boxers who have been important in the sport. Provides more detailed information on twelve of boxing's legends and fifteen of the greatest fights. Also covers other important contributors to boxing, such as promoters, managers, and trainers. Presents the rules and scoring, as well as a list of world championships arranged chronologically and by weight category. Illustrated with black-and-white and color photographs. Indexed.

701. Myler, Patrick. **A Century of Boxing Greats: Inside the Ring with the Hundred Best Boxers.** London: Robson Books, 1999. 394 pp. $15.00. ISBN 1-86105-258-8.

The author provides biographical detail on his selection of the twentieth century's 100 best boxers. Included for each boxer are nickname; championships won; dates and places of birth and death; career span in years; number of total contests won, lost, and so forth; and a detailed biographical essay that includes major events in the boxer's career as well as important lifetime events outside boxing. Illustrated with black-and-white photographs. Includes a brief bibliography.

702. Roberts, James B., and Alexander G. Skutt. **The Boxing Register: International Boxing Hall of Fame Official Record Book.** 3rd ed. Ithaca, N.Y.: McBooks Press, 2001. 640 pp. $24.95. ISBN 1-590130-20-0.

This guide to the history of boxing is the official record book of the International Boxing Hall of Fame in Canastota, New York. It provides rich details of the lives and careers of all the members of the hall of fame. Each individual's profile includes basic data, a photograph, information on the bouts and championships won, year of induction into the hall of fame, a descriptive essay on highlights of the person's career and life, and full statistics. Additional informative essays are included, as are photographs of items in the hall of fame museum. Indexed.

Instructional Source

703. Scott, Dana. **Boxing: The Complete Guide to Fitness and Training.** New York: Berkley Publishing Group, 2000. 127 pp. $12.95. ISBN 0-399-52601-3.

This guide to fitness and training for boxing is intended for anyone interested in boxing as a workout, regardless of level of expertise. There is a chapter on equipment and one on wrapping techniques. Other chapters focus on details of strategy and training, including movement in the ring and different boxing styles. Illustrated with black-and-white photographs. Includes a glossary and an index.

Web Sites

704. **Association Internationale de Boxe Amateur (AIBA).** http://www .aiba.net (accessed March 4, 2004).

The AIBA is the international governing body for boxing competition. Their site provides a directory of national boxing federations worldwide, as well as a news archive, press releases, results of competition, information on Olympic prequalifying tournaments, official documents and publications, rules and regulations, a list of AIBA approved equipment sources, a medical section, and much more.

705. **International Boxing Federation (IBF) / United States Boxing Association.** http://www.ibf-usba-boxing.com/ (accessed March 22, 2004).

This site is a joint venture of the IBF and the United States Boxing Association. It contains ratings of boxers and a list of fight results, but information about the organizations is incomplete.

706. **International Boxing Hall of Fame.** http://www.ibhof.com (accessed March 15, 2004).

This hall of fame's Web site contains a great deal of information, including articles on the history of boxing, biographical information on hall of fame members, archival information on Olympic medalists, the Boxing Writer's Association Award, and other championships, news, a gift shop, and much more.

707. **USA Boxing.** http://www.usaboxing.org (accessed March 26, 2004).

As the national governing body for men's and women's Olympic-style boxing, this organization maintains a comprehensive Web site, including a mission statement, history, athlete profiles, news, rankings, and results. Contains a calendar of events, and much more.

Fencing

Reference Sources

708. Evangelista, Nick. **The Encyclopedia of the Sword.** Westport, Conn.: Greenwood Press, 1995. 690 pp. $89.50. ISBN 0-313-27896-2.

In this complete source on fencing, the author presents "under one roof" the history, culture, language, technique, and influential persons in the world of fencing. In a traditional alphabetical arrangement, this rich and complex world is unfolded. Entries are clearly written and contain references. Appendices list types of swords, fencing masters, films, actors, and organizations.

709. Gaugler, William M. **A Dictionary of Universally Used Fencing Terminology.** Bangor, Maine: Laureate Press, 1997. 62 pp. $9.95. ISBN 1-884528-00-7.

Intended as a companion volume to *The Science of Fencing* by William M. Gaugler, this dictionary begins with an introduction to the history and origins of fencing and its terminology. The length of the definitions varies from one sentence to several pages. At the end of the volume is a bibliography of other classic works.

710. Morton, E. D. **The A to Z of Fencing.** Rev. ed. E. D. Morton, 1995. 312 pp. $24.95. ISBN 0952598108.

Previously published as *Martini A to Z of Fencing* (1988), this extensive source is a classic encyclopedia in fencing. It appears to be available for purchase via online booksellers.

Instructional Sources

711. Bower, Muriel. **Foil Fencing.** Sports and Fitness. 8th ed. New York: McGraw-Hill, 1997. 118 pp. $18.43. ISBN 0-697-25874-2.

This basic but comprehensive guide to fencing is intended for students of the sport, at the beginning level through advanced levels. Fencing is defined and a history of the sport is presented, followed by standard techniques and rules. Chapters are included on equipment, basic skills, beginning to bout, advanced techniques, conditioning, advanced bouting, and detailed rules. A glossary of fencing terms is included, as is an index. Illustrated with black-and-white photographs and diagrams.

712. Cheris, Elaine. **Fencing: Steps to Success.** Steps to Success Activity Series. Champaign, Ill.: Human Kinetics, 2002. 150 pp. $19.95. ISBN 0-87322-972-X.

Intended for beginning and developing fencers, as well as instructors, this manual divides the skills of fencing into nine distinct steps. Provided for each step are a detailed description of the skill or technique, illustrations, tips on how to correct errors, a series of drills, a success checklist, and ways to increase or decrease difficulty. Well illustrated with drawings and tables. Contains a brief history of fencing and a glossary.

713. Evangelista, Anita, and Nick Evangelista. **The Woman Fencer.** Terre Haute, Ind.: Wish Publishing, 2001. 288 pp. $16.95. ISBN 1-930546-48-3.

In an illustrated A to Z format, the authors provide the history of women in fencing, as well as a complete guide for the beginner, regardless of her age. This book covers all the basic concepts, equipment, techniques and strategies but also discusses women's health issues as they relate to fencing and provides biographies of prominent women fencers. Offers a glossary of terms and a bibliography of sources.

714. Evangelista, Nick. **The Art and Science of Fencing.** Lincolnwood, Ill.: Masters Press, 1996. 288 pp. $16.95. ISBN 1-57028-075-4.

More than a how-to book, this text on fencing explores the human element of the sport and includes significant historical detail to enliven the description of technique. It covers types of swords, schools, biographies of great fencers, and the psychology of fencing and includes definitions of terms, a list of films, and additional sources for further study. Illustrated with black-and-white photographs and drawings.

715. Garret, Maxwell R., Emmanuil G. Kaidanov, and Gil A. Pezza. **Foil, Saber, and Epee Fencing: Skills, Safety, Operations, and Responsibilities.** University Park, Pa.: Pennsylvania State University Press, 1994. 227 pp. $29.95. ISBN 0-271-01019-3.

The purpose of this book is to introduce the novice fencer to the sport but also to assist coaches, instructors, and more advanced students as they continue to learn about and teach fencing to others. Concepts are introduced, and active learning experiences are built around these to teach each skill and strategy. The rules of competition are included, as is information about conducting tournaments, officiating, and maintaining electrical equipment. It also provides information on fitness and safety. Illustrated with an abundance of photographs and drawings. Includes a glossary, a bibliography of sources, and an index.

716. Gaugler, William M. **The Science of Fencing: A Comprehensive Training Manual for Master and Student: Including Lesson Plans for Foil, Sabre and Epee Instruction.** Bangor, Maine: Laureate Press, 1997. 392 pp. $24.95. ISBN 1-884528-05-8.

Intended as a companion volume to *On Fencing* by Aldo Nadi, and useful with A Dictionary of Universally Used Fencing Terminology, this is an important, comprehensive work for teachers, coaches, and students. Detailed coverage of technique is provided in three parts: the foil, the sabre, and the epee. Within each part, a chapter on pedagogy is included. Illustrated with tables and many black-and-white photographs. Appendices include sample lessons, questions for review, contact information for organizations and equipment, and a table of terminology. Includes a glossary, a select bibliography, and an index.

717. Nadi, Aldo. **On Fencing.** Reprinted ed. Sunrise, Fla.: Laureate Press, 1994. 300 pp. $24.95. ISBN 1-884528-04-X.
   Originally published in 1943, this classic fencing reference covers the history of the sword and then describes in depth the philosophy and complex technique of fencing. Individual chapters cover the detail of footwork, parries, attack and counter-attack, and exercise and training for combat. A final chapter explores the essential characteristics of a fencing master teacher. Illustrated with eight black-and-white photographs.

Web Sites

718. **International Fencing Federation / Federation Internationale D' Escrime (FIE).** http://www.fie.ch/ (accessed March 15, 2004).
   The FIE is the international governing body for the sport of fencing. Its Web site contains rules, a handbook of specifications, a directory of national federations, a database of results, a calendar of events, history of the organization and of fencing, a rankings database, full text publications, a glossary of technical terms in fencing, information about equipment, links to other important sites, and much more.

719. **United States Fencing Association USFA.** http://www.usfencing.org (accessed March 11, 2004).
   This association site contains online news and press releases, as well as information on competitions and national rankings. Includes information for members and links to the Web sites of USFA committees, such as the Wheelchair Fencing Committee. Includes a U.S. Fencing Store and links to many other official bodies, such as the U.S. Olympic Committee and the NCAA. Also provides links to other fencing groups such as the FIE and the Canadian and Pan-American associations.

Martial Arts

Reference Sources

720. Corcoran, John. **The Martial Arts Sourcebook.** New York: HarperCollins, 1994. 434 pp. $18.00. ISBN 0-06-273259-5.
   The front cover indicates that this book is "the complete reference to the most frequently sought information on the martial arts." This sourcebook contains a variety of information, including description of the martial arts and styles of the world, Asian dynasties, official forms of karate and tae kwon do, and weapons of the world. It lists martial arts halls of fame and their members, other

award winners, and great masters. It includes the results of a number of international martial arts competitions and championships, a martial arts film and video guide, and a list of celebrity contacts. It also includes a business directory with contact information on associations, equipment and supply companies, book publishers, and marketing services.

721. Farkas, Emil, and John Corcoran. **The Overlook Martial Arts Dictionary.** Woodstock, N.Y.: Overlook Press, 1985. 301 pp. $13.95. ISBN 0-87951-996-7.

Intended for everyone's use, from the beginner to the black belt, this dictionary of martial arts terminology offers the phonetic pronunciation of the word, the language of origin, a literal translation of the term, cross-references to variant forms, and a concise definition. Arranged alphabetically and illustrated with black-and-white photographs throughout the text.

722. Frederic, Louis. **A Dictionary of the Martial Arts.** With Paul H. Crompton, ed. and trans. Rutland, Vt.: Tuttle, 1994. 276 pp. $19.95. ISBN 0-8048-1750-2.

Presented in traditional alphabetical arrangement, this dictionary of martial arts terminology offers a technical and historical treatment of terms in over forty martial arts. The entries vary in length depending on the term's significance and the level of detail required to adequately define it; some are chapter length and others are only one sentence. Well-illustrated with many black-and-white photographs and drawings.

723. Goodman, Fay. **The Ultimate Book of Martial Arts.** New York: Lorenz Books / Anness Publishing, 1998. 256 pp. $30.00. ISBN 1-85967-778-9.

This encyclopedia provides an excellent overview of many martial arts forms, including coverage of the most popular disciplines: Tae Kwondo, Iaido, Kendo, Shinto Ryu, Karate, Judo, Aikido, Kung Fu, Tai Chi, and Ju-Jitsu. Each discipline is covered in a chapter that begins with history and philosophy and also covers clothing and equipment, etiquette, warm-up exercises, and the technique. Both beginning and advanced technique is demonstrated step-by-step by experts. The work is beautifully illustrated with over 700 step-by-step color photographs.

724. Green, Thomas A., ed. **Martial Arts of the World: An Encyclopedia.** 2 vols. Santa Barbara, Calif.: ABC-CLIO, 2001. $185.00. ISBN 1-57607-150-2.

Edited by an anthropologist, this two-volume set with 894 pages presents signed, scholarly essays on the martial arts, focusing primarily on the history, philosophy, and evolution of martial arts through time. An appendix provides a timeline covering 30,000 years of martial arts history. Illustrated with black-and-white photographs. Includes bibliographical references and a useful index.

725. Nelson, Randy F. **The Martial Arts: An Annotated Bibliography.** Garland Reference Library of the Social Sciences, vol. 451. New York: Garland Publishing, 1988. 436 pp. $25.00. ISBN 0-8240-4435-5.

This comprehensive bibliography of martial arts will be important to scholars who want to do exhaustive research on the subject or to those who want to find a good book on a specific aspect of the martial arts. Contains nearly 2500 entries, approximately one-third of them annotated. Includes books, articles in periodicals, and chapters in books, in the following categories: general, philosophy, history, biographies/profiles, instruction and juvenile. Indexed by author and subject.

Instructional Sources

726. Clark, Angus. **The Complete Illustrated Guide to Tai Chi.** Boston: Element Books, 2000. 192 pp. $19.95. ISBN 1-86204-452-X.
Both informative and practical, this comprehensive guide to Tai Chi provides the history, origins, and philosophy of the ancient Chinese movement, as well as its seven qualities. It discusses the human body and how the various components, such as the skeleton, muscles, and sensory systems work together in movement. Introduces the fundamental steps and moves and then completes the short-form sequence of postures, which are illustrated with sequential sets of color photographs. Also discusses the broader picture, of using Tai Chi throughout life. Well-illustrated throughout with color photographs. Appendix includes information on styles and schools, a glossary, useful addresses, and a list of sources. Indexed.

727. Cochran, Sean. **Complete Conditioning for Martial Arts.** Champaign, Ill.: Human Kinetics, 2001. 175 pp. $17.95. ISBN 0-7360-0250-2.
This guide to conditioning for martial arts begins with fitness essentials and how to evaluate level of fitness before building a training program. Various elements of a training program are presented, such as activities for flexibility, joint-stabilization, strengthening, plyometrics, aerobic and anaerobic conditioning, and nutrition. Includes over eighty exercises specifically designed to improve the execution of martial arts techniques; these are illustrated with black-and-white photographs.

728. Kit, Wong Kiew. **The Complete Book of Tai Chi Chuan: A Comprehensive Guide to the Principles and Practices.** Boston: Tuttle, 2002. 317 pp. $16.95. ISBN 0-8048-3440-7.
This complete guide to Tai Chi Chuan provides an in-depth description of the history and philosophy of the art, as well as its benefits to one's spiritual, mental, and emotional development. It includes instructions for the basic set of movements, plus specific techniques for combat situations and thorough information on various styles of Tai Chi Chuan. Step-by-step line drawings illustrate the movements. Intended for beginning students or those who want a review. Includes sources for further reading and a list of addresses for organizations throughout the world. Indexed.

729. McFarlane, Stewart. **The Complete Book of T'ai Chi.** New York: Dorling Kindersley, 1999. 120 pp. $13.95. ISBN 0-7894-4259-0.
This well-illustrated instructional source demonstrates the fundamental exercises, postures, and movements of tai chi with step-by-step color photographs.

Also provides basic information on the history and philosophy of this ancient martial art, as well as the benefits to health and wellness. Indexed.

730. Park, Yeon Hee, Yeon Hwan Park, and Jon Gerrard. **Tae Kwon Do: The Ultimate Reference Guide to the World's Most Popular Martial Art.** Updated ed. New York: Facts On File, 1999. 218 pp. $29.65. ISBN 0-8160-3838-4.

Endorsed by the World Tae Kwon Do Federation (WTF), this comprehensive guide provides a history of the art, along with a philosophy for practitioners. The physical techniques are explained in detail and illustrated with over 750 black-and-white photographs that "walk through" every posture. Warm-up exercises are demonstrated first, then basic techniques, then the forms and sparring. Appendices contain the official rules of competition; the weight and belt classifications; a list of WTF-sanctioned national organizations throughout the world; contact information for the WTF and the United States Taekwondo Union; a list of terminology organized by broad subject (anatomy, commands, movements, etc.); and a Korean-English and English-Korean glossary of terms. Indexed.

731. Park, Yeon Hwan, and Jon Gerrard. **Black Belt Tae Kwon Do: The Ultimate Reference Guide to the World's Most Popular Black Belt Martial Art.** New York: Checkmark Books / Facts On File, 2000. 272 pp. $38.50. ISBN 0-8160-4240-3.

This volume is written by the same authors as Tae Kwon Do and is intended as a follow-up. It is written for advanced students of the martial art and is endorsed by the World Taekwondo Federation. Includes over 750 black-and-white photographs that illustrate the movements in a step-by-step manner. Chapters provide in-depth information on the philosophy of the art, practice routines and techniques, and on opening and running a Taekwondo school. Appendices explain the rules and terminology of competition. Includes a glossary of Korean and English terms.

732. Pedro, Jimmy. **Judo Techniques and Tactics.** Martial Arts. With William Durbin. Champaign, Ill.: Human Kinetics, 2001. 183 pp. $16.95. ISBN 0-7360-0343-6.

This basic instructional source provides the fundamentals of the art of judo and the benefits of its practice; intended for beginners or advanced students who want to review technique. Includes a brief history of judo, definitions of terminology, and chapters on competition and conditioning for enhanced performance. Illustrated with black-and-white photographs. Indexed.

Web Sites

733. **International Judo Federation (IJF).** http://www.ijf.org (accessed March 4, 2004).

In its role as the international governing body for judo competition, the IJF maintains a comprehensive Web site with news, a photo gallery, rules, statutes, an events calendar, and in-depth information on a variety of competitive events worldwide. They post a directory of national judo member organizations and make available for download publications such as a referee manual, referee rules, and antidoping rules. The site also contains information on the history of judo, research, women's judo, and techniques, as well as a hall of fame.

734. **United States Taekwondo Union (USTU).** http://www.ustu.org (accessed March 26, 2004).

The USTU is the official governing body for the United States. Their site contains an events calendar, rules, results, news, athlete biographies, and a referee textbook. Contains links to collegiate clubs and Taekwondo schools throughout the United States.

735. **USA Judo.** http://www.usjudo.org (accessed March 21, 2004).

This group is the national governing body for judo competition, and their Web site provides news, a calendar of events, results, a media guide, information for athletes, referees, coaches, and much more.

736. **USA National Karate-Do Federation.** http://www.usankf.org (accessed March 26, 2004).

This is the Web site of the national governing body for karate in the United States. It features news, a calendar of events, a media kit, information on different styles of karate, the results of international and U.S. tournaments, and a Hall of Fame.

737. **World Taekwondo Federation (WTF).** http://www.wtf.org/main.htm (accessed March 3, 2004).

WTF is the international governing body for Taekwondo and is recognized by the International Olympic Committee. Their site contains contact information for the member countries, arranged by region; a history of the organization; rules; a history and philosophy of Taekwondo; a calendar of events; a hall of fame; publications; and much more.

Wrestling

Reference Sources

738. Chapman, Mike. **Encyclopedia of American Wrestling.** Champaign, Ill.: Leisure Press, 1990. 533 pp. $16.78. ISBN 0-608-07080-7.

Though dated, this work may be useful for locating for research prior to 1990. Provides a chapter on the history of wrestling in America, then covers the Olympic games, World Championships and other world meets, the Amateur Athletic Union (AAU) National Freestyle Championships, the US. Freestyle Senior Open, the Greco-Roman Nationals, collegiate nationals, midlands championships, junior nationals, and junior world tournaments. Offers information on persons who have earned other special honors and awards and who have been inducted into the halls of fame.

739. Lentz, Harris M. **Biographical Dictionary of Professional Wrestling.** 2nd ed. Jefferson, N.C.: McFarland, 2003. 395 pp. $45.00. ISBN 0-7864-1754-4.

Entries provide basic biographical data about managers, promoters, and the wrestlers themselves and include a short essay describing the person's participation and accomplishments in the star-studded world of professional wrestling. Entries are arranged alphabetically by the person's name.

740. **NCAA Wrestling Rules and Interpretations.** 2004 ed. Indianapolis, Ind.: National Collegiate Athletic Association, 2003. 145 pp. $7.50. ISBN 0736-511X.

This annual rule book identifies the NCAA wrestling rules committee members and details major rule changes for the year, as well as all continuing rules and interpretations. Contains diagrams of playing areas, official signals, and official interpretations and rulings by which all NCAA institutions are required to abide when they hold contests. Also includes appendices that cover sports medicine topics such as weight management and body composition, blood-borne pathogens, dehydration, and weight-certification procedures. Illustrated with black-and-white photographs and diagrams. Indexed.

Instructional Source

741. Ledeboer, Suzanne. **A Basic Guide to Wrestling.** Updated Olympic ed. An Official United States Olympic Committee Sports Series. Glendale, Calif.: Griffin Publishing, 1998. 117 pp. $7.95. ISBN 1-882180-77-1.

This concise and informative guide to wrestling includes all that one needs to know to get started in the sport, either as a participant or a spectator. Contains chapters on the history of the sport, then goes on to cover the basic skills. Describes wrestling matches and various levels of competition, equipment and clothing, scoring and officiating, health and fitness for the sport, and safety and first aid. Black-and-white photographs of the 1996 Olympic champions accompany biographies; contains contact information for USA Wrestling, the national governing body and a glossary of terms.

Web Sites

742. **International Federation of Associated Wrestling Styles / Federation Internationale de Luttes Association (FILA).** http://www.fila-wrestling.com (accessed March 4, 2004).

FILA, the international governing body for wrestling competition, maintains a comprehensive Web site, providing a history of wrestling, definitions of the styles and techniques, in-depth information about the organization, news, rules, rankings, a hall of honor, and a national federation directory. The site also contains access to a database of information about wrestlers and competitions, a photo gallery, and information about qualifying for the Olympic Games.

743. **USA Wrestling.** http://www.usawrestling.org (accessed March 27, 2004).

The national governing body for wrestling maintains an informative Web site that contains news, results, rankings, schedules of events, athlete biographies, a photo gallery, a list of camps and clinics, and detailed information on competition for all ages and at all levels. Contains a 2002 Title IX Timeline for wrestling.

Track and Field, Multidisciplinary Sports, and Gymnastics

This chapter groups together information sources on track and field activities, multidisciplinary sports such as the triathlon, and gymnastics. There are far fewer traditional reference sources in these areas, perhaps because these sports haven't received the same media attention as baseball or football. But, they hold a fundamental place in sporting history and are featured prominently in the Olympic Games.

Track and Field

Reference Sources

744. Baldwin, David. **Track and Field Record Holders: Profiles of the Men and Women Who Set World, Olympic, and American Marks, 1946 through 1995.** Jefferson, N.C.: McFarland, 1996. 338 pp. $67.36. ISBN 0-7864-0249-0.

This biographical source contains brief profiles of nearly 700 men and women who set records in track and field. Many of the athletes are fairly obscure, so this is an important record of their accomplishments. There are separate sections for women and men; each is arranged by event, then by type of record (world, Olympic, U.S.), then chronologically. Biographies are presented the first time an individual is cited in the text, with cross-references used for subsequent references. Indexed.

745. Davis, Michael D. **Black American Women in Olympic Track and Field: A Complete Illustrated Reference.** Jefferson, N.C.: McFarland, 1992. 170 pp. $35.00. ISBN 0-89950-692-5.

This comprehensive reference work describes the accomplishments of over ninety African American women in Olympic track and field. The author provides a chronological checklist of women's participation in the Olympics, then presents detailed information on the individuals who won the honors and their record of Olympic participation and accomplishments. First-person interviews are included for twenty of the most prominent Olympians. Includes black-and-white photographs of many of the athletes. Indexed.

746. Lawson, Gerald. **World Record Breakers in Track and Field Athletics.** Champaign, Ill.: Human Kinetics, 1997. 467 pp. $24.95. ISBN 0-88011-679-X.

This comprehensive guide to accomplished athletes in track and field concentrates on events at the Olympic Games. Divided into two sections, it treats men and women separately, with one chapter devoted to each of the events. A history and description of the event is followed by a table that lists all the athletes who have held a world record in it. Also includes a short biography for each record holder. Black-and-white photographs are provided for many of the athletes. Indexed.

747. McNab, Tom, Peter Lovesey, and Andrew Huxtable, comps. **An Athletics Compendium: An Annotated Guide to the UK Literature of Track and Field.** Boston Spa, West Yorkshire, U.K.: British Library, 2001. 261 pp. $55.00. ISBN 0-7123-1104-1.

This ambitious work is an extensive annotated bibliography of books on track and field published in the United Kingdom and Ireland and is a continuation of a previous book, *The Guide to British Track and Field Literature, 1275–1968* (London: Athletics Arena, 1969). It is based primarily on the holdings of the British Library, supplemented with material from other libraries. The book is arranged by topic and includes sections on history and development; personalities; international competition; coaching; training; running; field events; officiating, organization and laws; facilities and equipment; physiology, psychology and fitness; injuries and sports medicine; literature and the visual arts; and a final section on reference works. Indexed by name, title, and subject.

748. **National Athletics Records.** 2003 ed. Mountain View, Calif.: Tafnews Press / Track & Field News, 2003. 208 pp. $24.95.

This reference contains the national track and field records of all countries in the world, from Afghanistan to Zimbabwe, including both men's and women's records.

749. **NCAA Men's and Women's Track and Field and Cross Country Rules.** 2004 ed. Indianapolis, Ind.: National Collegiate Athletic Association, 2004. $7.50. ISBN 0736-511X.

In this annual official rule book, the major rule changes for the year are noted. Covers the track and equipment specifications, time, scoring, and related information. Officials' signals are illustrated with drawings. Also illustrated with drawings of equipment and diagrams of the track. Indexed.

750. Tricard, Louise Mead. **American Women's Track and Field: A History, 1895 through 1980.** Jefferson, N.C.: McFarland, 1996. 746 pp. $75.00. ISBN 0-7864-0219-9.

This excellent historical work based on primary-source documents and interviews with athletes traces women's track and field from its beginnings in 1895 through 1980. Contains the results of Amateur Athletic Union women's championships since 1923. Five appendices provide additional information, including names of hall of fame enshrinees; Olympic gold medalists, 1928–1980; marathon winners; and chronologies of women's events. Includes a bibliography for each chapter and a detailed index.

751. **USA Track and Field Competition Rules.** 2003 ed. Indianapolis, Ind.: USA Track & Field, 2003. 239 pp. $13.00. ISSN 1546-5268.

This guide to competition rules is for track and field, long distance running, and race walking at the senior, junior, youth athletics, and master's levels. Contains the full official rules for all events. Includes diagrams with dimensions of the playing areas for all events. An appendix contains world records for men and women in all events, sample applications and forms, and a conversion table.

752. Zarnowski, Frank. **American Decathletes: A 20th Century Who's Who.** Jefferson, N.C.: McFarland, 2002. 316 pp. $75.00. ISBN 0-7864-1103-1.

This reference source provides biographical information on 319 twentieth-century American track and field athletes, highlighting their career records. The arrangement is alphabetical by athlete's name; criteria for inclusion is achievement based and is further defined in the book's preface. Each entry includes demographic information about the athlete, a timeline, a brief descriptive paragraph about the person's career, and a statistical record of the career. There is also a section on coaches, with a brief paragraph of career highlights included for each of twenty-six selected coaches. An appendix contains world and American decathlon rankings from 1912 to 2000. Includes a list of references and an index.

Instructional Sources

753. Carr, Gerry A. **Fundamentals of Track and Field.** 2nd ed. Champaign, Ill.: Human Kinetics, 1999. 304 pp. $21.95. ISBN 0-7360-0008-9.

An introductory guide to all track and field events, this source is a great tool for teaching beginners to run, jump, and throw. Includes step-by-step instructions, practice drills, troubleshooting tables, coaching tips, and safety information. Offers separate sections on track events, jumping events, and throwing events. Contains nearly 300 illustrations that demonstrate correct technique.

754. Jarver, Jess. ed. **The Hurdles: Contemporary Theory, Technique and Training.** 4th ed. Mountain View, Calif.: Tafnews Press / Track & Field News, 2004. 137 pp. $18.50.

This collection of twenty-eight scientific and technical articles is a guide to the most recent advanced thinking about hurdles technique and training throughout the world. It will be most appropriate for academic collections in exercise science or those libraries serving track and field coaches.

755. Jarver, Jess. **Sprints and Relays: Contemporary Theory, Technique and Training.** 5th ed. Mountain View, Calif.: Tafnews Press / Track & Field News, 2000. 160 pp. $18.95. ISBN 0-911521-56-9.

This collection of thirty-one recent articles on sprinting and relay racing is taken from the world's most important scientific track publications and journals. Covering basic factors such as speed development, stride, and energetics, and specific training procedures and concepts, it is a modern course on the latest thinking and research in the field. Best for academic collections or those serving track and field coaches.

756. Jarver, Jess, ed. **The Throws: Contemporary Theory, Technique and Training.** 5th ed. Mountain View, Calif.: Tafnews Press / Track & Field News, 2000. 179 pp. $18.50. ISBN 0-911521-58-5.

This collection of thirty-seven articles selected from the world's major technical journals is focused on the four throwing events—shot, discus, hammer, and javelin—but also includes articles on general concepts such as teaching, strength training, using tests, biomechanics, and weight training. All are scientific and technical in nature, and as such will be most appropriate for academic collections in exercise science or those libraries that serve track and field coaches.

757. Rogers, Joseph L., project coordinator. **USA Track & Field Coaching Manual.** With USA Track & Field. Champaign, Ill.: Human Kinetics, 2000. 316 pp. $21.95. ISBN 0-88011-604-8.

This coaching manual provides comprehensive, detailed, yet practical information on all the major track and field events. In twenty informative chapters written by expert coaches, it covers running, jumping, throwing, race walking, and multi-sport events. Each event is described in detail with extensive information on both technique and training. It is illustrated with black-and-white photographs and step-by-step drawings. A bibliography is included. This is the official coaching guide of USA Track & Field, the national governing body for track and field sports.

Web Sites

758. **International Association of Athletics Federations.** http://www.iaaf.org/ (accessed March 3, 2004).

The Web site of the international governing body for athletics (track and field) provides a directory of member federations (the national governing bodies) throughout the world. It also makes available news, results of competition, world rankings, a calendar of events, a history and definition of athletics and its subfields, a photo gallery, many links to related sites, and much more.

759. **USA Track and Field.** http://www.usatf.org (accessed March 27, 2004).

This is the national governing body for track and field, long distance running, and race walking. The Web site offers a calendar of events, records, results, official rules, athlete biographies, and the National Track and Field Hall of Fame, with members' biographies posted online.

Multidisciplinary Sports

Instructional Sources

760. Bernhardt, Gale. **Training Plans for Multisport Athletes.** The ultimate training series from VeloPress. Boulder, Colo.: VeloPress, 2000. 324 pp. $16.95. ISBN 1-884737-82-X.

Intended as a personal training guide, this volume will assist the individual who is planning to train for a triathlon. Includes training plans and specific workouts appropriate for the novice or for the experienced triathlete. General strength training, stretching, and nutrition information is included. Illustrated with many tables of information that detail expected performance. Indexed.

761. Friel, Joe. **The Triathlete's Training Bible: A Complete Training Guide for the Competitive Multisport Athlete.** Boulder, Colo.: VeloPress, 1998. 350 pp. $19.95. ISBN 1-884737-48-X.

This specialized training guide includes detailed chapters on techniques for training smarter, as well as the latest information on nutrition and fitness. Appendices include training worksheets and recommended swim, bike, and run workouts. Each chapter ends with a list of further references. Illustrated with many black-and-white tables, diagrams, and drawings. Contains a glossary and an index.

Web Sites

762. **International Biathlon Union (IBU).** http://www.biathlonworld.com (accessed March 19, 2004).

The IBU is the association of the national federations in the world and other organizations representing and interested in the sport of biathlon. This sport in its basic format combines free-technique cross-country skiing and small-bore rifle marksmanship. Its variations include, however, Roller Ski Biathlon, Cross-Running Biathlon, Mountain Bike Biathlon, and Archery Biathlon, among others. Biathlon is predominantly exercised as a winter sport, but summer biathlon is becoming more and more popular, especially in those parts of the world that do not have snow. Biathlon was admitted as an Olympic sport at the Olympic Winter Games in Squaw Valley in 1960.

763. **International Triathlon Union (ITU).** http://www.triathlon.org/ (accessed March 4, 2004).

The ITU is the international governing body for triathlon and multisport competition. Its Web site offers news, events, results, world rankings, championship details, profiles of elite men and women athletes, a brief history of triathlon, and much information about events and Olympic qualification. A comprehensive site.

764. **Union Internationale de Pentathlon Moderne (UIPM).** http://www .pentathlon.org (accessed March 4, 2004).

As the international governing body for the sport of modern pentathlon, the organization's Web site is very informative, with essays defining the pentathlon and its history at the Olympic Games. A newsletter is offered, information about the UIPM is provided, and links to national federation Web sites are given. Also included are official rules, a calendar of events, and world rankings.

765. **United States Modern Pentathlon Association.** http://usmpa.home .texas.net/ (accessed March 24, 2004).

This is the site of the national governing body for modern pentathlon competition. The Web site contains news, events, results, and more.

766. **United States Orienteering Federation (USOF).** http://www.us .orienteering.org (accessed December 7, 2004).

As the national governing body for orienteering in the United States, the USOF maintains an informative and well-organized Web site. It offers a directory of orienteering clubs in the United States, schedules for national and regional events, results of championships, education, club resources, equipment sources, and more.

767. **USA Triathlon.** http://www.usatriathlon.org (accessed March 27, 2004).

USA Triathlon is the national governing body for triathlon, duathlon, aquathlon, and winter triathlon activities. Their Web site contains news, rankings, events information, rules, and much more.

Gymnastics

Instructional Sources

768. Cooper, Phyllis, and Milan Tmka. **Teaching Basic Gymnastics: A Coeducational Approach.** 3rd ed. New York: Maxwell Macmillan International, 1994. 307 pp. $38.25. ISBN 0-02-324701-0.

An organized guide to the methods of teaching and spotting for beginning and intermediate gymnastic skills, this work provides a good introduction with an emphasis on safety. It covers biomechanics, conditioning, and skills in tumbling, pommel horse, still rings, balance beam, parallel bars, horizontal and uneven parallel bars, and other activities, such as pyramids and modern rhythmic gymnastics. Illustrated with drawings. Includes a bibliography and an index.

769. Hacker, Patricia, and Eric Malmberg / James Nance. **Gymnastics Fun and Games.** Champaign, Ill.: Human Kinetics, 1996. 136 pp. $15.95. ISBN 0-88011-557-2.

Intended for the elementary or middle school teacher who wants to safely introduce gymnastics activities into the curriculum, this guide offers thirteen warm-up and stretching activities, twenty-nine skill-development activities, and nine conditioning and endurance activities that kids will enjoy. Contains nearly fifty illustrations, plus a "game finder" for quick reference to specific activities by name, number, location in the book, activity type, skill development, or suggested grade level and complexity.

770. Jackman, Joan, and Bob Currier. **Gymnastic Skills and Games.** London: A & C Black, 1992. 128 pp. $19.95. ISBN 0-7136-3572-X.

With practical ideas that teachers or students can use, this guide illustrates how children can learn coordination, strength, and balance by using a wide range of enjoyable exercises. Activities are illustrated with sequential line drawings. Offers information on safety, warm-up, and competition, as well as fitness, strength, and mobility. Also offers advanced activities, such as artistic and rhythmic gymnastics. Indexed.

771. Malmberg, Eric. **Kidnastics: A Child-Centered Approach to Teaching Gymnastics.** Champaign, Ill.: Human Kinetics, 2003. 175 pp. $22.00. ISBN 0-7360-3394-7.

In an easy three-step instructional approach, this source advocates teaching children how to practice single skills, add multiple skills together in a sequence, and perform them for an audience. It utilizes traditional equipment and nontraditional equipment that can be adapted to offer different practice environments. Offers illustrated skills in rolling, jumping, balancing, vaulting, and hanging and climbing environments. The source is well illustrated with many black-and-white photographs and drawings of children in action. Provides a bibliography and a set of task cards.

772. Mitchell, Debby, Barbara Davis, and Raim Lopez. **Teaching Fundamental Gymnastics Skills.** Champaign, Ill.: Human Kinetics, 2002. 297 pp. $29.00. ISBN 0-7360-0124-7.

Although this is primarily a guide for teachers or coaches, it offers much specialized reference material related to gymnastics and will be useful to parents and students also. This work describes and illustrates the starting positions and movements that form the basis for further gymnastics skills. Provides detailed information on floor exercise, balance beam, springboard and vault, and bars. Each chapter presents a movement chart that outlines the progression of skills that are detailed. Illustrated with sequential drawings that show the progression of movements. Encourages a positive teaching philosophy and includes safety information to help prevent injuries.

Web Sites

773. Federation Internationale de Gymnastique (FIG). http://www.fig -gymnastics.com (accessed March 4, 2004).

This Web site of the international governing body for gymnastics offers a directory of affiliated federations worldwide. The site also includes news, official rules books, a calendar of events, publications, and more. Each of the individual disciplines is treated separately, with detailed information, athlete biographies, photos, and results.

774. USA Gymnastics. http://www.usa-gymnastics.org (accessed March 26, 2004).

As the governing body for gymnastics competition, this group's Web site describes the women's and men's programs and provides a calendar of events, athletes profiles, rules, educational material, history, a glossary of terms, a guide to the sport of gymnastics, a summer camp directory, and much more.

Chapter 12

Cycling and Equestrian Sports

Whether for transportation, fitness, adventure, or competition, riding bicycles and horses enables us to cover a distance and complete a task faster and more efficiently than walking or running. The information sources listed in this chapter cover cycling and equestrian activities. Because the rider is completely dependent on the mode of transportation, a number of the sources provide in-depth information on the care and maintenance of the bicycle or the horse.

Cycling

Reference Sources

775. Ballantine, Richard, and Richard Grant. **Richards' Bicycle Repair Manual.** 1st American ed. New York: Dorling Kindersley, 1994. 96 pp. $9.95. ISBN 1-56458-484-4.

This volume is a follow-up to *Richards' Ultimate Bicycle Book* (1992). Its subtitle, "Everything You Need to Know to Keep Your Bicycle in Peak Condition," sums up the content. Nicely illustrated with high-quality color photographs.

776. Ballantine, Richard, and Richard Grant. **Ultimate Bicycle Book.** New York: Dorling Kindersley, 1998. 192 pp. $13.95. ISBN 0-7894-2252-2.

A very browsable volume, this guide to bicycles describes the evolution of the bicycle and all its variations for adventure riding on mountain trails, racing, touring, working, everyday commuting, and recreation. Provides excellent coverage of the parts of bicycles and how they fit together and of general maintenance. Illustrated with over 700 color photographs that bring the explanation to life. Indexed.

777. Barnett, John. **Barnett's Manual : Analysis and Procedures for Bicycle Mechanics.** 5th ed. Boulder, Colo.: VeloPress, 2003. 1032 pp. $124.95. ISBN 1-931382-29-8.

Considered to be the benchmark for professional bicycle-repair mechanics, this is an extensive technical manual in four volumes, with over 700 illustrations and over 1000 pages. It includes techniques of repair on the latest technological innovations in bicycle design and mechanics and suggests the best tool choices for any type of work. The titles of the individual volumes are as follows: Vol. 1, *Introduction, Frames, Forks and Bearings*; vol. 2, *Wheels, Tires, and Drivetrain*; vol. 3, *Handlebars, Seats, Shift Systems, Brakes*; vol. 4, *Suspension and Appendix*.

778. Cuthbertson, Tom. **Anybody's Bike Book: A Comprehensive Manual of Bike Repairs.** Rev. ed. Berkeley, Calif.: Ten Speed Press, 1998. 228 pp. $14.95. ISBN 0-89815-996-2.

Intended for both the novice and the experienced cyclist, and anyone in between, this classic manual describes how to fix anything on a bicycle. Written in a casual, easy-to-understand style, it covers the information needed to buy a bike, keep it in good repair, and handle emergencies that occur while riding. Illustrated with good black-and-white drawings, the chapters cover the various parts of systems of a bike: brakes, handlebars, seat, wheels and tires, the chain, and so forth. Every point is categorized by the type of bike it applies to: cruiser, mountain bike, or road bike. Indexed.

779. **The Cyclists' Yellow Pages: The Directory of Bicycle Trip Planning, Maps and More.** 23rd (2002) ed. Missoula, Mont.: Adventure Cycling Association, 2002. 152 pp. $11.95.

This yearly publication comes with membership in the Adventure Cycling Association, a nonprofit group for recreational cyclists; it can also be purchased separately. The organization has developed an extensive national network of bicycle touring routes; the directory shows a map of these routes and provides detailed listings by state of relevant maps, tours, organizations, publications, and other information that will help cyclists plan a successful tour. International listings are also included. Each listing provides contact information, usually including a Web site or e-mail address and a phone number, and describes the source of information. Also contains useful articles on topics such as best frame materials for touring, what to pack on a trip, and how to pack a bike for shipment. Includes a section with classified ads as well as further listings for organizations, clubs, and bike shops. Illustrated with black-and-white photographs of cyclists on tour.

780. Gregor, Robert J., and Francesco Conconi, eds. **Road Cycling.** Handbook of Sports Medicine and Science. Malden, Mass.: Blackwell Science, 2000. 132 pp. $33.95. ISBN 0-86542-912-X.

This series is published under the auspices of the International Olympic Committee Medical Commission. The volume on road cycling covers the epidemiology of injury in the sport; physiological and nutritional aspects; preventive medicine; and information on the biomechanics of road cycling. The articles in the handbook are intended for use by physicians, trainers, and coaches but would also be useful for athletes or for parents of children who are participating in athletics. Illustrated with diagrams, tables, and black-and-white photographs. Each chapter contains a list of references for further reading. Indexed. This series is most appropriate for college and university collections in sports medicine.

781. Henderson, Bob. **The Haynes Bicycle Book: The Haynes Repair Manual for Maintaining and Repairing Your Bike.** Newbury Park, Calif.: Haynes North America, 1995. 192 pp. $19.95. ISBN 1-56392-137-5.

Well illustrated with many color photographs, this in-depth guide to bicycle repair and maintenance provides step-by-step procedures applicable to all bicycles. Also covers adjustments necessary to ensure proper fit of a bicycle to one's body, troubleshooting, and cleaning, replacing, and adjusting every part of the bicycle. Includes a glossary, a source list, and an index.

782. Langley, Jim. *Bicycling Magazine*'s **Complete Guide to Bicycle Maintenance and Repair for Road and Mountain Bikes: Over 1000 Tips, Tricks, and Techniques to Maximize Performance, Minimize Repairs, and Save Money.** 4th ed. Emmaus, Pa.: Rodale Press, 1999. 351 pp. $18.95. ISBN 1-57954-009-0.

Well organized and clearly written, this bike repair manual is easy to use. After an introductory chapter on home bicycle repair, the remaining chapters are arranged by the part of the bike being discussed. Includes coverage of frames, suspension, wheels and tires, hubs, crank sets, freewheels and cassettes, chains, shift levers, front and rear derailleur, headsets, brakes, etc. Includes a glossary of terms, a list of resources, and an index. Well-illustrated with black-and-white photographs and drawings.

783. Leccese, Michael, and Arlene Plevin. **The Bicyclist's Sourcebook: The Ultimate Directory of Cycling Information.** Rockville, Md.: Woodbine House, 1991. 355 pp. $16.95. ISBN 0-933149-41-7.

A directory of information sources on cycling, this work covers a wide variety of topics. Includes chapters on traveling with a bicycle and a directory of airlines, buses, and trains, along with their policies on taking a bicycle on board; choosing accessories, accompanied by a directory of manufacturers; kids' and a directory of manufacturers; a wide range of books and other publications, videos and posters; clothes; events; food and nutrition; custom-built frames and bicycles; traditional bicycle and mountain-bike manufacturers; bicycle organizations and advocacy groups; racing; safety; tools; touring; how to get started; and the history of cycling. Each of these chapters offers directory information. Also provides a glossary, a corporation index, and a subject index.

784. **The Official Tour de France Centennial: 1903–2003.** New York: Weidenfeld & Nicolson, 2003. 359 pp. $53.50; $24.95 (pbk.). ISBN 0-297-84358-3; 1-84188-239 (pbk.).

This beautifully illustrated, large-sized volume is produced in collaboration with *L'Equipe*, the French sports daily, and it includes a foreword by Lance Armstrong. The historic and action-oriented photographs from the Tour de

France's own archives will not disappoint readers. The book begins with a brief history of the race, then follows with a year-by-year summary of each event. For each race year there are statistics detailing the winners of the event and the various stages, along with a tour map. The table of contents is organized by year and winner's name. Additional statistics, such as for the green jersey and the polka-dot jersey, are provided at the end.

785. Smith, John M. **Cycling the USA.** Osceola, Wisc.: Motorbooks International, 1997. 224 pp. $14.95. ISBN 0-933201-84-2.

A directory of over 200 bicycle tours in the United States, this guidebook is intended for anyone interested in planning a tour and offers a good planning section, with additional information for visitors to the United States. The tours are arranged by region and state, and the book contains at least one detailed route for each state. Included for each tour are the distance, suggested number of days for the trip, the difficulty level, type of tour, information on getting to the starting point, available accommodations, helpful addresses, a map of the route, description of the route, and other suggested routes. An appendix identifies bicycle touring companies. Illustrated with black-and-white photos and maps. Contains a bibliography of sources and an index.

Instructional Sources

786. Burke, Edmund R. **Serious Cycling.** 2nd ed. Champaign, Ill.: Human Kinetics, 2002. 288 pp. $19.95. ISBN 0-7360-4129-X.

By using advanced scientific evidence, the author incorporates cycling physiology, biomechanics, nutrition, and injury prevention into a program of advanced training. Has fourteen chapters that provide the details of a plan for exercise, diet, training, and racing. Illustrated with black-and-white photographs and graphs. Indexed.

787. Burke, Edmund R., and Ed Pavelka. **The Complete Book of Long-Distance Cycling: Build the Strength, Skills and Confidence to Ride as Far as You Want.** Emmaus, Pa.: Rodale, 2001. 288 pp. $19.95. ISBN 1-57954-199-2.

No matter how far the journey, this comprehensive guide to long-distance cycling suggests more techniques and strategies to make the trip easier. Provides step-by-step training programs for three different distances with expert advice the whole way. Also includes information on fitness, nutrition, bicycle handling, equipment, and on dealing with a host of health issues that can occur during a long ride. Illustrated with black-and-white photographs and diagrams. Contains a glossary and an index.

788. Doughty, Simon. **The Long Distance Cyclists' Handbook.** Guilford, Conn.: The Lyons Press, 2001. 216 pp. $16.95. ISBN 1-58574-526-X.

This cycling handbook contains information on training, technique, and the logistics of planning a long trip, such as equipment and nutrition. Provides an overview of several specific long-distance cycling events. Illustrated with black-

and-white photos and diagrams. Includes a glossary of terms, lists of contact information for manufacturers and associations, a brief list of sources for additional reading, and an index.

789. Friel, Joe. **The Cyclist's Training Bible.** 3rd ed. Boulder, Colo.: Velo-Press, 2003. 296 pp. $22.95. ISBN 1-931382-21-2.

An excellent self-training source for cyclists, this guide presents a training program based on exercise science concepts. Regardless of gender, age, or racing experience, the program can be tailored to individual needs. Topics include periodization and planning, assessment of strength and fitness levels, maintaining a training diary, nutrition, supplements, stretching, and injury. Illustrated with charts, tables, and black-and-white photos. Appendices contain training plan worksheets, a maximum weight chart, weekly training journal, and glossary of terms. Indexed.

790. Lovett, Richard A. **The Essential Touring Cyclist: The Complete Guide for the Bicycle Traveler.** 2nd ed. Camden, Maine: Ragged Mountain Press, 2001. 160 pp. (Essential Series). $14.95. ISBN 0-07-136019-0.

For traveling via bicycle, this guide offers practical information that can be put to immediate use. It covers the selection of equipment for the bike and rider, basic riding skills, training for a tour, organized tours, loaded tours, and the challenges of riding in a variety of different environmental conditions. An appendix briefly describes sixty-five recommended tours and provides contact information. Illustrated with black-and-white photographs. Indexed.

791. Nasr, Kameel. **Bicycle Touring International: The Complete Book on Adventure Cycling.** Mill Valley, Calif.: Bicycle Books, 1992. 287 pp. $18.95. ISBN 0-933201-53-2.

A guide to international travel and touring by bicycle, this source provides information on the touring experience, choosing a bicycle, clothing and equipment for the trip, and extensive information on planning and preparation for an international trip. It also provides a directory of information specific to regions and countries of the world, first offering information on the general region, borders, climate, money, and bicycles, then providing further details on the specific countries in the region. The author provides good advice on what to expect in each area when traveling by bike. Illustrated with photographs. Appendices include an equipment packing list, prevailing wind patterns and weather tables, useful addresses, a bibliography and an index.

792. Pavelka, Ed. *Bicycling Magazine's* **Cycling for Health and Fitness: Use Your Machine to Get Strong, Lose Weight, and Feel Great.** Rev. & updated ed. Emmaus, Pa.: Rodale, 2000. 122 pp. $9.95. ISBN 1-57954-228-X.

In this brief fitness and training manual, basic elements are covered, such as choosing a bicycle, adjusting it to fit, conditioning with specific exercise, and eating well. It utilizes an easy-to-read question-and-answer and outline format to present the information. Illustrated with black-and-white photos. Contains a glossary and an index.

793. Pavelka, Ed, ed. *Bicycling Magazine*'s **Mountain Biking Skills: Tactics, Tips and Techniques to Master Any Terrain.** Emmaus, Pa.: Rodale, 2000. 117 pp. $9.95. ISBN 1-57954-250-6.

An informative guide for the beginner or the experienced mountain-bike rider, this source offers clear explanation of basic skills and many intermediate techniques. However, with chapter titles like "The Hour of Power" and "Get Over It!" it is difficult to discern the content. Thus, the index is more useful than the table of contents for finding information. The book includes random tips in sections called "Trail Mix" and "Ask Uncle Knobby." Provides a glossary of terms and an index.

794. Sloane, Eugene A. **Sloane's Complete Book of Bicycling.** 25th Anniversary ed. New York: Fireside / Simon & Schuster, 1995. 429 pp. $16.00. ISBN 0-671-87075-0.

This comprehensive manual provides detailed coverage of equipment, technology, and maintenance of all the parts of a bicycle, from the brakes to the saddle to the wheels. It provides practical information on choosing a bicycle, safety, typical bike accessories, the health benefits of cycling, and bike racing. Provides a glossary of terms, a bibliography, and an index. Illustrated with black-and-white photographs and drawings.

795. United States Olympic Committee. **A Basic Guide to Cycling.** An Official United States Olympic Committee Sports Series. Glendale, Calif.: Griffin Publishing, 1997. 117 pp. $7.95. ISBN 1-882180-51-8.

This guide provides basic information intended to help the novice user get started with the sport. Covers history, fundamentals of the sport, and information on the Olympics and other competitions, equipment, safety, and nutrition and training. Illustrated with drawings and black-and-white photographs. Includes a glossary and contact information for a number of cycling associations.

796. van der Plas, Rob. **Roadside Bicycle Repair: The Simple Guide to Fixing Your Road or Mountain Bike.** 3rd ed. San Francisco, Calif.: Bicycle Books, 1995. 96 pp. $7.95. ISBN 0-933201-67-2.

This small but very useful book provides step-by-step instructions for the most common bicycle repairs. Briefly describes types and parts of bicycles, as well as tools and useful spare parts to have on hand. This source covers preventive maintenance, then is arranged by type of repair needed (wheel, gearing, drive train, brake, steering, saddle, suspension, accessory). Clearly illustrated with diagrams and color photographs. Indexed.

Web Sites

797. **Adventure Cycling Association.** http://www.adventurecycling.org/ (accessed December 7, 2004).

The mission of this organization is "to inspire people of all ages to travel by bicycle." Accordingly, its Web site provides a great deal of relevant information to assist its more than 40,000 members with this goal. Travel routes, maps, tour information, and educational materials are joined with inspirational essays, an online store, a how-to department, portrait gallery, and discussion forums to inform, educate, and entertain users. The organization publishes *Adventure Cyclist* magazine; the Web site contains a developing online version of the *Cyclist's Yellow Pages*.

798. **International Cycling Union / Union Cycliste Internationale (UCI).** http://www.uci.ch (accessed March 4, 2004).

The mission of this international governing body is to promote and support all aspects of cycling, not just world cycling competition but also cycling as a healthy form of recreation and an efficient means of transportation. Its site provides a directory of national federations, a chronology of the organization, information on all the individual disciplines (road, track, cyclo-cross, bmx, etc.) with rules and regulations for each, along with news, press releases, a calendar of events, results and rankings, publications, archives, and links to other information. It even includes maps of race courses for the 2004 Olympic games. A very comprehensive site.

799. **United States Cycling Federation.** http://www.usacycling.org (accessed March 26, 2004).

As the national governing body for cycling, USA Cycling provides great information on its Web site about different types of cycling competition, championships, and other events, rankings, results, clubs and teams, and much more.

Equestrian Sports

Reference Sources

800. Belknap, Maria Ann. **Horsewords: The Equine Dictionary; the Ultimate Reference Book.** 2nd ed. North Pomfret, Vt.: Trafalgar Square Publishing, 2004. 581 pp. $24.95. ISBN 1-57076-274-0.

This comprehensive dictionary of terms and phrases covers all aspects of the horse and equestrianism, from abasia and Abats le Sultan to zebra and zigzag half pass. It concisely explains the meanings of thousands of unique horse-related words, both currently used terms and some that are quite antiquated, and includes many terms used almost exclusively by those in the veterinary world. This dictionary is useful as a current reference and as a beginning source for more in-depth research. Appropriate for both public and academic library collections.

801. Bryant, Jennifer O. **Olympic Equestrian: The Sports and the Stories from Stockholm to Sydney.** Lexington, Ky.: The Blood-Horse, 2000. 270 pp. $29.95. ISBN 1-58150-044-0.

The history of Olympic equestrian events is laid out in this informative book, which shows important developments over the years. Provides detailed description of three-day eventing, show jumping, and dressage, including official Olympic results, from the games in Stockholm in 1912 to Atlanta in 1996. Another chapter is devoted to the prospects at Sydney in 2000. Much of the behind-the-scenes preparation for Olympic competition is covered also, documenting the extreme dedication exhibited by the entire equestrian team in reaching their goals. Illustrated with beautiful color photographs. Indexed by people, horses, Olympic Games, sports and related topics, and organizations.

802. Duke, Jacqueline. **Thoroughbred Champions: Top 100 Racehorses of the 20th Century.** Lexington, Ky.: Eclipse Press / The Blood-Horse, 1999. 256 pp. $24.95. ISBN 1-58150-024-6.

This unique work contains the stories of the top 100 equine athletes, the thoroughbred horses, crafted by writers of the *Blood Horse*, thoroughbred horse racing's weekly magazine. The ranked list of 100 is chosen by a panel of experts, and each entry includes vivid detail about the horse's training and development during its years of racing, the horse's career accomplishments, and information about the horse's riders, trainers, and owners. The top 20 are treated first, with in-depth profiles, and the remaining 80 are covered in somewhat less detail. Illustrated with historic photographs.

803. Edwards, Elwyn Hartley. **The New Encyclopedia of the Horse.** Expanded and updated American ed. New York: Dorling Kindersley, 2000. 464 pp. $40.00. ISBN 0-7894-7181-7.

This encyclopedia offers comprehensive coverage of all aspects of the horse, including use and influence of the horse throughout history, extensive information on the history, physical characteristics, and temperament of various breeds, and horse management and equipment. One significant chapter, "The Sporting Horse," includes the history of racing and of other equestrian events, such as jumping, endurance riding, polo, rodeo, hunting, and Olympic competition. Beautifully illustrated with color photographs and maps throughout. Includes a glossary and an index.

804. Edwards, Elwyn Hartley. **The New Rider's Horse Encyclopedia.** 1st American ed. Irvington: Hydra Publishing, 2003. 256 pp. $29.95. ISBN 1-59258-001-7.

Quite similar to the author's other encyclopedic works on the horse, *The New Encyclopedia of the Horse*, this beautiful book is an excellent reference and a practical owner's manual. It covers the history of the horse in its various roles, provides descriptions and illustrations of all the major breeds of horses, and includes great information on owning a horse and using proper tack and equipment. One section details the sporting horse, describing competition ranging from steeplechasing and dressage to polo, rodeo, and Asian Games on horseback. Includes a ten-phase course of lessons that teach the fundamentals of riding, such as mounting and dismounting for the first time to jumping and riding cross-country. Illustrated with over 500 color photographs. It also includes a comprehensive glossary and an index.

805. Ennor, George, and Bill Mooney. **The World Encyclopedia of Horse Racing: An Illustrated Guide to Flat Racing and Steeplechasing.** London: Carlton, 2001. 224 pp. $45.00. ISBN 1-84222-244-9.

Contains international coverage of the world of horse racing and provides an overview of the early history of the sport. Includes over 200 color and black-and-white photographs. The major races are described, and for each year through 2000, the horse, jockey, and trainer are listed. Includes profiles of legendary horses, jockeys, and other greats of the game, such as owners and breeders. Contains chapters on gambling, scandals, and trivia, as well as a chronology of major events in horse racing from the year 1511 to 2001. Indexed.

806. Harris, Susan E., and Ruth Ring Harvie. **The United States Pony Club Manual of Horsemanship: Advanced Horsemanship, B/HA/A Levels.** Howell Equestrian Library. New York: Howell Book House / Hungry Minds, 1996. 477 pp. $24.99. ISBN 0-87605-981-7.

This illustrated manual builds on the fundamentals that were taught at the prior two levels, giving the intermediate rider the opportunity to advance his or her skills and utilize an advanced, classical technique. It also is intended for instructors who are looking for a comprehensive and organized presentation of material for their students. Includes information on stable management, competitive riding and schooling, and various other aspects of advanced horsemanship. An appendix contains the USPC Standards of Proficiency for rating at levels B, HA, and A. Indexed. USPC manuals are also available for levels D and C.

807. Harris, Susan E., and Ruth Ring Harvie. **The United States Pony Club Manual of Horsemanship: Basics for Beginners, D Level.** Howell Equestrian Library. New York: Hungry Minds, 1994. 305 pp. $19.99. ISBN 0-87605-952-3.

This illustrated official manual is intended as a first source for young people who are learning to ride, especially those who are members of the U.S. Pony Clubs, Inc., and want to meet the USPC's Standards of Proficiency. The text teaches how to become a careful rider and how to understand a horse or pony. Includes information on riding in a ring and in the open, beginning to jump, and horse care, handling, and safety. Also includes important information for parents. Indexed. USPC manuals are also available for levels C, B, HA, and A.

808. Harris, Susan E., and Ruth Ring Harvie. **The United States Pony Club Manual of Horsemanship: Intermediate Horsemanship, C Level.** Howell Equestrian Library. New York: Howell Book House / John Wiley, 1995. 361 pp. $19.99. ISBN 0-87605-977-9.

This illustrated manual is the official instruction guide for those students who have completed the beginning level and are ready to move on in their training to the intermediate level. It builds on material introduced in the D-level manual. Focus is on skills needed to ride independently and with correct form, and on the rider's taking on more responsibility for care and handling of the horse or pony. Appendices contain test requirements for a level-C rating, and sources for further reading. Indexed. USPC manuals are also available for levels D, B, HA, and A.

809. Kidd, Jane. **The International Encyclopedia of Horses and Ponies.** Howell Equestrian Library. New York: Howell Book House / John Wiley, 1995. 205 pp. $29.95. ISBN 0-87605-999-X.

This comprehensive encyclopedia identifies and describes over 100 breeds of horses. It traces the evolution of the horse over time and also describes their physical characteristics and behavior. Beautifully illustrated with over 450 color photographs.

810. Laffaye, Horace A. **The Polo Encyclopedia.** Jefferson, N.C.: McFarland, 2004. 413 pp. $49.95. ISBN 0-7864-1724-2.

This reference work consolidates coverage of the history and tradition of polo in one source, packing 10,000 alphabetically arranged entries into a single volume. The entries are concise, ranging in length from one sentence to several paragraphs, and cover the artists, authors, breeders, players, personalities, clubs, ponies, tournaments, rules, history and many other topics that together form the world of polo. Illustrated with over 100 small photographs and drawings.

811. Shambach, Barbara Wallace. **Equestrian Excellence: The Stories of Our Olympic Equestrian Medal Winners from Stockholm 1912 thru Atlanta 1996.** Boonsboro, Md.: Half Halt Press, 1996. 173 pp. $44.95. ISBN 0-939481-47-2.

Rich with history, this work chronicles the United States' participation in Olympic equestrian events. The work begins with a thorough explanation of the Olympic equestrian disciplines: dressage, the three-day event, and show jumping. What follows is a series of engaging essays that feature the horses and riders that earned medals between 1912 and 1996. The entries are arranged in order of the first year they won a medal and are listed in this way in the table of contents. There is also an alphabetical list of winners by name, as well as a useful list of medals won by U.S. riders, arranged by Olympiad.

Instructional Sources

812. Budd, Jackie. **A to Z of Horse Behavior and Training.** New York: John Wiley / Howell Book House, 2000. 288 pp. $24.95. ISBN 0-7645-6111-1.

Intended for both the novice and the accomplished rider, this work provides a comprehensive training program for horse and rider. Approaching training from the horse's point of view, it offers in-depth information on understanding the horse's behavior during the training process. Contains color illustrations and includes an alphabetical list of terms, methods, and definitions. Indexed.

813. Drummond, Jocelyn. **The Essentials of Horsemanship: Training, Riding, Care and Management.** Howell Equestrian Library. New York: John Wiley, 1998. 112 pp. $19.95. ISBN 0-87605-669-9.

A beginner's treat and also a good reference for seasoned riders, this guide to horsemanship contains all the details involved in caring for a horse: common problems, first aid, nutrition, fitness, clipping, shoeing, and saddlery. It also describes the steps involved with buying a horse, training it, riding on a course or cross-country, jumping, and competing. Beautifully illustrated with color photographs. Contains a glossary and an index.

814. Hastie, Stewart, and Johanna Sharples. **Horselopaedia: A Complete Guide to Horse Care.** Howell Equestrian Library. New York: Howell Book House, 1999. 256 pp. $14.95. ISBN 1-58245-063-3.

Primarily concerned with horse care and health, this handy reference book assists the reader in becoming more knowledgeable about keeping a horse healthy. Includes detailed information on choosing and buying a horse, stable management, health and sickness of the horse, tack and equipment, and training and competing.

815. Haw, Sarah. **The New Book of the Horse.** Howell Equestrian Library. New York: Howell Book House / Macmillan, 1993. 208 pp. $25.50. ISBN 0-87605-974-4.

This comprehensive reference is organized by topic into three sections: the horse, the horse and rider, and competitive riding. The first section provides information on breeding, rearing, and owning a horse, including stabling, maintaining a daily routine, tack and clothing for the horse, and the horse's health. The second section contains a complete illustrated range of riding techniques and the basics of leisure riding. The third details the specialized techniques of competitive riding: show-jumping, dressage, and eventing. This well-organized book is also beautifully illustrated with over 500 color photographs of horses and their riders in a variety of situations. Contains a good glossary of terms and an index.

816. Kidd, Jane, consultant. **Competitive Riding.** Newton Abbot, Devon, U.K.: David & Charles, 2000. 208 pp. $20.00 (est.). ISBN 0-7153-1086-0.

This beautifully illustrated equestrian source focuses entirely on competitive riding. It includes diagrams of training courses, arenas, and competition courses, and chapters provide in-depth coverage of schooling and jumping; mounted games; dressage; eventing; western riding; and endurance riding. Complete preparation for each type of activity is discussed in detail, along with information on taking proper care of the fitness and training needs of the horse. Contains many step-by-step photographs that illustrate specific competitive technique. Indexed.

817. Price, Steven D. **The Whole Horse Catalog: The Complete Guide to Owning, Maintaining, and Enjoying Horses.** Rev. and updated ed. New York: Fireside / Simon & Schuster, 1998. 351 pp. $20.00. ISBN 0-684-83995-4.

Appropriate for the novice or the experienced equestrian, this comprehensive reference guide contains information on selecting a horse, stabling, stable management, horse health, tack, apparel, a variety of equestrian activities, and even where to spend holidays with your horse! Also provides a host of other sources of information, both in the individual chapters and in a general chapter at the end that covers organizations, magazines and Web sites. Contains hundreds of illustrations. Indexed in detail.

818. Snyder-Smith, Donna. **The All-Around Horse and Rider.** Howell Equestrian Library. New York: John Wiley, 2004. 304 pp. $29.99. ISBN 0-7645-4974-X.

Intended for amateur adult riders, this one-stop guide covers modern innovations in horse handling, body awareness, and training methods that increase the strength and endurance of both the horse and the rider. Describes a set of basic lessons and stresses realistic goal setting to achieve success. Includes information on different types of competition and sources of further information. Contains profiles of real-life horses and their riders. Indexed.

Web Sites

819. **Federation Equestre Internationale (FEI).** http://www.horsesport.org (accessed December 7, 2004).

The FEI's Web site includes the following description:

> the FEI is the international governing body of Equestrian sport recognized by the International Olympic Committee. It is the organization which establishes rules and regulations for the conduct of international equestrian events in the Jumping, Dressage, Eventing, Driving, Vaulting and Endurance Riding disciplines. This includes the supervision and maintenance of the health and welfare of the horses taking part as well as the respect of the principles of horsemanship. The FEI was founded in 1921 and is based in Lausanne, Switzerland since 1991. It today counts some 130 member countries.

The site contains rules, a full calendar, and a results database. Links are provided to member federations.

820. **National Museum of Racing and Hall of Fame.** http://www.racing museum.org/ (accessed March 24, 2004).

Located in Saratoga Springs, New York, across from the historic Saratoga Race Course, the museum contains an equine art collection, trophies, silks, and Thoroughbred racing memorabilia. Contained within the site is a virtual tour of the museum and detailed information about the Official National Thoroughbred Racing Hall of Fame, including lists of horses, jockeys, and trainers who have been inducted.

821. **United States Equestrian Federation, Inc. (USEF).** http://www.esef.org (accessed February 24, 2004).

The USEF is the National Governing Body of equestrian sport in the United States, and as such it regulates competition in the United States, provides leadership to equestrian sport, and prepares athletes and their horses for the International Olympic Games. The site includes the organization's bylaws, the 2004 USEF Rule Book in PDF format, FEI Rule Books, and other guidelines. This comprehensive site also contains information on training and competition and includes many links.

822. **United States Equestrian Team (USET).** http://www.uset.com (accessed February 21, 2004).

USET's Web site includes the following description:

> The United States Equestrian Team, Inc. (USET) is a non-profit organization which represents the United States in international equestrian sports. For the past five decades the USET has carried the responsibility for selecting, training, equipping, and financing teams of the highest possible standard to represent the United States in Pan American and Olympic Games, World Championships, and other international competitions.

This comprehensive site contains schedules for upcoming events and results of past events, as well as many links to other sites.

823. **United States Polo Association (USPA).** http://www.us-polo.org/ (accessed March 14, 2004).

This site includes the official rules of play, a directory of polo clubs, links to information about all kinds of tournaments, the history of polo and the USPA, the USPA Collegiate Handbook, and much more. Features an interactive polo experience and many links to other sites.

824. **United States Pony Clubs, Inc. (USPC).** http://www.ponyclub.org (accessed February 24, 2004).

This site, maintained by one of the major junior equestrian associations in the world, offers information to its members and those interested in learning to ride. The focus is on safety, teaching basic techniques, and sharing information about opportunities and events. The organization offers an online bookstore, many links to other organizations and sources of information, official USPC rule books in PDF format, and much more.

Chapter 13

Extreme Sports and Motor Sports

Faster, farther, higher, and more adventurous, the extreme sports go to the next level, offering a more exciting experience than ever. A selection of information sources is offered in this area and also in skate boarding, in-line skating, and in motor sports, specifically automobile racing and motorcycle racing.

Extreme Sports

Reference Sources

825. Goyer, Norm. **Air Sports: The Complete Guide to Aviation Adventure.** New York: McGraw-Hill, 2004. 242 pp. $24.95. ISBN 0-07-141051-1.

This guide to flight-related sports provides the details of a number of activities, including soaring, sky diving, paragliding, hang gliding, powered parachuting, ballooning, ultralight piloting, gyrocopter flying, and remote-controlled airplane flying. Each entry includes training requirements, time and cost estimates, and safety precautions. Each chapter includes many sources of other information. Well illustrated with black-and-white photographs. Indexed.

826. Malafronte, Victor A., and F. Davis Johnson. **The Complete Book of Frisbee: The History of the Sport and the First Official Price Guide.** Alameda, Calif.: American Trends, 1998. 287 pp. $19.95. ISBN 0-9663855-2-7.

Though not really an extreme sport, Frisbee definitely has a place in the world of sport, so it is included here. This source, which is illustrated with color photographs, provides a history of the design and production of the Frisbee and lists Frisbee games with the details of their development. It also has a chapter on collecting the historical Frisbee Pie Pan. Contains a comprehensive guide to all types of collectible Frisbees, along with prices, and a listing of major collectors worldwide. Appendices contain a list of major Frisbee events, a glossary of terms, resources, and a bibliography. Indexed.

827. McMenamin, Paul. **Ultimate Adventure: National Geographic Ultimate Adventure Sourcebook.** Washington, D.C.: National Geographic Society, 2000. 384 pp. $35.00. ISBN 0-7922-7591-8.

Organized alphabetically by activity, this book contains great information on twenty-five types of adventure activities. From alpine mountaineering to horseback riding to sailing to wind surfing, each travel adventure is described in detail, with recommended outfitters and guides, directions and maps to the locations, equipment needed, and more. Each chapter begins with introductory material and ends with a section on further resources, such as travel tips, contact information for training, online sources, and lists of books, periodicals, and videos. Also contains a chapter on travel planning and a general directory of outfitters. Indexed.

828. Tomlinson, Joe. **The Ultimate Encyclopedia of Extreme Sports.** Reprinted ed. London: Carlton Books Ltd., 1999. 192 pp. $19.95. ISBN 1-85868-718-7.

This colorfully illustrated encyclopedia provides brief coverage of many extreme sports. Arranged by type of sport environment (air, land, water), this guide gives a good introduction and many critical facts about the sports, including many definitions of terms. Coverage includes everything from speed sailing to tightrope walking to barefoot water skiing. Indexed.

829. Youngblut, Shelley, editorial director. **Way Inside ESPN's X Games.** New York: Hyperion / ESPN Books, 1998. 255 pp. $18.95. ISBN 0-7868-8292-1.

This unique source contains brief descriptions of aggressive in-line skating, sky surfing, skateboarding, downhill in-line skating, street luge, barefoot jumping, bicycle stunt, sport climbing, wakeboarding, and big-air snowboarding. The informally written entries each feature a history of the sport, profiles of persons involved, descriptions of equipment, a glossary of terms specific to the activity, and explanations of tricks and judging. An appendix provides X Games results for 1995 to 1997. Well illustrated with many color photographs of the competitors in action and just hanging out.

Instructional Sources

830. Jay, Jackson. **Skateboarding Basics.** New Action Sports. Mankato, Minn.: Capstone Press, 1996. 48 pp. $21.26. ISBN 1-56065-374-4.

This basic guide to the sport of skateboarding describes the history of the sport, as well as the equipment used and the techniques employed to stay safe and advance in the sport. Classed as juvenile literature, it will be most appropriate for collections that serve younger readers. Illustrated with color photographs. It contains a glossary of terms and a brief list of other books to read and associations to consult for more information. Indexed.

831. Murdico, Suzanne J. **Street Luge and Dirtboarding.** The World of Skateboarding. New York: Rosen Publishing Group, 2003. 48 pp. $26.50. ISBN 0-8239-3647-3.

This brief book provides a guide to two variations on the skateboard: street luge and dirt boarding. Includes history of the sports, the basics of equipment, and racing strategy. Discusses major competitions, such as the X Games and the Gravity Games, and profiles several colorful personalities who are stars in these sports. Illustrated with color photographs. Contains a glossary of terms, a list of sources for more information and books for further reading, and a bibliography. Indexed.

832. Poynter, Dan, and Mike Turoff. **Parachuting: The Skydiver's Handbook.** 9th ed. Santa Barbara, Calif.: Para Publishing, 2004. 402 pp. $19.95. ISBN 1-56860-087-9.

This classic guide to parachuting provides a brief history of the sport and describes in detail the progression of events leading to opening the parachute. Appropriate for the beginner or the advanced jumper. Also discusses emergencies and specialized jumps. Includes information on equipment and safety. Illustrated with black-and-white photographs and drawings. Contains an extensive list of other resources, a very comprehensive glossary of terms, and an index.

832a. Werner, Doug. **In-Line Skater's Start-Up: A Beginner's Guide to In-Line Skating and Roller Hockey.** San Diego, Calif.: Tracks Publishing, 1995. 159 pp. $14.98. ISBN 1-884654-04-5.

This guide to in-line skating covers the basic techniques in an easy-to-understand style. It recommends appropriate gear, tips for safety, and instructions on stopping, turning, and all the other tricky transition moves required in in-line skating. The second part of the book provides detailed information on the sport of roller hockey, including the techniques of play. Includes a glossary of terms, a list of resources, and a bibliography. Illustrated with black-and-white photographs. Indexed.

Web Sites

833. **EXPN.com.** http://expn.go.com/ (accessed March 11, 2004).

This is the online version of ESPN's action sports network: the site covers skateboarding, snowboarding, surfing, in-line skating, BMX, MotoX, and X Games. Includes photos, events, tricks and tips, athlete columns, biographies, videos, and contests. News stories are separated by sport. A comprehensive site.

833a. **International Inline Skating Association.** http://www.iisa.org (accessed February 10, 2004).

The IISA is a non-profit trade association that represents regular in-line skaters. The IISA conducts educational and safety programs in in-line skating and promotes the benefits and pleasures of in-line skating for sport, recreation, fitness, and vitality. The site contatins an events calendar, club directory, and information on equipment, instruction and links to other sources.

834. **United States Parachuting Association (USPA).** http://www.uspa.org (accessed March 5, 2004).

The USPA maintains an informative Web site, making available a history of skydiving and details about how to start, choosing a school, various techniques, equipment, safety, and regulation. The site contains news, an events calendar, much information on various levels of competition, world records and awards, and links to other sites. Publications are also available to download from the site, such as the *Skydiver's Competition Manual* and the 2004 edition of *Skydiver's Information Manual.*

835. **World Flying Disc Federation.** http://www.wfdf.org/ (accessed March 30, 2004).

This site contains everything you ever wanted to know about Frisbee, disc golf, ultimate, and related topics. Events, rules, links, world records, and much more.

Motor Sports

Reference Sources

836.   Bennett, Jim. **The Complete Motorcycle Book: A Consumer's Guide.** 2nd ed. New York: Facts On File, 1999. 272 pp. $30.75. ISBN 0-8160-3853-8.

In this consumer's guide to buying, riding, and caring for motorcycles, the author provides essential information and advice on buying, riding, and caring for motorcycles. It includes evaluative reviews of many top brands and comparison between different types of motorcycles. In-depth information on mechanics is included, as is advice on taking appropriate safety measures. Illustrated with over 100 black-and-white photographs. Contains a comprehensive glossary and an index.

837. Burt, William M. **Stock Car Race Fan's Reference Guide: Understanding NASCAR.** Osceola, Wisc.: MBI Publishing, 1999. 192 pp. $19.95. ISBN 0-7603-0509-9.

This informative source contains a fifty-year history of NASCAR, from its beginnings through 1998. It offers coverage of the racers, teams, races, career records, season records, statistics, and profiles of the tracks. A well-illustrated volume, it contains 50 black-and-white photographs and over 250 color photographs.

838.   Coble, Don, and Lee Buchanan. **Insider's Guide to the NASCAR Tracks: The Unofficial, Opinionated, Fan's Guide to the Nextel Cup Circuit.** Guilford, Conn.: Insider's Guide, 2004. 271 pp. $12.95. ISBN 0-7627-2723-3.

In this travel guidebook to stock-car racing, tracks are reviewed one-by-one, on the basis of statistics, classifications, and the track's personality and special features, and what type of racing action to expect, where to sit, and what to watch for are also noted. For the NASCAR novice and experienced fans alike, it includes options for dining, lodging, camping, directions to tracks, and listings of nearby attractions. Full of insider information and anecdotes. Illustrated with maps.

839. Fleischman, Bill, and Al Pearce. **The Unauthorized NASCAR Fan Guide.** 2004 ed. Farmington Hills, Mich.: Visible Ink, 2004. 600 pp. $14.95. ISBN 1-57859-161-9.

This guide to the NASCAR world contains the year's race results, a driver register, team directory, and the top drivers of all time. It also includes information on the history of NASCAR, as well as year-by-year summaries of the races and race results from 1949 to 2003. Offers instructions on how to watch a NASCAR race and provides a track directory and an all-time list of car numbers and drivers. Illustrated with 200 photos and illustrations.

840. Golenbock, Peter, and Greg Fielden, eds. **The Stock Car Racing Encyclopedia.** New York: Macmillan, 1997. 984 pp. $39.95. ISBN 0-02-860859-3.

Beginning with a relatively brief but very informative history of stock-car racing, this substantial reference work goes on to document drivers' and owners' career and single-season records, and winners by car manufacturer. Next, a year-by-year statistical summary is presented, listing each driver, the starts, poles, finish, laps, laps and races led, Winston Cup points awarded, and cash awarded. Also includes the number of laps completed and led, miles led and driven, and races led during the year. The next section covers the drivers' individual statistics, followed by the owners' statistics. Illustrated with a high-quality set of black-and-white photographs. A directory of the tracks is provided, arranged alphabetically by state, followed by an index of the tracks. Finally, a chronological listing of races with selected race histories is included.

841. Golenbock, Peter, and Greg Fielden, eds. **NASCAR Encyclopedia.** St. Paul, Minn.: MBI, 2003. 984 pp. $39.95. ISBN 0-7603-1571-X.

Its cover says that this book is "the complete record of America's most popular sport." This massive volume is an update of the editors' comprehensive earlier work. Contains all the statistics on drivers, owners, cars, races, and tracks: a complete record of NASCAR participation in one volume. Illustrated with forty color and sixty black-and-white photographs.

842. McCarter, Mark. **The Racetracks Book: A Journey around the Tracks Where Stock Cars Roar.** St. Louis, Mo.: Sporting News Books, 2003. 229 pp. $34.95. ISBN 0-89204-704-6.

This colorful and well-illustrated guide provides a tour of twenty-six of the most prominent stock-car racetracks in the United States. Illustrated with hundreds of color photographs, including panoramic shots of each track. Historic events are noted, contributing to the overall history that is provided for each track.

843. **NASCAR Record and Fact Book.** 2004 ed. St. Louis, Mo.: Sporting News Publishing, 2004. 408 pp. $16.95.

Intended as an annual guide for racing fans, this encyclopedia is the officially licensed NASCAR source. It covers every NASCAR season from 1948 to the present, and looks ahead to the next season. It provides driver-by-driver biographies and career statistics; complete team information, including crew chief and owner statistics; detailed 2003 season results; historical listings of each race, with winners and key statistics clearly outlined; and season-by-season breakdowns for the NASCAR Busch Series and NASCAR Craftsman Truck Series. Also contains the 2004 race schedules.

844. Poole, David, Woody Cain, and Jason Mitchell. **Legends of NASCAR: Defying Time . . . Defining Greatness.** Chicago: Triumph Books, 2003. 144 pp. $17.95. ISBN 1-57243-557-7.

In this biographical source, six of the greatest NASCAR drivers—on Bill Elliott, Dale Jarrett, Terry Labonte, Mark Martin, Ricky Rudd, and Rusty Wallace—are profiled in detail.

845. Wilson, Hugo. **The Ultimate Motorcycle Book.** 1st American ed. New York: Dorling Kindersley, 1993. 192 pp. $30.00. ISBN 1-56458-303-1.

This beautifully illustrated volume provides a guide to over 200 U.S. and imported motorcycles and presents a history of motorcycles, including their use in World War II and for racing, touring, motocross, and customizing. Illustrated with color photographs. Intended for a teen audience, this source is best for high school and public libraries.

Web Sites

846. **Federation Internationale de l'Automobile.** http://www.fia.com/ (accessed December 7, 2004).

Recognized by the International Olympic Committee as the governing body for all world motor sports, including Formula One. The site provides the FIA statutes, its organizational structure, international sporting calendars, a list of affiliated members worldwide arranged alphabetically by country, and links to other sites, including the Gran Prix encyclopedia online.

847. **Motorsports Hall of Fame of America.** http://www.mshf.com/ (accessed January 9, 2004).

Hall of fame inductees, "Heroes of Horsepower," since 1989 are listed for air racing, drag racing, motorcycles, open wheel, power boats, sports cars, and stack cars, plus an at-large and historic inductee for each year. The museum itself is located in Novi, Michigan, and maintains a collection of artifacts, including vehicles, and photographs. The Web site contains a great deal of news and information and offers a discussion forum.

847a. **International Motorsports Hall of Fame and Museum.** http://www.motorsportshalloffame.com (accessed April 1, 2004).

This comprehensive site offers much information for visitors traveling to the site and to online visitors. Provides a virtual tour, hall of fame database with biographical information and photos of the members, a library, the museum, news, a photo gallery, and much more.

Mountaineering, Fishing, Camping, and Hiking

The sources in this chapter provide information on the type of outdoor activities that a great many people engage in simply for a weekend's recreation. However, there are competitive aspects of these sporting activities, especially mountaineering and fishing. This chapter lists information sources on mountaineering and rock climbing, fishing, camping, and hiking.

Mountaineering

Reference Sources

848. Child, Greg, comp. **Climbing: The Complete Reference to Rock, Ice, and Indoor Climbing.** New York: Facts On File, 1997. 264 pp. $19.95. ISBN 0-8160-3653-5.

With its over 1000 entries arranged alphabetically from A to Z, this encyclopedia describes the greatest mountain ranges and rock-climbing cliffs of the world. It also identifies techniques of climbing, types of equipment, and major figures in the world of mountain climbing. Appendices show major features of mountains and glaciers, provide a key to standard climbing symbols and abbreviations, and outline a comparison of international rating systems. Illustrated with over sixty black-and-white drawings and photographs. Contains a bibliography and an index.

849. Hattingh, Garth. **Climbing: The World's Best Sites.** New York: Rizzoli International, 1999. 160 pp. $50.00. ISBN 0-8478-2226-5.

This attractive volume offers seasoned advice on the techniques and equipment necessary to climb the world's tallest and most challenging peaks. Filled with descriptive detail and the personal accounts of noted climbers themselves, the reader is allowed a view that most will never see firsthand. Includes rock and ice climbing and sport climbing as well as hiking routes. Contains a chronology of important first ascents. Illustrated with topographic maps, diagrams, and many beautiful color photographs. Contains a bibliography, a glossary, and an index.

850. Jones, Chris. **Climbing in North America.** Seattle, Wash.: The Mountaineers, 1997. 365 pp. $24.95. ISBN 0-89886-481-X.

With lively details, this history of mountaineering in the United States and Canada covers from the earliest years through the 1970s, focusing both on the ranges and the people who climbed them. Considered a classic among mountaineers, this is a reprinted edition of the 1976 original that was published for the American Alpine Club by the University of California Press. References are included at the end of each chapter. Illustrated with black-and-white photographs.

851. Kelsey, Michael R. **Climber's and Hiker's Guide to the World's Mountains and Volcanos.** 4th ed. Provo, Utah: Kelsey Publishing, 2001. 1248 pp. $36.95. ISBN 0-944510-18-3.

This guide to the world's climbing destinations is arranged geographically, with separate chapters devoted to Europe; Africa; Asia; the Pacific; North America; Mexico, Central America, and the Caribbean; and South America. There is also a bibliography of other, more specific guidebooks for these geographic areas. The table of contents serves as an index to the nearly 450 entries. Each entry contains a map of the area on one page and a description of the major highlights on the facing page. Most entries also contain one black-and-white photograph of a typical sight in the area.

852. Salkeld, Audrey, ed. **World Mountaineering.** Boston: Bulfinch Press / Little, Brown, 1998. 304 pp. $50.00. ISBN 0-8212-2502-2.

A beautifully illustrated guide to fifty-two of the world's most famous mountain peaks, this oversized volume presents each peak with vivid description by an expert climber who is known to have specialist knowledge of the area. For each mountain, a locator map is given, as are an introduction to the area and its features, a detailed description of the topography, a historical time line of the mountain's climbing highlights, main climbing routes, route photographs with route lines numbered, other practical information, and an evaluation of prospects for future climbing. Includes technical grading information, a glossary, and an index.

Instructional Sources

853. Cinnamon, Jerry. **The Complete Climber's Handbook.** 2nd ed. Camden, Maine: Ragged Mountain Press, 2000. 314 pp. $22.95. ISBN 0-07-135755-6.

This handbook, which is illustrated with drawings and black-and-white photographs, provides detailed information on all aspects of climbing, from selecting proper equipment to staying protected in ice and snow. Includes a thorough explanation of movement, typical climbing locations and tools, and safe movement in extreme environmental conditions. Appendices contain additional information on first aid, fitness, lightning, and pulley-system basics. Contains great information for beginners as well as experts. Indexed.

854. Fyffe, Allen, and Iain Peter. **The Handbook of Climbing.** Rev. ed. London: Pelham Books, 1997. 390 pp. $34.95. ISBN 0-7207-2054-0.

Endorsed by the British Mountaineering Council, this comprehensive handbook describes the principles and techniques of climbing and the expert use of equipment to move about on rock, snow, and ice. Also includes information on training, psychological skills, navigation, and first aid. Illustrated with many drawings, as well as color and black-and-white photographs. Contains an extensive glossary and an index.

855. Graydon, Don, and Kurt Hanson. **Mountaineering: The Freedom of the Hills.** 6th ed. Seattle, Wash.: The Mountaineers Books, 1997. 528 pp. $35.00; $24.95 (pbk.). ISBN 0-89886-426-7; 0-89886-427-5 (pbk.).

This standard text on mountaineering provides complete coverage of the concepts, techniques, and challenges to be found in mountain climbing. New to this edition is a section of chapters on the mountain environment, including geology, weather, and the climber's impact. Illustrated with black-and-white photographs and drawings. Appendices cover rating systems and a list of supplementary references. Indexed.

856. Hattingh, Garth. **The Climber's Handbook.** Mechanicsburg, Pa.: Stackpole Books, 1998. 160 pp. $21.95. ISBN 0-8117-2706-8.

This handbook is beautifully illustrated with color photographs, drawings, and diagrams, providing immense motivation for the reader. Chapters detail the variety of environments encountered, as well as equipment and techniques used in this challenging sport. Appendices include descriptive information on expeditions, basic navigation, first aid and rescue, rock-climbing grading systems, and a list of international mountaineering associations with contact information. Contains a glossary, a bibliography, and an index.

857. Hill, Pete, and Stuart Johnston. **The Mountain Skills Training Handbook.** Newton Abbot, Devon, U.K.: David & Charles, 2000. 160 pp. $26.99. ISBN 0-7153-1091-7.

Recommended by the United Kingdom's Association of Mountaineering Instructors, this informative handbook is intended as a reference to be taken along and used when actively learning the techniques and working with equipment. Useful for teachers and for those who are teaching themselves. Illustrated with many color photographs, diagrams, and drawings. Indexed.

Web Site

858. **American Alpine Club.** http://www.americanalpineclub.org/ (accessed February 27, 2004).

This nonprofit organization is dedicated to "promoting climbing knowledge, conserving mountain environments and serving the American climbing community." Their Web site offers excellent information, including access to the online catalog for their library in Golden, Colorado; a newsletter; information on ranches and huts in various climbing locations; information on grants available for expeditions; full text of recent issues of *American Alpine News* and a catalog of AAC Press publications to order online; and detailed information about AAC's conservation projects.

Fishing

Reference Sources

859. Bailey, John. **The Complete Guide to Fishing: The Fish, the Tackle, and the Techniques.** Guilford, Conn.: Lyons Press, 2003. 160 pp. $19.95. ISBN 1-58574-782-3.

The front cover indicates that this book is "a fully illustrated manual detailing all aspects of fishing, for everyone from novice to expert." This guide to angling covers bait, lure, and fly fishing within the context of the natural environment and provides instruction on the techniques involved in each. Beautifully illustrated with 300 color photographs taken all over the world. Contains a glossary of knots and an index.

860. Bailey, John. **The New Encyclopedia of Fishing.** 1st American ed. New York: Dorling Kindersley, 2001. 288 pp. $40.00. ISBN 0-7894-8399-8.

The cover indicates that the book is "the complete guide to the fish, tackle and techniques of fresh and saltwater angling." This comprehensive fishing encyclopedia contains gorgeous color photographs, maps, and drawings that illustrate the detail of equipment, fish, and angling techniques. Appendices contain a glossary, a general subject index, and an additional index of scientific names of some 250 species of fish.

861. Griffin, Steve A. **The Fishing Sourcebook: Your One-Stop Resource for Everything to Feed Your Fishing Habit.** Old Saybrook, Conn.: Globe Pequot Press, 1996. 218 pp. $18.95. ISBN 1-56440-752-7.

This informative volume on fishing provides advice and direction on fishing methods, equipment, organizations, and sources for the latest fishing products and gadgets. Includes description of freshwater and seawater fish, an overview of tackle, baits, and techniques, and listings of state and provincial fishery agencies, clubs, videos, books, and supply houses.

862. McClane, Albert Jules. **McClane's New Standard Fishing Encyclopedia and International Angling Guide.** New York: Gramercy Books, 1998, 1974. 1156 pp. $75.00. ISBN 0-517-20336-7.

This source contains over 6000 entries, presented in alphabetical order. Some terms simply are defined, while other topics are treated in several pages.

Content includes methods of angling, types of fish, and geographic areas that should be of particular interest to anglers, equipment, and biographies of important persons in the world of angling. A very comprehensive encyclopedia, similar in content to *Ken Schultz's Fishing Encyclopedia*. Illustrated with color and black-and-white photographs and drawings.

863. Miles, Tony, Martin Ford, and Peter Gathercole. **The Practical Fishing Encyclopedia: A Comprehensive Guide to Coarse Fishing, Sea Angling and Game Fishing.** London: Lorenz Books / Anness Publishing, 1999. 256 pp. $40.00. ISBN 0-7548-0283-3.

This comprehensive encyclopedia is divided by topic into three sections: coarse fishing, sea angling, and game fishing. With references to the rivers Thames and Trent, this volume is definitely written from a U.K. perspective. Most of the notes on habitat and location of fish species refer to the United Kingdom, though some international locations are also included. Beautifully illustrated with color photographs and drawings that show everything from fish, bait, and tackle to proper angling attire and tying knots. Indexed.

864. Schultz, Ken. **Ken Schultz's Fishing Encyclopedia: Worldwide Angling Guide.** Foster City, Calif.: IDG Books Worldwide, 2000. 1916 pp. $60.00. ISBN 0-02-862057-7.

An incredible angling encyclopedia, this extremely informative volume contains over 2000 entries presented in alphabetical order, with more than 1400 color photographs and drawings. Covers both freshwater and saltwater sport fishing and describes in detail over 500 fish species from all over the world. Discusses tackle and fishing technique as well as broader boating issues. The author was an editor at *Field & Stream* for twenty-six years; he worked with over 100 contributors and artists to compile this amazing bible of angling. Also provides a conversion chart for weights and measures.

865. Schultz, Ken. **The World Atlas of Saltwater Fishing.** New York: Lyons Press, 2000. 208 pp. $40.00. ISBN 1-58574-192-2.

Arranged by geographic area, this work offers a survey of diverse locations throughout the world that are noted for saltwater fishing. Included are the east and west coasts of North America, and locations in Africa, the Caribbean, South America, Australia, New Zealand, and Europe. For each location, the author reviews the primary types of game fish that can be found, as well as special fishing techniques and other information unique to the area or type of fishing. Includes many useful tips that will increase the success of both the beginner and the experienced angler. Illustrated with color photographs, diagrams, and maps.

866. Weiss, John. **The Bass Angler's Almanac: More Than 650 Tips and Tactics.** New York: Lyons Press, 2001. 296 pp. $29.95. ISBN 1-58574-214-7.

This collection of tips and tactics for bass fishing is intended for all anglers, regardless of experience level. The brief entries are arranged in eighteen topical chapters and include a variety of subjects, such as bass biology; reading maps and using sonar; habits of the fish in a variety of environments; how water chemistry, weather, and temperature influence bass behavior; and how to select the most appropriate rods, reels, and lines for catching bass.

867. Wright, Leonard M. **The Complete Fisherman.** Guilford, Conn.: Lyons Press, 2004. 485 pp. $16.95. ISBN 1-59228-426-4.

Intended for beginners and expert anglers alike, this is a comprehensive encyclopedia that covers all aspects of fishing. Written by authors and editors from *Field & Stream* magazine, this substantial source contains chapters on how to find the fish, tying fishing knots for both saltwater and freshwater fishing, baits and rigs, how to catch largemouth bass, fly fishing for trout, and tackle care and repair.

Web Site

868. **American Sportfishing Association.** http://www.asafishing.org/ (accessed December 8, 2004).

The ASA is the sport fishing industry's trade association. Their mission is to "safeguard and promote the enduring social, economic, and conservation values of sport fishing in America." Their Web site contains much information, including statistics on participation and economic impact, news, and information on shows, other events, and conservation.

Camping and Hiking

Reference Sources

869. **The Official Guide to America's National Parks.** 12th ed. With the National Park Foundation. New York: Fodor's Travel Publications, 2004. $19.00. ISBN 1-4000-1375-5; ISSN 1532-9771.

Previously entitled *The Complete Guide to America's National Parks*, this is the official visitor's guide of the National Park Service. The guide begins with a set of regional maps of the United States that clearly indicate the location of national parks, monuments, and historic sites. An alphabetical, state-by-state directory is presented next. For each state, parks are listed alphabetically; entries include a brief description of the park or site, what to see and do, information on planning a visit (camping, lodging, and fees), directions, and sources for additional information. Usually updated every other year.

870. Smith, Darren L., and Penny J. Hoffman. **Parks Directory of the United States.** 4th ed. Detroit, Mich.: Omnigraphics, 2004. 1008 pp. $180.00. ISBN 0-7808-0663-8.

This directory provides valuable information on 4960 national and state parks, historic sites, national trails, wildlife sanctuaries, conservation organizations, heritage areas, and other designated recreational areas in the United States that are administered by national and state park agencies, plus Canadian national parks. Listings contain full contact information, Web address, location, acreage, and a description of facilities and special features. State maps are included to help locate the areas. Offers a master index, as well as indexes by geographic area, classification, and special features. An important reference tool for most large public and academic libraries.

871. Sparano, Vin T. **Complete Outdoors Encyclopedia.** New York: Thomas Dunne Books / St. Martin's Griffin, 2000. 830 pp. $22.95. ISBN 0-312-26722-3.

Unique because of its extensive coverage of diverse outdoor sporting activities under one cover, this reference source covers fishing, hunting, firearms and shooting sports, camping, boating, first aid, archery and bow hunting, sporting dogs, fish species, big game, small game, and upland game and waterfowl. Other topics include survival, backpacking, nutrition, all-terrain vehicles, water sports, and GPS. Illustrated with over 1000 drawings and diagrams. Contains a listing of private organizations and government information sources. Indexed.

872. Townsend, Chris, and Annie M. Aggens. **Encyclopedia of Outdoor and Wilderness Skills: The Ultimate A–Z Guide for the Adventurous.** Camden, Maine: International Marine / Ragged Mountain Press, 2003. 400 pp. $22.95. ISBN 0-07-138406-5.

Over 450 alphabetically arranged entries cover the gamut of wilderness topics in an easy-access format: terrains, climates, and situations for all types of wilderness activity, from mountain biking to hiking to kayaking, and other topics, from anchors to bears to crevasse rescue and from fog to "leave no trace" to switchbacks. Illustrated with photographs and drawings. Indexed.

873. **Trailer Life Directory: Campgrounds, RV Parks, and Services.** 2004 ed. Ventura, Calif.: Trailer Life Books, 2004. 1952 pp. $24.95. ISBN 0-934798-73-7.

The directory offers listings for over 15,500 campgrounds, RV parks, service centers, LP gas stations, and other attractions. This edition identifies modem-friendly campgrounds and RV parks with easy online access for campers, as well as special music events. Listings include location; directions; opening and closing dates if not year-round; daily rates and extra charges; hookup facilities; number and kind of sites available; pull-throughs; amenities such as security, laundry, dump stations, and swimming pool, spas, and other types of recreation; patio availability; pet restrictions; elevation, if over 2500 feet. Evaluations and ratings are included, as are color state maps to help RVers plan their travels.

874. **Woodall's North America Campground Directory.** 2004 ed. Ventura, Calif.: Woodall's Publications, 2004. 1952 pp. $21.95. ISBN 0-7627-2772-1.

This directory is known for its accurate information and reliable rating system. Includes listings for over 15,000 privately owned and public campgrounds. Listings include descriptions of facilities, driving directions, camping fees, telephone numbers, pet restrictions, phone/modem hookup availability, handicap accessibility, county information (for weather warnings), e-mail addresses for parks, and much more. Arranged by geographic region, and then by state or province, with a general description of travel information and attractions at the beginning of each section. This edition also includes a guide to seasonal sites that only operate for a brief period or seasonally during the year.

Instructional Sources

875. Harvey, Mark W. T., and Peter Simer. **The National Outdoor Leadership School's Wilderness Guide: The Classic Handbook.** Rev. and updated ed. New York: Fireside / Simon & Schuster, 1999. 268 pp. $15.00. ISBN 0-684-85909-2.

In this expert guide to the great outdoors, comprehensive chapters cover the details of planning an expedition, choosing equipment, dressing appropriately, using good camping technique, travel technique, leadership behavior, using maps and compasses, emergency procedures, weather, cooking, and being responsible to the land. Appendices provide an equipment list and suggested reading. Illustrated with drawings and photographs. Indexed.

876. McManners, Hugh. **The Backpacker's Handbook.** New York: Dorling Kindersley, 1995. 160 pp. ISBN 1-56458-852-1.

Especially good for beginners, this well-illustrated guide offers all the basic information needed to get started on a backpacking adventure. It provides tips on improving fitness level before a trip and describes all the equipment needed. It offers clear and concise information on weather-travel conditions, using a map and compass, moving over difficult terrain, staying safe, finding food, and building emergency shelters. Illustrated with excellent color photographs, charts, and maps.

877. McManners, Hugh. **The Complete Wilderness Training Book.** 1st American ed. New York: Dorling Kindersley, 1994. 192 pp. $29.95. ISBN 1-56458-488-7.

Whether you're getting back to basics or need survival skills for an adventure in the great outdoors, this source will lead you in the right direction. Describes all the basic equipment needed, from clothing and footwear to tools and ropes. Includes good information on choosing a campsite, building shelter, building a fire, finding water and food, navigation and traveling in unfamiliar surroundings, staying safe, and surviving in extreme conditions or for long periods. Illustrated with over 950 color photographs and drawings that vividly show the tools, techniques, and strategies of wilderness survival. Includes a glossary of terms and an index.

878. Roswal, Glenn M., Karen J. Dowd, and Jerry W. Bynum. **Including People with Disabilities in Camp Programs: A Resource for Camp Directors.** Martinsville, Ind.: American Camping Association, 1997. 145 pp. $30.95. ISBN 0-87603-156-4.

An excellent resource for those involved in directing camps, this resource provides an overview of inclusion, discusses the Americans with Disabilities Act (ADA) and medical considerations, and presents a general camp inclusion model. It also provides model activity programs for specific sports and activities, such as adventure programs, archery, canoeing, equestrian activities, fishing, golf, outdoor adventure trips, sailing, swimming, and winter activities. Excellent resources are included for further information, and a glossary defines selected disability terms.

879. Townsend, Chris. **The Backpacker's Handbook.** 3rd ed. Camden, Maine: International Marine / Ragged Mountain Press, 2004. 400 pp. $19.95. ISBN 0-07-142320-6.

This very comprehensive and well-written handbook, now in its third edition, offers just about everything a backpacker needs. Appropriate for beginners or the experienced, detailed information is included on navigating the basic trail and also on the complex conditions to be found and tackled in unexplored areas. Contains information for all terrains and hiking styles, covers adventure trekking and long-distance and low-impact methods. Offers advice on gear of every type, cooking and nutrition on the trail, safety, and shelter. Contains good illustrations. Appendices contain an equipment checklist, a list of suggested readings, useful contact information, and a metric conversion chart. Indexed.

Web Sites

880. **American Hiking Society.** http://www.americanhiking.org/ (accessed June 11, 2004).

A very useful collection of information can be found on this Web site, including an online "trail finder," news and resources, events, and volunteer opportunities.

881. **National Park Service.** http://www.nps.gov (accessed June 11, 2004).

This site offers an alphabetical list of all national parks and also a search option by geographic location or topic, with links to the individual parks' sites. Entries offers information on history, culture, education, nature, and science activities available at the parks, as well as type of facilities and services.

Health and Wellness

Chapter 15

Featured in this chapter are information sources that contribute to the body of literature aimed at increasing personal wellness. This goal of wellness can be accomplished by focusing on nutrition, medical aspects of exercise, assessing fitness level, and training for specific fitness results. Sources are grouped according to the following topics: medicine, nutrition, tests, training, facilities, and general exercise and fitness.

Medicine

882. Bracker, Mark D., ed. **The 5-Minute Sports Medicine Consult.** The 5-Minute Consult. Philadelphia, Pa.: Lippincott Williams & Wilkins, 2001. 631 pp. $69.95. ISBN 0-7817-3045-7.

Intended to help clinicians quickly assess problems and also to serve as an educational guide for patients, this reference provides concise sports-medicine information on over 280 topics. Arranged alphabetically, the topics are grouped into three main categories: general musculoskeletal topics; population-specific musculoskeletal injuries; and general medicine. Each entry includes the basics, diagnosis, acute treatment, long-term treatment, common questions and answers, and miscellaneous information that includes a bibliography. An appendix includes home-exercise guidelines for common injuries. Illustrated with black-and-white photographs and drawings. Indexed.

882a. Brukner, Peter, Karim Khan, and John Kron. **The Encyclopedia of Exercise, Sport and Health.** Crow Next, NSW: Allen & Unwin, 2004. 501 pp. $45.00. ISBN 1-7411-4058-7.

With A to Z coverage of approximately 2000 topics in exercise, sport, and health, this comprehensive reference source is suitable for both public and academic libraries. Written in an easy-to-understand style, the entries describe and explain terms and concepts that are of interest to everyone, regardless of age, athletic ability, or fitness level. Coverage includes fitness, training, nutrition, psychology, injuries, illness, prevention strategies, alternative therapies, and di-

223

agnosis and treatment of injury. Includes a list of sources for further reading. Well illustrated with over 200 photographs and over 70 line drawings. Indexed.

883. Micheli, Lyle J., and Mark Jenkins. **The Sports Medicine Bible: Prevent, Detect, and Treat Your Sports Injuries through the Latest Medical Techniques.** New York: Harper Perennial, a Division of HarperCollins, 1995. 339 pp. $23.95. ISBN 0-06-273143-2.

Intended to help the recreational athlete prevent, identify, and treat sports injuries, the author provides excellent information in an easily understood format. In promoting the prevention and rehabilitation of injuries, the first five chapters present general information about fitness, strength and flexibility, and self-treatment. The remaining sixteen chapters detail common injuries to specific areas of the body; for example, the feet, shoulders and upper arm, hand and finger, head and neck, and so forth, as well as injuries common to specific populations, and information on the role of nutrition. The book also includes charts listing symptoms for both acute and overuse injuries. Well illustrated with drawings that show rehabilitative exercise technique and the anatomy of body-specific body parts. Indexed.

884. Moffat, Marilyn, and Steve Vickery. **Book of Body Maintenance and Repair.** With the American Physical Therapy Association. New York: Henry Holt, 1999. 288 pp. $19.95. ISBN 0-8050-5571-1.

Written from the physical therapist's viewpoint, this fitness book features practical information on staying physically fit, as well as hundreds of at-home stretches and exercises. Illustrated with 500 line drawings. Part 1 consists of nine chapters, each focused on a specific part of the body: the back, neck, jaw, shoulder, elbow, wrist and hand, hip, knee, ankle and foot. The details stress prevention of injury and noninvasive home treatment that can be done when injury occurs. Part 2 features chapters written on basic concepts in kinesiology and physiology that affect the body's overall health, such as posture, gait, body mechanics, weight, strength, flexibility, and work. Part 3 is an illustrated collection of almost 200 exercises that build strength, endurance, and flexibility. Appendices offer additional information on first aid and cardiovascular conditioning.

885. Shannon, Joyce Brennfleck. **Sports Injuries Sourcebook.** 2nd ed. Health Reference Series. Detroit, Mich.: Omnigraphics, 2002. 614 pp. $78.00. ISBN 0-7808-0604-2.

Titles in this reference series are intended for the general reader who seeks basic consumer health or medical information, so are appropriate for the public, college, or university library. Topics include sports-related injuries by age group, including common injuries, injuries related to specific sports, and the diagnosis, treatment, and rehabilitation of injuries. Also includes tips for conditioning and training, injury prevention for specific sports, a glossary, and a list of additional resources.

Nutrition

886. Applegate, Liz. **Encyclopedia of Sports and Fitness Nutrition.** Roseville, Calif.: Prima, 2002. 411 pp. $22.95. ISBN 0-7615-1378-7.

This informative guide to nutrition contains four sections. The first covers the basics of fitness nutrition, along with the benefits and goals of a healthy fitness plan, while the second details all the products we consume, including vitamins and minerals. The third section discusses and illustrates appropriate eating at every age group and specific types of diets. The last section is an alphabetically arranged encyclopedia on nutrition topics as varied as aerobics, energy, heart disease, swimming, and weight gain. Indexed.

887. Clark, Nancy. **Nancy Clark's Sports Nutrition Guidebook.** 3rd ed. Champaign, Ill.: Human Kinetics, 2003. 406 pp. $18.95. ISBN 0-7360-4602-X.

Designed to help readers make nutritious food choices to manage stress, lose body fat, build muscle, and boost energy, this is a popular sports nutrition guide. Arranged in four sections, the first covers the basics of nutrition and meal design, the second is focused on sports nutrition for peak performance, the third covers weight management, and the fourth provides healthy recipes. Illustrated with drawings and many data tables. Appendices provide sources for additional information. Indexed.

888. Kent, Michael. **Food and Fitness: A Dictionary of Diet and Exercise.** New York: Oxford University Press, 1997. 377 pp. $59.50. ISBN 0-19-863147-2.

Arranged alphabetically and with detailed entries of varying lengths, this work is more encyclopedia than dictionary. It defines and explains the complex terms and concepts of nutrition, exercise and fitness, offering precise scientific information on everything from aerobic-training threshold to folic acid to obesity to zero fat diet. Appendices provide additional information on recommended daily allowances, reference nutrient intakes (RNIs), composition of selected foods, ratings and energy expenditure for a variety of sports and activities, and a table outlining the benefits of specific exercise for flexibility, strength, upper body and lower body. Illustrated with occasional drawings throughout the text. Indexed.

889. Maughan, Ronald J., and Louise Burke, eds. **Sports Nutrition.** Handbook of Sports Medicine and Science. Malden, Mass.: Blackwell Science, 2002. 200 pp. $36.95. ISBN 0-632-05814-5.

This series is published under the auspices of the International Olympic Committee Medical Commission. The volume on sports nutrition covers the athlete's nutrition needs for training, energy demands, fuels used in exercise, hydration issues, eating strategies in competition, weight management, and sport-specific nutrition information. The articles in the handbook are intended for use by physicians, trainers, and coaches but would also be useful for athletes or for parents of children who are participating in athletics. Illustrated with diagrams, tables, and black-and-white photographs. Each chapter contains a list of references for further reading. Indexed. This series is most appropriate for college and university collections in sports medicine.

890. Rosenbloom, Christine A., ed. **Sports Nutrition: A Guide for the Professional Working with Active People.** 3rd ed. With the Sports, Cardiovascular and Wellness Nutritionists Dietetic Practice Group of the American Dietetic Association. Chicago: The American Dietetic Association, 2000. 759 pp. $69.00. ISBN 0-88091-176-X.

For food, nutrition, and other health professionals who work with active people of all ages and ability levels, this authoritative source is an essential reference. It is also an appropriate source for athletes themselves who want to enhance their performance. Topics include nutrient and fluid needs of active people, ergogenic aids, nutrient and body-composition assessment, fitness evaluations, and guidelines for working with special populations, such as Olympic athletes, those in high school, vegetarians, those with hypertension, or those who are pregnant or physically disabled. It also provides sport-specific nutrition guidelines for nineteen sports activities, such as swimming, hockey, rowing, and basketball. This is an essential reference for academic collections that support programs in sports nutrition or exercise physiology; and it is also appropriate for health-science libraries. Illustrated with photos, tables, and graphs. Indexed.

891. Ryan, Monique. **Complete Guide to Sports Nutrition.** The Ultimate Training Series from VeloPress. Boulder, Colo.: VeloPress, 1999. 324 pp. $16.95. ISBN 1-884737-57-9.

Practical nutrition information is presented in this source, and current sports nutrition guidelines are clarified. Features menu and meal-planning guidelines, food strategies, weight management recommendations, as well as full discussion of the basic components of a sports diet. Illustrated with data tables and black-and-white photographs of athletes.

892. Ryan, Monique. **Sports Nutrition for Endurance Athletes.** Boulder, Colo.: VeloPress, 2002. 326 pp. $19.95. ISBN 1-931382-15-8.

The nutritional challenges of sports participation are tackled in this guide. Sport-specific guidelines provide nutrition recommendations to increase endurance and improve performance in such sports as adventure racing, cross-country skiing, cycling, cyclo-cross, distance running, mountain biking, swimming, and triathlon. The detailed information is presented in a concise, understandable format. Also discusses weight and body composition, nutritional ergogenic aids, and creating the optimal diet. Appendices provide a glycemic index of foods, facts about vitamins and minerals, a comparison of sports-nutrition products, and sample menus. Includes data tables, a bibliography, and an index.

892a. Sawyer, Thomas H., Michael G. Hypes, and Joe Brown. **A Guide to Sport Nutrition: For Student-Athletes, Coaches, Athletic Trainers, and Par-**

ents. Champaign, Ill.: Sagamore Publishing, 2003. 342 pp. $36.95. ISBN 1-57167-494-2.

This comprehensive source assists the athlete, coach, trainer, or parent by providing in-depth nutrition information based on scientific research. The book's twenty-four chapters are arranged in five sections: nutrition, energy, and exercise; macronutrients; micronutrients; weight gain and weight loss; and nutritional concerns of special populations and situations (for example: osteoporosis, the female athlete, the aging athlete, the vegetarian athlete). Nine appendices provide additional information on such topics as selecting low-fat food and comparing fluid replacement value of different beverages, and include a list of organizations and other sources of information. Includes a glossary of terms. Indexed.

Tests

892b. Brodie, David A., ed. **A Reference Manual for Human Performance Measurement in the Field of Physical Education and Sports Sciences.** Mellen Studies in Education. Lewiston, N.Y.: Edwin Mellen Press, 1996. 238 pp. $89.95. ISBN 0-7734-8788-3.

This reference manual describes thirty tests that are used by persons studying kinesiology and human movement to measure human performance. Aspects of performance include muscle strength, speed, power, flexibility, endurance, and coordination. The tests are covered in eight sections: kinanthropometry, muscle function, anaerobic and explosive power, aerobic capacity, local muscular endurance, speed and agility, test batteries, and others. Each entry provides information to describe the purpose of the test, common usages, equipment needed, procedure, special notes, validity and reliability, scoring, and references from scientific literature. Illustrated with charts and graphs.

892c. Collins, D. Ray, and Patrick B. Hodges. **A Comprehensive Guide to Sports Skills Tests and Measurement.** 2nd ed. Lanham, Md.: Scarecrow Press, 2001. 303 pp. $43.95. ISBN 0-8108-3884-2.

This source reviews eighty-six performance tests that measure skills required in twenty-eight sports. It is arranged by sport and each chapter begins with an introduction to the sport. Tests are arranged in chronological order according to the date they were developed. Each entry includes a statement of purpose for the test; brief description; education application; time required to administer the test; personnel, equipment, facilities, and space required; directions for administering the test; scoring method; validity and reliability; and additional comments. Each chapter includes a list of references. Illustrated with diagrams, charts, and drawings.

893. Kirby, Ronald F., ed. **Kirby's Guide to Fitness and Motor Performance Tests.** Cape Girardeau, Mo.: BenOak Publishing, 1991. 458 pp. $95.00. ISBN 0-9629098-3-1.

This reference provides comprehensive information on 193 tests of the following components of fitness and motor performance: agility, balance, cardio respiratory endurance, coordination, flexibility, kinesthesis, muscular endurance, power, reaction time, speed, and strength. Each test is described, then reviewed by an expert. Though dated, it is still an excellent starting source for students and professionals who are looking for tests that measure specific fitness components. Includes a bibliography and an index.

894. Ostrow, Andrew C., ed. **Directory of Psychological Tests in the Sport and Exercise Sciences.** 2nd ed. Morgantown, W.Va.: Fitness Information Technology, 1996. 533 pp. $39.00. ISBN 1-885693-06-0.

In its twenty chapters, this respected source provides summaries of over 300 psychological assessment tools that are specific to sport and exercise. Each chapter groups together tests that measure a specific psychological construct, such as confidence, aggression, leadership, anxiety, or motivation. Entries contain the source, purpose, description, construction, reliability, validity, norms, and availability of the test, as well as references to the test's use in research. Indexed by subject, title, test acronym, and test author. An electronic version, available by individual or institutional subscription, covers 1965 to the present, with new test summaries added continually.

Training

895. Alter, Michael J. **Sport Stretch: 311 Stretches for 41 Sports.** 2nd ed. Champaign, Ill.: Human Kinetics, 1998. 221 pp. $17.95. ISBN 0-88011-823-7.

This illustrated a handbook of stretching techniques and routines offers advice and information on muscle structure, the benefits of stretching, injury management, and how to add a stretching program to an existing workout. Twelve fundamental stretches are shown, followed by twenty-eight additional stretches that isolate specific muscle groups. Specific stretching routines are presented for twenty-eight sports such as archery, diving, figure skating, jogging, swimming, and weight lifting. Instructions for 311 stretches are accompanied by drawings and arranged by major muscle group. Includes a list of references.

896. American College of Sports Medicine. **ACSM Fitness Book: A Proven Step-by-Step Program from the Experts.** 3rd ed. Champaign, Ill.: Human Kinetics, 2003. 175 pp. $16.95. ISBN 0-7360-4406-X.

This concise guide introduces a comprehensive fitness plan that individuals can adopt and continue with, regardless of present fitness level. Fitness tests are included to help gauge one's present level of fitness and make a plan to increase it. Step-by-step instructions, sample exercise programs, and basic information on nutrition, weight control, and motivation are also included. Illustrated with color photographs, many informative charts, and drawings. Indexed.

897. Brooks, Douglas S. **The Complete Book of Personal Training.** Champaign, Ill.: Human Kinetics, 2004. 589 pp. $59.00. ISBN 0-7360-0013-5.

This detailed book provides a great deal of practical information applicable to starting a business in personal training. Includes comprehensive information on fitness-program design, the science behind exercise, working with clients to establish goals, working with special populations, and much more. Includes references to many additional sources of information. Illustrated with black-and-white photographs. Indexed.

898. Burke, Edmund R., ed. **Precision Heart Rate Training.** Champaign, Ill.: Human Kinetics, 1998. 211 pp. $15.95. ISBN 0-88011-770-2.

Introducing the basic concepts of heart rate training, the editor explains why and how to train with a monitor. The details are then presented on how to design and use such training programs in seven different sports and activities. Includes programs and guidelines for walking, running, cycling, in-line skating, multisport training, circuit training, and group exercise. Illustrated with black-and-white photographs and data tables.

899. Earle, Roger W., and Thomas R. Baechle, eds. **NSCA's Essentials of Personal Training.** With the National Strength & Conditioning Association. Champaign, Ill.: Human Kinetics, 2004. 676 pp. $69.00. ISBN 0-7360-0015-1.

This text is the primary preparation source for the NSCA's Certified Personal Trainer examination. For colleges and universities that support related programs, this is an essential source. As a reference tool, it offers a huge body of practical information that is supported by scientific evidence on health, fitness, and exercise technique. Illustrated with over 240 color photographs and drawings that explain the proper technique for stretching, resistance training, aerobic-endurance training, and plyometrics. Includes detailed information on anatomy, physiology, biomechanics, nutrition, exercise psychology, health and fitness evaluation, exercise-program design, clients with special needs, and legal and safety issues. Study tools are included, as is a comprehensive glossary. Indexed.

900. National Institute on Aging. **Fitness over Fifty: An Exercise Guide from the National Institute on Aging.** New York: Healthy Living Books, 2003. 134 pp. $15.95. ISBN 1-57826-136-8.

This guide to getting started with exercise is for men and women aged fifty and over. It provides a set of twenty-five exercises that build strength, flexibility, vitality, and balance to help people remain active and independent as they age. Includes safety tips, ways to stay motivated, tips on stretching and increasing flexibility, and sample exercise and nutrition record-keeping methods. Previously published as *Exercise: A guide from the National Institute on Aging* (2002). Illustrated with over 100 black-and-white photographs. Indexed.

901. Prentice, William E. **Get Fit, Stay Fit.** 3rd ed. New York: McGraw-Hill, 2004. 290 pp. $25.71. ISBN 0-07-255734-6.

This informative fitness text is intended to be used with a course but also works well for an individual who wants to begin a personal fitness or exercise program. The content is presented concisely and covers lifestyle, cardio-respiratory fitness, muscular strength, endurance, power, stretching, nutrition, and safety. Each chapter begins with objectives and ends with suggested readings, Web sites, and a summary. Includes an extensive food-composition table in the appendix. Provides over twenty fitness tests and other lab activities to evaluate fitness level. Illustrated with black-and-white photographs and many tables and graphs.

902. Schmottlach, Neil, and Jerre L. McManama. **Physical Education Activity Handbook.** 10th ed. San Francisco, Calif.: Benjamin Cummings / Pearson Education, 2002. 449 pp. $67.00. ISBN 0-205-34401-1.

Meant to serve as a teaching and reference tool for teachers, sports enthusiasts, and students, this source contains introductory chapters on the mechanical and psychological aspects of skill development and on the basic principles of physical fitness. It also reviews the basic skills, equipment, playing areas, rules, and terminology associated with twenty-five physical activities, such as badminton, field hockey, gymnastics, aerobic dance, softball, and yoga. Each chapter provides step-by-step instructions for performing the fundamental strokes or moves, with photographs that illustrate the movements. Chapters also offer lists of additional resources, including Web sites, for each activity. This is a revised edition of *Physical Education Handbook*, 9th ed. (1997).

903. Sharkey, Brian J. **Fitness and Health.** 5th ed. Champaign, Ill.: Human Kinetics, 2002. 437 pp. $24.95. ISBN 0-7360-3971-6.

This comprehensive guide demonstrates how to improve and maintain health through an enjoyable program of regular physical activity. The method is based on scientific research, but the text is written in language that is easy for anyone to comprehend. It discusses the benefits of activity, offers a health-risk analysis, and provides the information needed to develop an aerobic-fitness program and to increase muscular strength, endurance, and flexibility. The source also provides facts to help with diet and weight control and to improve performance at work and in sport activities. Illustrated with many photographs and data tables.

904. Sloan, Jim. **Staying Fit over Fifty: Conditioning for Outdoor Activities.** Seattle, Wash.: Mountaineers Books, 1999. 224 pp. $19.95. ISBN 0-89886-668-5.

This handbook is intended to help the reader understand fitness and the role of exercise during the aging process. Both training and nutrition are covered, as is the effect of exercise on the brain. In-depth information is provided for individual sports: running, cycling, rowing (plus kayaking and canoeing), swimming, skiing, walking, snowshoeing, and climbing. The book includes many practical tips and provides advice on equipment, techniques, workouts, mental approaches, and injuries. Includes lists of other resources.

Facilities

905. Burke, Edmund R. ed. **Complete Home Fitness Handbook.** Champaign, Ill.: Human Kinetics, 1996. 250 pp. $14.95. ISBN 0-87322-994-0.

Want to achieve total fitness without leaving your home? This handbook describes how to develop a personal fitness program and choose the best home equipment, depending on your fitness goals and budget. Includes information on safety, nutrition, conditioning and weight control, stretching, and fitness testing. For each type of equipment, provides basic instructions on use and a range of exercises that can be utilized to create a fitness program. Covers weight machines, free weights, stationary bikes, stair climbers, treadmills, and ski machines. Illustrated with black-and-white photographs.

906. Leavy, Hannelore R., and Reinhard R. Bergel. **The Spa Encyclopedia: A Guide to Treatments and Their Benefits for Health and Healing.** Clifton Park, N.Y.: Thomson / Delmar Learning, 2003. 132 pp. $34.95. ISBN 1-56253-868-3.

This encyclopedia discusses the origins of the spa, explains how to choose a good spa, and provides a directory of some of the best ones. It also defines and describes over seventy spa treatments with in-depth information and step-by-step procedures so the reader knows what to expect. Offers information on the health benefits of each type of treatment.

907. Swiac, Christine. **Fodor's Healthy Escapes.** 8th ed. New York: Fodor's Travel Publications / Random House, 2003. 346 pp. $20.00. ISBN 1-4000-1089-6.

A great resource to help find the perfect health-conscious vacation, this directory reviews 288 spas, resorts, and retreats that are available in the United States, Hawaii, Canada, Mexico, and the Caribbean. Access to the information is provided by geographic region, by resort name, and by type of resort. Entries provide information on lodging, dining, services, facilities, and type of activities offered. A glossary of spa terminology is provided.

908. Tharrett, Stephen J., and James A. Peterson, eds. **ACSM's Health/Fitness Facility Standards and Guidelines.** 2nd ed. With the American College of Sports Medicine. Champaign, Ill.: Human Kinetics, 1997. 211 pp. $39.00. ISBN 0-87322-957-6.

Reflecting the consensus among industry organizations and fitness associations, this work presents six general standards for health and fitness facilities and then expands to define approximately 400 guidelines that further recommend the specifications, policies, and procedures used to operate the facilities. Includes guidelines for specific activity areas, such as pools, exercise classrooms, playing courts, and running tracks, as well as nonactivity areas such as laundry, locker room, and control-desk areas. Appendices provide additional information, such as a sample preventive maintenance schedule, dimensions and markings for activity areas, safety checklist, acoustical guidelines, and information on the Americans with Disabilities Act. Illustrated with drawings. Contains a bibliography and an index.

General Exercise and Fitness

909. Anshel, Mark H., ed. **Dictionary of the Sport and Exercise Sciences.** Champaign, Ill.: Human Kinetics, 1991. 163 pp. $27.00. ISBN 0-87322-305-5.

In this comprehensive reference, the language of the sport and exercise sciences is identified and defined. It includes approximately 3000 terms from nine subdisciplines: adapted physical education, biomechanics, exercise physiology (including body composition and cardiac rehabilitation), motor control, motor development, motor learning, sport pedagogy, sport psychology, and sport sociology. Terms are defined clearly, cross-references are given, and occasional small illustrations are included.

910. Copeland, Barry. **Funding Sources in Physical Education, Exercise and Sport Science.** Morgantown, W.Va.: Fitness Information Technology, 1995. 135 pp. $19.00. ISBN 0-9627926-7-5.

Divided into three parts, this directory of funding sources provides the contact person or agency's name, address, and phone number, as well as the application deadline, type of funding, and amount of funding available. The first part identifies research funding in athletics, coaching, dance, exercise physiology, nutrition, and similar areas. Part two identifies funding for project development in physical education, sports medicine, women's studies, youth sport, and similar areas. And part three identifies internships, fellowships, and scholarships in physical education, exercise, and sport science.

911. Fentem, P. H., N. B. Turnbull, and E. J. Bassey. **Benefits of Exercise: The Evidence.** Manchester, U.K.: Manchester University Press, 1990. 344 pp. $90.00. ISBN 0-7190-2430-7.

Though dated now, this is a classic source of scientific and medical evidence that exercise is beneficial to health. The bibliography concentrates on sources published between 1978 and 1988; it was compiled by utilizing Medline, Current Contents, and similar scholarly indexes. The content includes general exercise capacity, cardiovascular function, respiratory function, connective tissues, metabolic function, reproductive function, psychological function, and general health. Indexed by keywords, global keywords, and author.

912. Gledhill, Kristen M., ed. **Fitness and Exercise Sourcebook.** Health Reference Series. 2nd ed. Detroit, Mich.: Omnigraphics, 2001. 646 pp. $78.00. ISBN 0-7808-0334-5.

Titles in this reference series are intended for the general reader who seeks basic consumer health or medical information and so are appropriate for the public, college, or university library. Topics include general fitness and exercise, diet, fitness for specific populations, those with specific medical conditions such as cancer or arthritis, and specific types of exercise activities, such as bicycling, skating and walking. The comprehensive chapters are written by experts in the field and contain substantial lists of other sources to consult. A final chapter is also included to lead the reader to additional information available from the federal government and the private sector. Contains a glossary of terms and a subject index.

913. Herron, Nancy L., ed. **The Leisure Literature: A Guide to Sources in Leisure Studies, Fitness, Sports, and Travel.** Englewood, Colo.: Libraries Unlimited, 1992. 181 pp. $30.00. ISBN 1-56308-062-1.

This work brings together the literature of leisure, fitness, sport, and travel/tourism and provides a guide for researchers, librarians, students, faculty, and professionals working in these areas. Each chapter corresponds to one of the four areas and consists of an introduction to the discipline and an annotated list of the most frequently used sources, arranged from general to specific. Includes a variety of types of sources. Appendices provide a list of degree programs in the four areas, important publishers, and associations. Indexed by author/title and subject.

914. Karolides Jr., Nicholas, and Melissa Karolides. **Focus on Fitness: A Reference Handbook.** Teenage Perspectives. Santa Barbara, Calif.: ABC-CLIO, 1993. 470 pp. $46.25. ISBN 0-87436-662-3.

Intended primarily for the teen market, this source provides a comprehensive overview of health and fitness topics. Chapters cover fitness and body types, emotional fitness and stress, measuring health-related fitness, energy systems and exercise benefits, aerobic activities and exercise, exercise injuries, nutrition for healthy living, eating disorders and overtraining, and motivation for fitness. Includes a bibliography and an index.

915. National Association of Sport and Physical Education. **2001 Shape of the Nation Report: Status of Physical Education in the USA.** Reston, Va.: American Alliance for Health, Physical Education, Recreation and Dance, 2002. 30 pp. $10.00. ISBN 0-88314-742-4.

This report provides current information on the status of physical education in each of the states and the District of Columbia. It is meant to be used as an advocacy tool when communicating with state policymakers and others about the value of providing physical-education programs. The report includes an executive summary with results and recommendations for action and background information on the need for physical activity and education. It features a state-by-state summary, reporting on who teaches physical education, student requirements, enforcement, standards, class size, curriculum, and contact information for the physical education director or consultant in each state's Department of Education.

916. University of California at Berkeley. **The New Wellness Encyclopedia.** Boston: Houghton Mifflin, 1995. $27.50. ISBN 0-395-73345-6.

A home-reference encyclopedia, this guide to wellness is intended to help prevent disease and maintain health and well-being. Covers longevity and the health risks that influence wellness, as well as nutrition, self-care, and environmental and safety factors that are typical in modern life. Offers a good chapter on the role of exercise and the basic elements of fitness. Provides specific information on a number of common aerobic activities, such as cycling, ice skating, running, and swimming, and discusses the most effective techniques and best equipment. Provides additional information on maintaining strength and flexibility.

Web Sites

917. **Aerobics and Fitness Association of America (AFAA).** http://www .afaa.com (accessed September 6, 2004).

As a fitness education organization, the AFAA offers workshops and certification programs in a large number of fitness career areas. Their Web site provides access to study materials and much other information.

918. **American Alliance for Health, Physical Education, Recreation and Dance (AAHPERD).** http://www.aahperd.org/ (accessed January 2, 2004).

AAHPERD is a professional organization that is an alliance of six organizations: the American Association for Health Education, American Association for Leisure and Recreation, American Association for Active Lifestyles and Fitness, National Association for Girls and Women in Sport, National Association for Sport and Physical Education, and National Dance Association. The Web site provides a diverse array of information about programs, advocacy issues, professional development, and links to related organizations, state AAHPERD associations, and publications.

919. **American College of Sports Medicine (ACSM).** http://www.acsm.org (accessed April 2, 2004).

The ACSM's mission is to "advance and integrate scientific research to provide educational and practical applications of exercise science and sports medicine." Their Web site is very informative, containing details of membership, certification, professional education, grants and research initiatives, news, and opportunities to order publications and learn more about fitness and health.

920. **American Council on Exercise (ACE).** http://www.acefitness.org (accessed March 3, 2004).

The ACE Web site provides excellent information and news about exercise, nutrition, and other aspects of fitness. It offers education and professional certification programs, online directories of health and fitness clubs and fitness professionals, and 100 "fit facts" information sheets in PDF format.

921. **American Orthopaedic Society for Sports Medicine (AOSSM).** http:// www.sportsmed.org (accessed December 8, 2004).

The AOSSM is a national organization of orthopedic surgeons specializing in sports medicine. A major part of their mission is education and research, and their Web page offers much information. Includes a searchable directory of sports medicine specialists.

922. Food and Nutrition Information Center at the National Agricultural Library (FNIC). http://www.nal.usda.gov/fnic (accessed December 8, 2004).

The FNIC site provides a directory to accurate and complete nutrition information, including in-depth coverage of the Food Guide Pyramid, printable educational materials, dietary guidelines, resource lists, and access to a number of databases maintained by the NAL.

923. National Association for Health and Fitness. http://www.physical fitness.org (accessed December 8, 2004).

This nonprofit organization exists to improve the quality of life of people in the United States by promoting fitness activities, sports, and healthy lifestyles and by supporting Governor's and State Councils on physical fitness in every U.S. state. The Web site provides detailed information on the many fitness programs the organization supports, reports and guidelines, and links to other health-and-fitness information.

924. National Strength and Conditioning Association (NSCA). http://www .nsca-lift.org (accessed March 12, 2004).

The NCSA is a professional organization for strength and conditioning coaches, personal trainers, exercise physiologists, athletic trainers, researchers, educators, sport coaches, physical therapists, and others involved in health and fitness areas. Their Web site helps disseminate information to members and provides a directory of personal trainers, links to publications and meetings, a career center, and continuing education and certification opportunities.

925. President's Council on Physical Fitness and Sports. http://www.fitness .gov (accessed December 8, 2004).

The President's Council on Physical Fitness and Sports encourages Americans of all ages to become physically active and get involved in sports and fitness activities. The Web site makes available many publications in PDF and HTML formats and indicates other sources of information useful to individuals who want to become more active or fitness leaders who are planning programs.

Chapter 16

Specific Exercise and Fitness Activities

Instructional in nature, the sources in this chapter describe specific exercise and fitness activities. Information sources are included on aerobics, pilates, running, walking, water aerobics, weight training, jump rope, and yoga. Selected Web sites are also included where appropriate.

Aerobics

926. Bishop, Jan Galen. **Fitness through Aerobics.** 6th ed. San Francisco, Calif.: Benjamin Cummings / Pearson Education, 2004. 205 pp. $16.50. ISBN 0-8053-5455-7.

Intended for adult courses in aerobics, step aerobics, or aerobic dance, this source teaches the moves and methodologies for performing all types of aerobic-dance exercises, as well as the strength and flexibility exercises that contribute to proper technique. Features complete coverage of new trends in aerobics and fitness, along with information on standard aerobic dance, warm-up/cool-down activities, flexibility, injury prevention, and methods for teaching different types of students. Offers a list of Web sites and worksheets.

927. Brink, Lynne G. **Fitness Aerobics.** Fitness Spectrum Series. Champaign, Ill.: Human Kinetics, 1996. 169 pp. $14.95. ISBN 0-87322-471-X.

Intended for all readers, regardless of fitness level or experience, this guide to fitness aerobics provides useful information in a practical format. Introductory chapters cover equipment, determining fitness level, and warming up. Then six sample workouts are presented, each with a differing level of duration and intensity, accompanied by a progress chart. Appendices provide an illustrated directory of aerobics moves and a list of appropriate music. Illustrated with color photographs and many colorful workout charts.

928. Mazzeo, Karen S. **Fitness through Aerobics and Step Training.** 3rd ed. Belmont, Calif.: Thomson / Wadsworth, 2002. 184 pp. $22.95. ISBN 0-534-57396-7.

Intended for individuals beginning an aerobics or step-training program, this source presents the latest fitness research available. Offers information on motivation and goal setting, safety, posture, fitness testing, warm-up, and the details of three aerobic-exercise options: aerobics, step training, and fitness walking. Also includes a program for strength training and chapters on stress management and relaxation, nutrition, and weight management. Illustrated with black-and-white photographs and drawings. Indexed.

Pilates

929. Selby, Anna, and Alan Herdman. **Pilates' Body Conditioning: A Program Based on the Techniques of Joseph Pilates.** Hauppauge, New York: Barron's Educational, 2000. 143 pp. $16.95. ISBN 0-7641-1627-4.

This book on the Pilates method of exercise and physical fitness contains beautiful color photographs that illustrate every page and, along with the clear, detailed text, make the exercise regimen very easy to understand. Includes a self-help questionnaire for each chapter, methods for reviewing progress, and a statement of goals for each level of the program. Provides a glossary of terms and a list of useful addresses. Illustrated with captioned, step-by-step, full-color photographs.

930. Siler, Brooke. **The Pilates Body: The Ultimate at Home Guide to Strengthening, Lengthening, and Toning Your Body—Without Machines.** New York: Broadway books, 2000. 194 pp. $18.00. ISBN 0-7679-0396-X.

This work begins with a review of the philosophy of Joseph Pilates. It includes archival black-and-white photos of Pilates and shows the entire mat-work sequence of the Pilates method. Provides instructions for over sixty exercises, arranged in beginning, intermediate, and advanced categories. Each exercise is clearly described and illustrated in two pages. The book offers step-by-step instructions for each exercise and is illustrated with drawings and black-and-white photos. Includes a list of certified Pilates instructors, arranged geographically, and a brief glossary of terms.

Running

931. Benyo, Richard, and Joe Henderson. **Running Encyclopedia: The Ultimate Source for Today's Runner.** Champaign, Ill.: Human Kinetics, 2002. 417 pp. $24.95. ISBN 0-7360-3734-9.

With over 1000 alphabetically arranged entries, this encyclopedia provides a comprehensive history of the sport of road racing. Contains profiles of the runners, the coaches, the races, and training techniques used, as well as milestone events in the history of running. Marathon winners and hall of fame members are listed. Throughout the book are excerpts from Joe Henderson's *Running Commentary* newsletter. Illustrated with over 100 black-and-white photographs. Includes an extensive supplemental index of persons and subjects that are mentioned in entries and sidebars.

932. Burfoot, Amby. ***Runner's World* Complete Book of Running: Everything You Need to Know to Run for Fun, Fitness, and Competition.** Emmaus, Pa.: Rodale Press, 2004. 312 pp. $17.95. ISBN 1-57954-929-2.

This is a classic, comprehensive source for those interested in beginning to run or for accomplished runners who seek to improve their performance. It includes detailed information on how to begin, choose the best shoes, eat the best foods, and train and condition for maximum performance. Features specific information for women runners and for those who are training for a marathon. Includes color illustrations.

933. Chase, Adam W., and Nancy Hobbs. **The Ultimate Guide to Trail Running.** Guilford, Conn.: Lyons Press, 2001. 240 pp. $18.95. ISBN 1-58574-228-7.

This guide to trail running features detailed information on equipment, finding trails, nutrition on the trail, hill strategy, avoiding injury, training, weather, safety, and physical conditioning. Includes an appendix on competing at the international level. Also offers a bibliography, a list of useful Web sites, and an index.

934. Derderian, Tom. **Boston Marathon: The First Century of the World's Premier Running Event.** Centennial Race ed. Champaign, Ill.: Human Kinetics, 1996. 635 pp. $21.95. ISBN 0-88011-479-7.

Arranged in a year-by-year chronological format, this history of the Boston Marathon provides an overview of each decade, then the results for each year, along with a detailed essay describing significant persons and events surrounding the race. Includes many a personal anecdote and scandal and provides good coverage of women's entrance into the marathon in the 1960s. Provides a simple list of winners, a bibliography of sources, and an index. Illustrated with black-and-white photographs.

935. Fordyce, Bruce. **Marathon Runner's Handbook.** Champaign, Ill.: Human Kinetics, 2002. 160 pp. $19.95. ISBN 0-7360-4420-5.

A handbook with essential facts for marathon runners, this source contains detailed information on training, stretching, nutrition, injuries, clothing and shoes, and racing. Illustrated with color photographs.

936. Glover, Bob, and Shelly-lynn Florence Glover. **The Competitive Runner's Handbook: The Bestselling Guide to Running 5Ks through Marathons.** 2nd ed. New York: Penguin Books, 1999. 672 pp. $19.00. ISBN 0-14-046990-7.

The revised and expanded edition of this classic running handbook contains the official training program for the New York City Marathon and the New

York Road Runner's Club classes, as well as specific training programs for runners at all levels. Includes information on speed training and on the psychological aspects of competitive running. Also provides advice on health and nutrition, the environment, and on running form and shoes. Indexed.

937. Hawley, John A., ed. **Running.** Handbook of Sports Medicine and Science. Malden, Mass.: Blackwell Science, 2000. 96 pp. $33.95. ISBN 0-632-05391-7.

This series is published under the auspices of the International Olympic Committee Medical Commission. This volume on running covers the epidemiology of injury in the sport; physiological and nutritional aspects; preventive medicine; and information on the biomechanics of running and improving the runner's performance. The articles in the handbook are intended for use by physicians, trainers, and coaches but would also be useful for athletes or for parents of children who are participating in athletics. Illustrated with diagrams, tables, and black-and-white photographs. Each chapter contains a list of references for further reading. This series is most appropriate for college and university collections in sports medicine. Indexed.

938. Henderson, Joe. **Marathon Training: A 100-Day Program to Your Best Race.** 2nd ed. Champaign, Ill.: Human Kinetics, 2004. 248 pp. $17.95. ISBN 0-7360-5191-0.

This guide to marathon training describes a fifteen-week training program and includes daily training logs. It is meant to be used day by day as the runner trains. The program can be customized at three levels: cruiser, pacer, and racer. Includes a directory of major marathons in the United States and Canada, arranged by state or province, with contact information, Web site when available, and the month the race is held. Indexed.

939. Higdon, Hal. **Marathon: The Ultimate Training Guide.** Revised and updated ed. Emmaus, Pa.: Rodale, 1999. 230 pp. $15.95. ISBN 1-57954-171-2.

Intended for runners of all experience levels, this popular marathon guide offers a good introduction for the beginner, as well as great information for a seasoned marathon participant looking to maximize peak performance. The source offers realistic training schedules, information on nutrition, motivation, and safety, and strategies for preparing for the race day.

940. Lebow, Fred, and Gloria Averbuch. **The New York Road Runner's Club Complete Book of Running and Fitness.** 3rd ed. New York: Random House Reference, 1999. 558 pp. $18.00. ISBN 0-679-78010-6.

A comprehensive guide to running, walking, and fitness, this source provides many anecdotes but also in-depth information on training techniques and racing, with separate chapters devoted to the seven typical race distances: the mile, the 5K, the 10K, ten miles to the half marathon, the marathon, ultramarathon, and cross-country. Also includes coverage of motivation, nutrition and hydration, health and medicine, running equipment, aging and exercise, and women's health issues. Provides a resource list and an index. Illustrated with photographs, drawings, and charts.

941. MacNeill, Ian. **The Beginning Runner's Handbook.** Rev. and updated ed. Vancouver, BC: Greystone Books, 2001. 170 pp. $12.95. ISBN 1-55054-861-1.

This training guide details a safe thirteen-week walk/run program aimed at the beginning runner. Focuses on an incremental approach to avoid injury and build skills gradually. Includes information on psychology and motivation, nutrition, stretching, and strengthening. Includes a training log and outlines for a walking program and an advanced running program. Contains a bibliography and an index.

942. Noakes, Tim. **Lore of Running.** 4th ed. Champaign, Ill.: Human Kinetics, 2002. 930 pp. $27.95. ISBN 0-87322-959-2.

This classic book on running is unusual in its extensive coverage and also in that the author backs up every assertion with scientific evidence. It provides comprehensive information on the physiology, training aspects, and injuries of running and also covers racing and the people and events that have shaped the sport over time. The contents are arranged in four sections: physiology and biochemistry of running; training basics; transferring training to racing; and running health. Illustrated with black-and-white photographs, drawings, and many tables of data. The author's complete, 100-page bibliography is accessible on the publisher's Web site.

943. Pfitzinger, Pete, and Scott Douglas. **Advanced Marathoning.** Champaign, Ill.: Human Kinetics, 2001. 237 pp. $19.95. ISBN 0-7360-3431-5.

This marathon training source focuses on efficient and effective techniques to help runners meet their goals. Detailed information is provided on the elements of training, nutrition and hydration, balancing training and recovery, tracking progress, and developing an effective race-day strategy. Contains a series of specific training schedules tailored to a variety of goals. Includes a pace chart, lactate threshold charts, a VO2max chart, a glossary, and a list of references for further reading. Illustrated with black-and-white photographs, drawings, and graphs. Indexed.

944. Salazar, Alberto. **Alberto Salazar's Guide to Road Racing: Championship Advice for Faster Times from 5K to Marathon.** Camden, Maine: Ragged Mountain Press, 2003. 286 pp. $16.95. ISBN 0-07-138308-5.

A training guide for runners, this work provides information on basic principles of running, base training, running form, speed training, nutrition, weight control, avoiding injury and treating injury when it happens, preparing for races, stretching, weight training, cross-training, and goal advancement. Includes a pace chart of common workout and racing distances. Indexed.

945. Scott, Dagny. *Runner's World* **Complete Book of Women's Running: The Best Advice to Get Started, Stay Motivated, Lose Weight, Run Injury-Free, Be Safe, and Train for Any Distance.** Emmaus, Pa.: Rodale Press, 2000. 308 pp. $24.95. ISBN 1-57954-118-6.

This informative handbook provides a supportive approach for the beginning woman runner; organized training schedules for more advanced runners and those who want to run competitively; an incremental training schedule for moving from walking to jogging to running within six weeks; a similar incremental schedule for advanced runners; information on nutrition, weight loss, body image, safety, and motivation geared specifically for women; additional information for specific populations (older, younger, or pregnant); and stretching and strength-training exercises illustrated with step-by-step black-and-white photographs. Indexed.

946. Weddington, Michael, and Barry Perilli. **National Road Race Encyclopedia.** Glendale, Calif.: Griffin Publishing, 1997. $24.95. ISBN 1-882180-73-9.

In this directory of 100 road races held in 33 U.S. states, the authors provide four pages of valuable information for each selected race; arrangement is alphabetical by name of race. In addition to the excellent descriptive information about the race, the authors include the top 100 finishers by gender and the top 20 divisional finishers with time and year. Races are included based on the number of participants; thus, this is a good source of information about the races that are selected, but be aware that many smaller, regional races are not included. Indexed by state.

Walking

Reference Source

946a. American Volkssport Association. **Starting Point 2004: The AVA Guide to 1,400+ Walking Trails in America.** Universal City, Tex.: American Volkssport Association, 2004. Unpaged. $15.00. ISBN 0-9644794-9-4.

This directory of over 1400 self-guided walking and biking trails throughout the United States is arranged by state. Each entry provides the trail's starting point, address, driving directions to the trail from major highways and streets, hours of operation, trail length and difficulty level, trail points of interest, and local host club name and club contact information. Events in the book are noncompetitive, and are sanctioned by the American Volkssport Association.

Instructional Sources

947. American Heart Association. **The Healthy Heart Walking Book.** New York: Macmillan, 1995. 181 pp. $14.95. ISBN 0-02-860447-4.

This guide to getting started with walking as a form of exercise discusses the health and wellness benefits of maintaining a high fitness level and offers tips on staying motivated. It also presents a program for advanced walking and discusses diet, injuries, and assessment tools.

948. Fenton, Mark. *Walking Magazine*'s **The Complete Guide to Walking for Health, Weight Loss, and Fitness.** New York: Lyons Press, 2001. 261 pp. $24.95. ISBN 1-58574-190-6.

In a motivating, step-by-step format, the author presents a structured approach to developing a walking program and staying with it and gives compelling reasons to exercise, along with a simple plan will make the program work. He discusses strength training and stretching, options for indoor and outdoor movement, the role of diet, and a progression toward more speed and longer workouts. Also covers race walking and long-term care of the body. Illustrated with color photographs. Includes week-by-week progress charts, a list of other resources, and a detailed index.

949. Iknoian, Therese. **Fitness Walking.** Fitness Spectrum Series. Champaign, Ill.: Human Kinetics, 1995. 161 pp. $17.95. ISBN 0-87322-553-8.

Intended for beginners as well as seasoned walkers, this guide to the fitness benefits of walking offers an organized and understandable approach. It begins with information on the preparation, including equipment, basic technique, warm-up and cool-down. Next, a series of different workouts are defined and arranged by color code from easiest to most challenging. A detailed workout plan is offered for each of six intensity levels. Includes a chapter on cross-training and one on charting progress. Well-illustrated with color photographs throughout.

950. Malkin, Mort. **Aerobic Walking: The Weight-Loss Exercise; A Complete Program to Reduce Weight, Stress, and Hypertension.** New York: John Wiley, 1995. 232 pp. $19.95. ISBN 0-471-55672-6.

Offering an eight-week aerobic-walking program that is structured around the key concepts of diet, exercise, and motivation, the author presents a very easily understood plan. Detailed discussion is given on walking technique, motivation, an aerobic diet, and principles of health, safety, and long-term maintenance of the program. Includes references and an index.

951. Rosato, Frank. **Jogging and Walking for Health and Fitness.** 4th ed. Englewood, Colo.: Morton Publishing, 2000. 146 pp. $21.95. ISBN 0-89582-546-5.

In this basic guide to jogging and walking for health and fitness, the author's objective is to introduce readers to the benefits of sustained exercise. Provides an overview of physical fitness, motivational techniques, and basic principles of participation in walking and jogging, physiological adaptations, and the role of exercise in preventing heart disease and in reducing the effects of other chronic diseases such as cancer, osteoarthritis, asthma, and stress. Also covers nutrition and prevention of injury. Illustrated with photos, drawings, and data tables. An appendix provides useful Web addresses and includes a glossary. Indexed.

952. Rudner, Ruth. **Walking.** Champaign, Ill.: Human Kinetics, 1996. 121 pp. $13.95. ISBN 0-87322-668-2.

Most appropriate for the beginner, but containing some details that experienced walkers will appreciate, this guide provides information on apparel, form, fitness, and safety and illustrates a series of preparatory stretches. It also offers brief information on trails and other good places to walk in the United States, Canada, the United Kingdom, Europe, and Australia. Includes a chapter on more advanced forms of walking. An appendix provides sources of further information. Well illustrated with color photographs and maps. Indexed.

953. Seiger, Lon H., and James L. Hesson. **Walking for Fitness.** 4th ed. Winning Edge. Boston: McGraw-Hill, 2001. 224 pp. $16.25. ISBN 0-07-235386-4.

Intended as a college-level walking text, this excellent source would be appropriate for any adult who wants to begin a walking program. The authors present an approach that emphasizes safety and personal fitness. They begin with a discussion of the walking trend and the health benefits of walking. They provide information on choosing appropriate clothing, shoes, and other equipment, then proceed to safety considerations, warming up, cooling down, and flexibility. They introduce several fitness-walking tests and provide specific walking programs and walking techniques. Includes information on nutrition, weight and body fat, wellness, and motivational strategies. Illustrated with black-and-white photographs, data tables, and diagrams. Appendices include an exercise log and further resources. Indexed.

954. Spilner, Maggie. *Prevention*'s **Complete Book of Walking: Everything You Need to Know to Walk Your Way to Better Health.** Emmaus, Pa.: Rodale Press, 2000. 292 pp. $24.95; $14.95 (pbk.). ISBN 1-57954-398-7; 1-57954-236-0 (pbk.).

This comprehensive encyclopedia of walking for fitness introduces the tools and techniques that increase the walker's distance, speed, comfort, and safety. A six-week program is offered that utilizes the expertise of a movement therapist to enhance the walker's posture, gait, and biomechanics. Features three workout plans, including a training plan for a 5K event, advice on choosing well-fitting shoes and other fitness equipment, and explanation of yoga poses that support a walker's stride. According to the front cover of the book, "lose weight, look younger, feel stronger, get energized. Featuring Suki Munsell's Dynamic Walking Method."

Web Sites

955. **America Walks.** http://www.americawalks.org (accessed March 28, 2004).

"The National Coalition of Local Advocacy Groups Dedicated to Promoting Walkable Communities."

956. **American Volkssport Association.** http://www.ava.org (accessed December 8, 2004).

The AVA's Web site offers access to their network of 350 walking clubs and more than 3000 walking events that are held each year in all 50 states. Contains a tutorial, a new walker's program, a youth walking program, and much more.

957. **Pedestrian and Bicycle Information Center.** http://www.walkinginfo
.org/ (accessed December 8, 2004).

The Pedestrian and Bicycle Information Center is a clearinghouse of information intended to help communities make walking and cycling viable transportation options, and it maintains a very comprehensive and informative Web
site. It provides coverage of many aspects of walking, including fitness and
health, but also community solutions, engineering, education, costs and benefits, and research and development.

Water Aerobics

958. Baum, Glenda. **Aquarobics: The Training Manual.** New York: Saunders,
1998. 213 pp. $34.95. ISBN 0-7020-2234-9.

Designed to show therapists and fitness instructors how to teach aquarobics to a wide variety of people, this manual can also be useful to the serious
student herself. Includes over 100 exercises that can be done in the water to assist in the rehabilitation of injured or disabled patients. Contains clear description and many practical examples of aquatic-therapy techniques.

959. Case, LeAnne. **Fitness Aquatics.** Fitness Spectrum. Champaign, Ill.:
Human Kinetics, 1997. 176 pp. $17.95. ISBN 0-87322-963-0.

This guide to water exercise workouts features sixty color-coded workouts,
organized according to the length and intensity of the exercise into six training
ranges. Illustrated with color photographs and diagrams.

960. Huey, Lynda, and Robert Forster. **The Complete Waterpower Workout
Book: Programs for Fitness, Injury Prevention, and Healing.** New York:
Random House, 1993. 371 pp. $19.95. ISBN 0-679-74554-8.

This detailed guide to water-fitness workouts provides a number of workouts that serve different purposes and are designed to meet different goals. It
offers a general waterpower workout, plus one for deep water, as well as a dance-
specific and a sport-specific waterpower workout. The book also offers a warm-
down program. The second half of the book deals with using water workouts as
rehabilitation exercises and offers variations for specific situations (lower body,
upper body, post-surgical). Illustrated with 200 black-and-white photographs.
Indexed.

961. Katz, Jane. **Aqua Fit: Dr. Jane Katz's Water Workout Program with
Yoga, Pilates, Tai Chi, and More.** New York: Broadway Books, 2003. 185 pp.
$12.95. ISBN 0-7679-1482-1.

The noted aquatics author uses a holistic approach to offer a soothing and
strengthening program for total body fitness. Exercises are drawn from yoga,
Pilates, and tai chi, as well as land sports such as skiing and golf. Also includes
high-intensity challenges, such as deep-water running and cross-training for athletes. Each exercise is illustrated with a drawing and step-by-step instructions.

Offers workouts of different lengths, with warm-ups and cool-downs. Accessories such as fins and kickboards are utilized to vary the workouts.

962. Katz, Jane. **The Aquatic Handbook for Lifetime Fitness.** Boston: Allyn & Bacon, 1996. 310 pp. $32.00. ISBN 0-205-17207-5.

Arranged in a modular format, this handbook of swimming as a form of exercise begins with a history of aquatics, then moves through the process of becoming comfortable in the water and learning the stroke techniques, as well as other aquatic-fitness activities. Intended to be used with all ages, either in a group setting or for individual purposes. Illustrated with photographs and drawings. Appendices contain sample personal records and sources of aquatic information. Indexed.

963. Spitzer, Terry-Ann, and Werner W. K. Hoeger. **Water Aerobics for Fitness and Wellness.** 3rd ed. Belmont, Calif.: Thomson / Wadsworth, 2002. 170 pp. $22.95. ISBN 0-534-58106-4.

The authors provide guidelines for developing an effective program of water aerobics, and they examine fitness assessment, including specific tests of cardio-respiratory endurance, muscular strength, flexibility, and body composition. The basic principles of water exercise are presented, along with special considerations and equipment. Many examples of both shallow- and deep-water exercise are detailed and illustrated, and discussion is included on the complementary strategies of good nutrition, weight management, and a healthy lifestyle. Illustrated with black-and-white photographs. Includes a bibliography and an index.

Weight Training/Lifting

Instructional Sources

964. Baechle, Thomas R., and Barney R. Groves. **Weight Training: Steps to Success.** 2nd ed. Champaign, Ill.: Human Kinetics, 1998. 182 pp. $17.95. ISBN 0-88011-718-4.

Twelve progressive steps are presented to guide the reader through the development of a program of weight training. Each step builds on the previous one, from lifting fundamentals to exercises for specific muscles to maximizing a personalized program. Illustrated with sequential drawings. Provides a glossary of terms and a good orientation to weightlifting equipment.

965. Berger, Richard A. **Introduction to Weight Training.** 2nd ed. Englewood Cliffs, N.J.: Prentice Hall, 1992. 184 pp. $26.00. ISBN 0-13-484098-4.

This basic source on weight training begins with a discussion of muscle structure and function and factors that determine strength. This sets the stage for thorough coverage of the principles of training with weights. Health and safety considerations are presented, along with a program for basic lifts with barbells and dumbbells. Long-range training programs are outlined, as are exercising without special equipment, circuit training, and strength training. Illustrated with drawings. Indexed.

966. Fahey, Thomas D. **Basic Weight Training for Men and Women.** 5th ed. New York: McGraw-Hill, 2004. 225 pp. $37.00. ISBN 0-07-255688-9.

In this basic guide to weight training, the practical and scientific bases are presented in a jargon-free style. Includes comprehensive information on health and wellness benefits, training advantages, how to get started, and full chapters on the specific areas of the body that can be developed, such as chest and shoulders, arms, back, abdominal muscles. Offers exercises to develop speed and power and a chapter on nutrition. Line drawings illustrate the techniques. Includes a glossary of terms, a list of references, and an index.

967. Goldenberg, Lorne, and Peter Twist. **Strength Ball Training.** Champaign, Ill.: Human Kinetics, 2002. 191 pp. $17.95. ISBN 0-7360-3828-0.

The 69 Swiss-ball and medicine-ball exercises presented in this clearly written guide target all the major muscle groups and include exercises for core stabilization, flexibility, and strength. Illustrated with over 140 black-and-white photographs that demonstrate the steps in sequential fashion. Specific muscle groups are treated in separate chapters. Functional strength-ball training programs for ten sports are included. Includes a brief bibliography.

968. Hesson James L. **Weight Training for Life.** 7th ed. Belmont, Calif.: Thomson / Wadsworth, 2004. 176 pp. $22.95. ISBN 0-534-63702-7.

Intended as a text for college students in a weight-training activity course, this book is perfect for beginners who want credible exercise information. Using techniques consistent with the recommendations of the National Strength and Conditioning Association and the American College of Sports Medicine, it covers muscle structure and function, warm-up and stretching, safety, and a beginning program of weight training. Next, a series of exercises are provided that focus on specific muscles and areas of the body. Also provides information on nutrition and offers an advanced program and motivational strategies. Illustrated with color photographs. Appendices provide additional sources of information. Indexed.

969. Kraemer, William J., and Keijo Hakkinen, eds. **Strength Training for Sport.** Handbook of Sports Medicine and Science. Malden, Mass.: Blackwell Science, 2002. 200 pp. $33.95. ISBN 0-632-05568-5.

This series is published under the auspices of the International Olympic Committee Medical Commission. This volume complements the others in the series and covers both basic concepts and theoretical background for sport-specific strength training and program design. Sample strength-training programs are presented for a variety of sports. The articles in the handbook are intended for use by physicians, trainers, and coaches but would also be useful for athletes or for parents of children who are participating in athletics. Illustrated with diagrams, tables, and black-and-white photographs. Each chapter contains a list of references for further reading. This series is most appropriate for college and university collections in sports medicine. Indexed.

970. Rasch, Philip J. **Weight Training.** 5th ed. Sports and Fitness series. Dubuque, Iowa: Brown and Benchmark, 1990. 114 pp. $9.60. ISBN 0-697-10417-6.

This guide to weight training discusses the role of diet and nutrition, safety measures, and a basic program of training for men and women. Covers advanced methods and use of dumbbells also. Each chapter ends with a list of references. Illustrated with black-and-white photographs. Appendices illustrate the muscles of the human body and summarize their actions and exercises. Includes a glossary. Index by name and by subject.

971. Sandler, David. **Weight Training Fundamentals.** Sports Fundamentals. Champaign, Ill.: Human Kinetics, 2003. 152 pp. $14.95. ISBN 0-7360-4488-4.

This beginner's guide to weight training provides sequential instructions and accompanying photographs to demonstrate basic exercises that tone and strengthen muscles. Offers exercises for warm-up, stretch, and cool-down, as well as specific routines to develop the chest, upper back, shoulders, trapezins, triceps, biceps, forearms, abdominals, lower back, gluteal and hip muscles, quadriceps, hamstrings, and calves. Assists with developing an individual program. According to the cover, this book is "a better way to learn the basics."

972. Schwarzenegger, Arnold. **The New Encyclopedia of Modern Bodybuilding.** 2nd ed. With Bill Dobbins. New York: Simon & Schuster, 1999. 800 pp. $50.00. ISBN 0-684-84374-9.

A hefty source at 800 pages, this encyclopedia provides a history of bodybuilding and in-depth information on the fundamentals and getting started in a training program. Offers basic training principles, stretching exercises, and advanced and competitive training, then moves in to specific exercise routines for building particular muscles. Demonstrates hundreds of exercises, discusses competition, health, nutrition and diet, and injuries. Illustrated with hundreds of black-and-white photographs of famous bodybuilders with incredibly huge muscles. According to the cover, the book is "the bible of bodybuilding." Indexed.

973. Sisco, Peter, ed. *Ironman*'s **Ultimate Bodybuilding Encyclopedia.** With *Ironman* magazine. Lincolnwood, Ill.: Contemporary Books, 1999. 451 pp. $19.95. ISBN 0-8092-2811-4.

This volume contains articles and photos that are reprinted from *Ironman* magazine, and it features many famous bodybuilders, including Arnold Schwarzenegger. It offers coverage of the major topics of interest in bodybuilding, including training for specific muscle groups (abdominals, arms, chest, shoulder, and legs), mental aspects of bodybuilding, nutrition, injuries, and drugs, as well as many tips and tricks to improve mass and power. Illustrated with black-and-white photographs. Indexed.

974. Wolff, Robert. **Bodybuilding 201.** New York: Contemporary Books / McGraw-Hill, 2004. 228 pp. $18.95. ISBN 0-07-141321-9.

Aimed at intermediate and advanced weight-training enthusiasts who want to move to the next level of training, this book follows from *Bodybuilding 101*, by the same author. Contains step-by-step exercises, tips, workouts, and additional information on stretching, exercises for specific muscle groups, body type, and nutrition. Illustrated with nearly 200 black-and-white photographs.

Web Sites

975. **International Weightlifting Federation (IWF).** http://www.iwf.net (accessed March 4, 2004).

The international governing body for weightlifting competition maintains an informative Web site with a directory of national federations throughout the world. Also available on the site are a history of the sport, a handbook, rules, news, a list of publications, an events calendar, results and rankings, information on equipment, a photo and multimedia gallery, and links to other information, including information related to the Olympics.

976. **USA Weightlifting.** http://www.usaweightlifting.org (accessed March 27, 2004).

USA Weightlifting is the national governing body for Olympic weightlifting in the United States. Its Web site contains rules, athlete biographies, qualifying totals, news, records, rankings, results, an events calendar, weightlifting basics and lifts, the USAW rulebook, a club directory, and many links.

Jump Rope

977. Lee, Buddy. **Jump Rope Training.** Champaign, Ill.: Human Kinetics, 2003. 157 pp. $16.95. ISBN 0-7360-4151-6.

According to its cover, the book contains "techniques and programs for improved fitness and performance." Using this training method, the user will master jump-rope skills and build aerobic endurance. Includes techniques to use the jump rope to warm-up and cool-down; gain speed and quickness; develop agility, coordination, and balance; increase strength and power; and condition for specific sports and fitness goals.

977a. Marrott, Barbara. **Getting a Jump on Fitness.** New York: Barricade Books, 1997. 155 pp. $14.95. ISBN 1-56980-102-9.

Written by a certified personal trainer, this source presents a practical fitness plan for readers of all fitness levels. A variety of individual workout plans are given, utilizing only a jump rope in many interesting ways to improve cardiovascular health, muscular strength, endurance, flexibility, and coordination. Includes a selected bibliography.

977b. Solis, Ken M. **Ropics: The Next Jump Forward in Fitness.** Champaign, Ill.: Leisure Press, 1992. 137 pp. $12.95. ISBN 0-88011-444-4.

This detailed guide to jumping rope for increased fitness provides thirty-four techniques and variations, from basic to advanced levels. It describes how to modify the exercise plan depending on age, fitness level, or specific goals. It offers many additional tips on topics such as choosing the right rope, using music to enhance the workout, and strategies to stay motivated. Appendices list jump rope organizations and sources for purchasing accessories. Includes a glossary of terms and a selected bibliography.

Yoga

978. Ansari, Mark, and Liz Lark. **Yoga for Beginners.** New York: Harper-Collins, 1998. 96 pp. $21.95. ISBN 0-06-273648-5.

In this practical guide to yoga for beginners, the authors present a manageable set of instructions to help the reader learn the basic postures, breathing techniques, and other exercises of yoga. The goal is for beginners to feel the benefits of stretching, moving, and breathing to relieve tension. An intermediate program is also offered, as is a guide to meditation and the mental aspects of yoga. This is a brief presentation, but with very good information. Well illustrated with sequential color photographs, the book's cover includes an easel so it can stand on its own at the readers' eye level.

979. Christensen, Alice. **The American Yoga Association's Beginner's Manual.** Rev. and updated ed. New York: Fireside / Simon & Schuster, 2002. 238 pp. $15.00. ISBN 0-7432-1941-4.

This comprehensive beginner's manual offers basic information for getting started with yoga, plus three ten-week programs of exercise. Provides extensive information on diet and nutrition, as well as special routines for pregnancy, improved sports performance, and stress relief. Instructions for each asana in the three exercise programs are illustrated with over 300 sequential black-and-white photographs. Contains a glossary, list of other sources, and an index.

980. Coulter, H. David. **Anatomy of Hatha Yoga: A Manual for Students, Teachers, and Practitioners.** Honesdale, Pa.: Body and Breath, 2001. 623 pp. $40.00. ISBN 0-9707006-0-1.

A very technical presentation of yoga and human anatomy, this work provides extremely detailed description. The chapters focus on fully describing elements of the movements and postures, breathing, abdominopelvic exercises, standing postures, backbending postures, forward bending postures, twisting postures, the headstand, the shoulder stand, and techniques of relaxation and meditation. Illustrated with 230 black-and-white photographs and over 120 diagrams and anatomical charts.

981. Feuerstein, Georg. **The Shambhala Encyclopedia of Yoga.** Boston: Shambhala Publications, 1997. 537 pp. $24.95. ISBN 1-57062-555-7.

While this extensive dictionary of over 2000 alphabetically arranged entries is devoted primarily to the spiritual aspects of yoga, it also does an excellent job of providing complete definitions of the physical aspects. Black-and-white photographs or drawings are usually included to illustrate the postures being defined. Includes a bibliography of sources for further reading. A previous version by the same author was issued under the title *Encyclopedic Dictionary of Yoga* (New York: Paragon House, 1990).

982. Iyengar, B.K.S. **Yoga: The Path to Holistic Health.** London: Dorling Kindersley, 2001. 416 pp. $40.00. ISBN 0-7894-7165-5.

Intended for every age and level of ability, this substantial, comprehensive volume features a holistic approach to yoga, bringing together the physical, mental, and emotional aspects of health. Early chapters discuss stress and how yoga can be used to increase fitness and health, as well as the philosophy of yoga. Asanas are clearly described and vividly illustrated, with the specific health benefits outlined for each. Asanas for stress are described in detail, as are asanas used to treat specific health conditions in the body's systems, such as the heart and circulation, nervous system, and hormonal system. Includes a twenty-week yoga course, an anatomy guide, a glossary, and a list of asanas with translation. Illustrated with over 1900 high-quality color photographs. Indexed.

983. Kirk, Martin, and Brooke Boon. **Hatha Yoga Illustrated: For Greater Strength, Flexibility, and Focus.** Photographs by Daniel DiTuro. Champaign, Ill.: Human Kinetics, 2004. 233 pp. $24.95. ISBN 0-7360-5122-8.

Illustrated with over 600 color photographs that demonstrate seventy-seven standard hatha yoga poses, this book provides practical information to help users achieve success. Each pose is presented with instructions given in step-by-step format and is illustrated with a series of photographs. In many cases, a gentle variation is also provided for beginners. It also contains a list of suggested readings, contact information for schools, sources for yoga props and clothing, an alphabetical list of asanas, and an illustrated index.

984. Meaux, Kia. **Dynamic Yoga.** 1st American ed. New York: Dorling Kindersley, 2002. 160 pp. $14.95. ISBN 0-7894-8064-6.

Describes the development of this style of Hatha yoga and provides beautiful color photographs to illustrate the poses throughout the work. This is an excellent visual resource for the techniques and postures that are described. Provides three different programs of exercise, tailored to all fitness levels. Contains a brief glossary of Sanskrit terms and an index.

985. Sivananda Yoga Center, The. **The Sivananda Companion to Yoga.** New York: Fireside, 2000. 192 pp. $16.00. ISBN 0-684-87000-2.

A standard text for both students and teachers of yoga, this source offers easy-to-follow instructions and high-quality illustrations that guide the reader. Encourages yoga as an exercise for everyone throughout the life cycle, including pregnant women, children, and the elderly. Covers the basic poses, breathing, diet, and meditation, and then offers a range of variations and new asanas for further practice. Includes a glossary and an index.

986. Townley, Wyatt. **Yoganetics: Be Fit, Healthy, and Relaxed One Breath at a Time.** New York: HarperCollins, 2003. 173 pp. $15.95. ISBN 0-06-050224-X.

Intended for students of all levels and traditions, this relaxed guide to yoga is a combination of easily understood text and excellent photographs that give an added visual dimension to the exercises. The amount of text that accompanies each photograph is not overwhelming, so it is possible to read, see, and then easily do the exercise without confusion. Offers workouts for beginning and intermediate levels, as well as exercises that can be done "beyond the mat," for instance when sitting at a desk. Illustrated with over 120 high-quality black-and-white photographs.

987. Vishnu-devananda, Swami. **The Complete Illustrated Book of Yoga.** New York: Three Rivers Press / Random House, 1988. 359 pp. $18.00. ISBN 0-517-88431-3.

This book, a classic text written by a noted authority and originally published in 1960, provides detailed explanation and discussion of the philosophy of yoga and also demonstrates the fundamental postures. Provides chapters that discuss breathing, diet, relaxation, and spiritual awareness. Illustrated with 146 black-and-white photographs.

AUTHOR INDEX

Reference is to entry number.

TITLE INDEX

Reference is to entry number.

SUBJECT INDEX

Reference is to entry number.

About the Author

MARY BETH ALLEN is Applied Life Studies librarian at the University of Illinois at Urbana-Champaign.